Manchester Medieval Sources Series

series advisers Rosemary Horrox and Ja

This series aims to meet a growing need amongst students and teachers of medieval history for translations of key sources that are directly useable in students' own work. It provides texts central to medieval studies courses and focuses upon the diverse cultural and social as well as political conditions that affected the functioning of all levels of medieval society. The basic premise of the new series is that translations must be accompanied by sufficient introductory and explanatory material, and each volume, therefore, includes a comprehensive guide to the sources' interpretation, including discussion of critical linguistic problems and an assessment of the most recent research on the topics being covered.

THE LIVES OF THOMAS BECKET

MANCHESTER
UNIVERSITY PRESS

Medieval Sources*online*

Complementing the printed editions of the Medieval Sources series, Manchester University Press has developed a web-based learning resource which is now available on a yearly subscription basis.

Medieval Sources*online* brings quality history source material to the desktops of students and teachers and allows them open and unrestricted access throughout the entire college or university campus. Designed to be fully integrated with academic courses, this is a one-stop answer for many medieval history students, academics and researchers keeping thousands of pages of source material 'in print' over the Internet for research and teaching.

titles available now at Medieval Sources*online include*

John Edwards *The Jews in Western Europe, 1400–1600*

Paul Fouracre and Richard A. Gerberding *Late Merovingian France: History and hagiography 640–720*

Chris Given-Wilson *Chronicles of the Revolution 1397–1400: The reign of Richard II*

P. J. P. Goldberg *Women in England, c. 1275–1525*

Janet Hamilton and Bernard Hamilton *Christian dualist heresies in the Byzantine world, c. 650–c. 1450*

Rosemary Horrox *The Black Death*

Graham A. Loud and Thomas Wiedemann *The history of the tyrants of Sicily by 'Hugo Falcandus', 1153–69*

Janet L. Nelson *The Annals of St-Bertin: Ninth-century histories, volume I*

Timothy Reuter *The Annals of Fulda: Ninth-century histories, volume II*

R. N. Swanson *Catholic England: faith, religion and observance before the Reformation*

Jennifer Ward *Women of the English nobility and gentry, 1066–1500*

visit the site at *www.medievalsources.co.uk*
for further information and subscription prices

THE LIVES OF THOMAS BECKET

selected sources translated and annotated by Michael Staunton

Manchester University Press
Manchester and New York

distributed exclusively in the USA by Palgrave

Published by Manchester University Press
Oxford Road, Manchester M13 9NR, UK
and Room 400, 175 Fifth Avenue, New York, NY 10010, USA
http://www.manchesteruniversitypress.co.uk

Distributed exclusively in the USA by
Palgrave, 175 Fifth Avenue, New York, NY 10010, USA

Distributed exclusively in Canada by
UBC Press, University of British Columbia, 2029 West Mall, Vancouver, BC, Canada V6T 1Z2

British Library Cataloguing-in-Publication Data
A catalogue record for this book is available from the British Library

Library of Congress Cataloging-in-Publication Data applied for

ISBN 0 7190 5454 0 *hardback*
       0 7190 5455 9 *paperback*

First published 2001

10 09 08 07 06 05 04 03   10 9 8 7 6 5 4 3 2

Typeset in Monotype Bell
by Koinonia Ltd, Manchester
Printed in Great Britain
by Bell & Bain Ltd, Glasgow

CONTENTS

SERIES EDITOR'S FOREWORD

Astonishingly, and uniquely for any medieval subject, no fewer than fourteen Lives of Thomas Becket were produced within twenty years of his death. One, by a woman, seems now, alas, definitively lost. The rest, including as much of another now-lost Life as has survived incorporated in a fourteenth-century Icelandic saga, are the subject-matter of Michael Staunton's book in the Manchester Medieval Sources series. Given Becket's historical interest, and hence the Lives' importance as evidence of a life that has often baffled medieval as well as modern commentators, the lack of modern translations of most of these texts has long been regretted. Michael Staunton's book fills the gap admirably. With lucid translations, he supplies an introduction and commentary that will make these works, not easy, for they are, as he rightly insists, 'sophisticated and complex', but accessible to thoughtful and attentive readers. Appropriately, since Becket caused so much contention in life, this book also contains some contemporary critical views of Becket. Such inclusivity is timely: modern judgements on Becket are – at last – ceasing to be polarised between hagiography and exposé. Michael Staunton provides the wherewithal to stimulate and support new readings and richer understandings of the man and his context: a twelfth century that, for good as well as ill, contributed a very great deal to the making of Europe.

Janet L. Nelson
Kings College London

PREFACE

The story of Thomas Becket is one of the best-known in English history, but few have read it in the words of those who knew him best. It is not that material is lacking – rather, that the collection of twelfth-century Lives and letters is vast (almost two million words in total), and very little of it has been translated. It is hoped that this book will allow students and scholars an accessible form in which to read what Thomas's intimates, admirers and critics had to say about his life and death, his personality and character, and his world.

The selection of material was by no means easy, but it was made less difficult by the nature of the Lives. They tend to begin at the beginning of Thomas's life and proceed in a quite consistent manner up to his death and its aftermath. They devote most attention to the seven and a half years when Thomas was archbishop, and particular attention to his last days, and I have echoed this emphasis. Some biographers, Edward Grim or 'Roger of Pontigny' for instance, provide very good broad narratives, but for the most important and dramatic events I have usually used the more detailed accounts of eyewitnesses such as William Fitzstephen or Herbert of Bosham. My main intention has been to tell the story, but I have also included more reflective extracts and material which illustrates features of contemporary life. It is also hoped that this collection will provide an insight into the Lives themselves. I have included all the main biographers, but the proportion included of each writer gives a general reflection of their importance as historical and literary works as I saw it.

The most difficult decision concerned the inclusion of letters. I originally intended to intersperse extracts from the Lives with contemporary correspondence but eventually decided against it. I feared not only that the inclusion of correspondence would have pushed the word count far beyond the desired limit, but also that it might obscure the nature and meaning of the sources. The Thomas that correspondents wrote of in the 1160s is an entirely different creature to the subject of the posthumous Lives: while one was a flawed and embattled archbishop, the other was a saint whose works had been vindicated. Still, considering that the inclusion of the Lives alone would give an unduly biased viewpoint, I tried to provide balance with a separate section entitled 'Dissenting Voices'.

I have provided quite a lot of introductory commentary. The story and the issues often require explanation and interpretation, and it is sometimes necessary to fill in the gaps left by the biographers. It sometimes seems that everything that needs to be said about Thomas has been said, but this is not so. It is hoped that by reading about him in the words of his biographers, others will be encouraged to investigate further the unresolved features of his life.

All translations are my own, except for those of Garnier's Life which I took from Janet Shirley's *Garnier's Becket*, and the Icelandic Saga which was translated by Haki Antonson. I am very grateful to both of them.

Many people helped in the production of this book. My first thanks are to Jennifer O'Reilly of University College Cork who introduced me to the subject and has given me support ever since. I am also very grateful to those who helped me in my research into the subject while at Cambridge, in particular Gillian Evans and Christopher Brooke. This book was written in the highly supportive atmosphere of the Department of Mediaeval History, St Andrews, and I am indebted to far too many people to mention. Chris Given-Wilson, Brian Briggs, and Philip Burton of the Classics Department very kindly looked over some difficult passages, though it must be said that any mistakes are my own. Kris Towson's technical expertise was essential to the production of the maps, and Haki Antonson was of invaluable assistance, not only for providing the translation from Icelandic and reading over drafts, but also for numerous discussions of the material. The staff of Manchester University Press have been encouraging, sympathetic and efficient throughout. Finally I would like to thank those who have provided the longest and most valuable support in the writing of this book, my family and Oonagh Smyth.

ABBREVIATIONS

Barlow   F. Barlow, *Thomas Becket* (London, 1986).

Councils and Synods   Councils and Synods With Other Documents Relating to the English Church, I AD 871–1204, Part 2, 1066–1204 (Oxford, 1981), eds D. Whitelock, M. Brett, and C. N. L. Brooke.

Garnier   Guernes de Pont-Sainte-Maxence, ed. E. Walberg (Lund, 1922).

CTB   The Correspondence of Thomas Becket, Archbishop of Canterbury, 1162–70 (Oxford, 2000), ed. A. Duggan.

LCGF   The Letters and Charters of Gilbert Foliot (Cambridge, 1967), eds A. Morey and C. N. L. Brooke.

LJS   The Letters of John of Salisbury, vol. II (Oxford, 1979), eds W. J. Millor and C. N. L. Brooke.

Morey and Brooke   A. Morey and C. N. L. Brooke, *Gilbert Foliot and his Letters* (Cambridge, 1965).

MTB   *Materials for the History of Thomas Becket, archbishop of Canterbury,* eds J. C. Robertson and J. B. Sheppard (RS, London, 1875–85).

Saga   Thómas Saga Erkibyskups, ed. E. Magnusson (RS, London, 1875–83).

Smalley   B. Smalley, *The Becket Conflict and the Schools* (Oxford, 1973).

Warren   W. L. Warren, *Henry II* (London, 1973).

York

Knaresborough

Beverley

Lincoln

Catley

Haverholme

Boston

Stafford

Grantham

Eye

Wabridge

Forest

Northampton

Bedford

Gloucester

Woodstock

Berkhamstead

Oxford

Harrow

London

Windsor

Marlborough

Reading

Southwark

Rochester

Merton

Canterbury

Sandwich

Bletchingley

Saltwood

Dover

Tonbridge

Clarendon

Winchester

Hythe

Romney

Southampton

Hastings

Pagham

Pevensey

ENGLISH   CHANNEL

England: places mentioned in the text

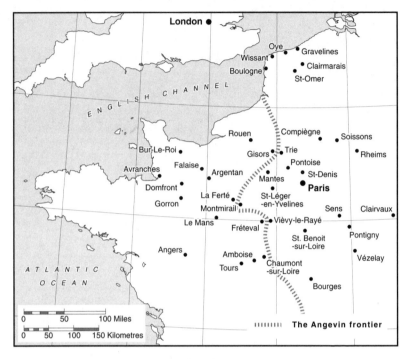

Northern France: places mentioned in the text

INTRODUCTION

Thomas of Canterbury was no ordinary saint, and on that his admirers
and critics can agree. In the wake of his murder on 29 December 1170
he was hailed by many as the greatest saint of his age, one who
emulated the patriarchs of the early church, and even Christ. But even
as thousands testified to his miraculous powers and visited his tomb,
and his memory was honoured by his own church, by the pope and by
his enemies during life, doubts remained. It was not long since he had
been widely regarded as an arrogant troublemaker whose personal
inadequacies had damaged not only the interests of the crown, but
those of the Church which he claimed to espouse. It seemed to some
then, and many since, that his glory had been achieved solely by virtue
of his death, not his life. Both admirers and critics have approached
his life through the prism of his death, whether as confirmation of its
greatness, or a distraction from its flaws. But Thomas's life would still
have been remarkable, even without its violent end. This was the son
of a London merchant, who had risen first to one of the highest
administrative positions in the land, and then to its highest ecclesiastical office. His rift with his former friend the king, and the progress
of the dispute which led to public confrontation and prolonged exile,
was keenly followed all over the Christian world. As the shock of his
murder reverberated around Europe, many of those touched by these
events began to write their accounts of what they regarded as the
most important episode of their age. They sought to tell the story, not
only of Thomas's glorious death but also of his life, and to show that
one was the true fulfilment of the other.

We probably know more about Thomas's life than that of any other
Englishman of the middle ages. The twelfth-century Latin Lives com-
prise four weighty volumes of the Rolls Series and the letter
collection a further three, and that is before we take into account the
French verse Lives, the Icelandic Saga and the numerous other notices
in contemporary histories. These works provide eyewitness testimony
to his character, conversation and way of life and a very detailed
account of the turbulent years as archbishop from 1163 to 1170. Like
that of Abelard and Heloise, or Richard III, Thomas's story is
dramatic and extraordinary in itself and at the same time illustrative
of its time and place. There are few texts in which one can find such

precise and evocative descriptions of, for example, high and low-level politics in the secular and ecclesiastical worlds, or the development of a saintly cult. But while the Lives are superior historical records, they are more than that. They are works of history and biography, but also of hagiography. They are partisan accounts, written by some of the most learned people of their time, many of whom were steeped in knowledge of theology and canon law. They are more sophisticated and complex works than many have imagined, and as such they present both challenges and opportunities to the historian.

The dispute

At the centre of the dispute is the personality of Thomas himself. It has often been said that Thomas's personality and character are elusive, but perhaps it is more accurate to say that they are complex and sometimes contradictory. After all, there is general agreement that he was highly capable, and could inspire others, and that he was also rash and often arrogant. Against him is Henry II, a young and energetic king supposedly led astray by uncontrollable temper and poor counsel. Much of the sharpness of the dispute derives from the volatile relationship between these two men, former friends, whose forcefulness and obstinacy pushed them further apart once the rift had emerged. But that was not the only personality clash to define the dispute. Archbishop Roger of York and Bishops Hilary of Chichester and Gilbert of London make vivid appearances in the Lives as fomenters of envy towards the bishop and discord towards the Church, and the conflict was brought to its conclusion by laymen who had long harboured grudges against the archbishop. Prominent roles were also played by King Louis VII of France and Pope Alexander III, who often had to walk a tightrope between Thomas and Henry. But if we follow those biographers who knew him best, the greatest personal conflict was within Thomas himself as he struggled to adapt himself to his changing roles and the different challenges which he faced at every step, right up to his death.

The personalities involved gave the dispute its character, but there were always serious underlying issues present. They derived from the conflicting duties and ambitions of an archbishop of Canterbury and an English king in the mid-to-late twelfth century. Thomas and his biographers claimed that he was advancing the cause of the Church, but this was a multifaceted phenomenon with overlapping and sometimes conflicting components. It was the archbishop's duty to defend and advance the fortunes of his see, the English Church, and the Church at large.

One ought not to overlook the importance of Canterbury rights to the Becket dispute. The earliest recorded disputes in which Thomas was involved as archbishop relate to his attempts to retrieve Canterbury properties; it was the usurpation of Canterbury's right to crown the young king that led first to the settlement at Fréteval and the excommunication and suspension of the bishops involved; this in turn led to their complaint to the king, which prompted Thomas's murder by men under the overall command of those who had taken Canterbury lands during the archbishop's exile.

The crisis of 1163–64 was based around the protection of the liberty of the English Church. Henry's customs were principally an attempt to reassert the crown's control over jurisdiction which had lapsed since the reign of his grandfather, Henry I, mainly because of the laxity of royal control during the reign of Stephen, and the burgeoning influence of papal jurisdiction which had affected all of Europe. The most important specific issues were those of 'criminous clerks' – men in religious orders who had committed a serious felony whom Henry believed had been treated too leniently by Church courts – and appeals to the pope. Whether Thomas's opposition was legally grounded is a matter for debate, but it was certainly his duty as the leader of the English Church to defend the rights he had inherited from his predecessors in that office, and he was supported, at least at first, by the majority of the English clergy. However, it was equally Henry's duty to protect and advance the privileges which his royal ancestors had possessed.

But by the late twelfth century such matters did not involve the English clergy alone. The second half of the previous century had seen, with 'the Investiture Contest' between Pope Gregory VII and Emperor Henry IV, the first great clash between ecclesiastical and secular power, and even had the dispute between Thomas and Henry remained a domestic affair, the concepts of priestly and royal power were bound to play a part. Was the Becket dispute, then, a clash of powers, or even ideologies? Undoubtedly the clash of personalities and the individual disputes exposed fault-lines which had already been there between a confident post-Gregorian Church and an English monarchy that was intent on exploiting its rights to the full. There is some discussion in the Lives and the letters of the theoretical relationship between spiritual and secular power, but it may seem surprising that there is not more. Thomas's principal critics during his life came from within the Church and were, to put it simply, on the same side, but they also recognised the importance of the Church's relationship with the crown. Gilbert Foliot and others did not criticise Thomas for defending the Church: rather, they claimed that through his reckless-ness and his personal inadequacies he had endangered it. Their counsel was to retreat from his path of outright opposition to the king, not because the king ought to be obeyed before the Church, but because there was an appropriate time for opposition and for co-operation. Thomas, on the other hand, argued that the time was at hand to follow in the footsteps of the righteous defenders of the Church, and speak out against sinners.

This is perhaps the most fundamental reason why those involved in the dispute were so difficult to reconcile: they had quite different notions of the nature of the dispute itself. Gilbert Foliot is reported as saying that the dispute was a trivial and unimportant one which might have been easily settled had a restrained approach been taken. Between this position and the view that the issues came down to a battle between good and evil, in which its participants followed in the footsteps of Old Testament prophets and tyrants, Christ and the pharisees, the saints and the Church's persecutors, there could be no middle ground.

The Lives

What is most striking about the Lives of St Thomas is that there are so many of them, and that they were written so quickly. This is a testimony to the strength of the cult, and the fascination that Thomas's story held. It is also of great benefit to the historian.

Three of those who knew Thomas best wrote posthumous biogra-phies, his clerks John of Salisbury, William Fitzstephen and Herbert of Bosham. Though John's Life is short and often superficial, the other two are highly informative works which are of great value as independent historical records. Other writers had more limited con-tact with their subject: William of Canterbury and Benedict of Peterborough were monks of Christ Church, Canterbury, witnesses to his martyrdom and custodians of his shrine; 'Roger of Pontigny', if we accept his identity as a monk of that Cistercian house,[1] knew Thomas

1 See below, pp. 9–10.

during his exile; Edward Grim did not meet Thomas until December
1170, but his attempt to protect Thomas from his murderers' blows
gained him a place in history. Though the other biographers had no
personal knowledge of Thomas,[2] they had easy access to information
about him. All of the biographers included here wrote within twenty
years of Thomas's death, and most within ten.[3] They were familiar
with what has become known as 'Canterbury legend': the stories which
grew up around Thomas after his death, based on witness testimony.
Most also had access to the relevant correspondence, and Garnier, at
least, undertook investigative journalism, interviewing witnesses
including Thomas's sister. In addition, many of the writers borrowed
from each other.

Although these writers can be as guilty of exaggeration and biased
interpretation as any other contemporary hagiographers, in terms of
historical detail their accounts are generally believable, with little
deliberate distortion of events and a strong degree of precision. This
is not surprising: these were important events, fresh in their minds,
and familiar to many of their readers. While there is occasional
disagreement about dates, places and sequence, it is not difficult to
construct an accurate picture of the events of 1162–70, at least, from
the Lives and the letters. The Lives give us a remarkable insight into
Thomas's everyday life as chancellor and archbishop. They also give
us comprehensive narratives of the most important public occasions
in which Thomas was involved: the councils of Westminster and
Northampton, the meeting with the pope at Sens, the peace negotiations at Montmirail and Montmartre, and the murder (although
information on the Council of Clarendon and the excommunications
at Vézelay is regrettably scarce).

The Lives, then, provide a great deal of what the modern historian
wants to know. However, it is important to remember that this was
not the writers' principal intention. Motives for writing tend to be
mixed, and are impossible to pin down precisely, but one may wonder
why so many people wanted to write about Thomas. After all, his cult
had gained popular and official recognition in a remarkably short
time, before most of the Lives were even written, thereby removing
one of the most common purposes of hagiography: the establishment

2 If we discount the dubious claims of the Lambeth Anonymous and Garnier's
sighting of him as chancellor.

3 The Icelandic Saga is an exception, but this was based on the lost Life by Robert
of Cricklade, written in 1173–74.

of the subject's sanctity. One of the driving forces was obviously the widespread interest in the subject, affording a ready audience. But another powerful motive remained: to explain Thomas's controversial life. That is the very title of Alan of Tewkesbury's work – the *Explanatio* – and Thomas's life took some explaining. How could one reconcile the image of the glorious martyr with the apparently proud and vain chancellor who was made archbishop through the pressure of secular power, and in that role abandoned the cause of ecclesiastical liberty by submitting to the king's customs, abandoned his flock by fleeing to the continent, and caused havoc for his king and his church while in exile?

The biographers looked to Christian tradition. This was not difficult for them: all were churchmen – either clerks or monks – some were very learned in theology, others in canon law. As one of Thomas's supporters is reported as saying to the French king when he suggested that Thomas should have remembered the reading 'Be ye angry and sin not', 'Perhaps he would have remembered this verse if he had heard it as often as we have in the canonical hours'.[4] Christian tradition, in the form of the bible, theology, hagiography, history and canon law, provided a range of examples which could be applied to Thomas: the holy man who lived in the public eye but hid his inner sanctity; the convert who by God's grace was inspired to put off the old man and put on the new; the sinner who rose up more strongly after a fall; the righteous exile who fled in the body, but advanced, as a pilgrim, in the spirit; the defender of Christ and the Church who spoke with authority to princes and great men; the righteous man who stood alone against evil. For the biographers, the manner of Thomas's death was not an aberration which could be dissociated from the manner of his death: it was – and this is the word they often use to describe it – the *consummation* of his conversion, his pilgrimage and his struggle.

The biographers

Thomas's biographers share much. They were writing around the same time, they all benefit from Canterbury tradition, and many borrow from each other, so it is not surprising that they tend to similarity in structure and in detail. Nevertheless, these are individual works, each

4 See below, p. 127.

with its own character. There is some debate about the sequence in which they are written, but it is possible to place them in broad chronological order.[5]

Edward Grim

Though it is neither the most informative nor the most sophisticated of the Lives, Edward Grim's is one of the most important. A clerk from Cambridgeshire, he happened to be in Canterbury Cathedral to witness Thomas's murder. His heroic attempt to shield the archbishop from the knights' blows earned him a place in the saint's legend, and in many visual representations of the martyrdom. Written very early, 1171–72, it was very influential, and formed the basis of the Lives by Garnier and 'Roger of Pontigny'. The structure of Grim's Life is mirrored by many of the others: after a brief and hagiographical account of Thomas's years before he became archbishop it is more detailed from 1162 onwards, and provides a good description of the early dispute; the section on Thomas's exile is covered much less fully, but his return to England, his murder and posthumous acclaim receive far more attention. He is often uncertain on detail, placing the young king's coronation four years too early, for example, but his account of the murder is probably the best. [1, 11, 22, 30, 35, 51, 58]

John of Salisbury

As a close ally of Thomas and one of the foremost intellectuals of his era, John was ideally suited to write a Life of Thomas. The author of, among other works, the *Policraticus* and a *Life of St Anselm*, he served as a clerk in the papal court, as well as in the courts of Archbishops Theobald and Thomas of Canterbury. He became archbishop of Chartres in 1176 and died in 1180. A prolific letter-writer, he played an important role in the Becket dispute. His work is in fact a disappointment, consisting of an expanded version of a letter he wrote in the immediate aftermath of the murder.[6] The view that John's Life was written in 1173–76 and was almost entirely derivative has recently been challenged,[7] but whatever its date, John's main contribution to the hagiography is his letters, not only the one which formed the basis of his Life, but the others which contained arguments on Thomas's

5 On the relation between the Lives and their dates, see E. Walberg, *La tradition hagiographique de S Thomas Becket avant la fin du XIIe siècle* (1929), or for a more accessible summary, Barlow, pp. 1–9.

6 *LJS* no. 305, pp. 724–39.

7 Barlow, p. 4.

behalf which were later taken up by others. [5, 14]

'The Lambeth Anonymous' (Anonymous II)

One of the more curious Lives of Thomas is found in one manuscript in Lambeth Palace Library. Although the author claims to be an eyewitness in the preface, the claim is not repeated, and the Life does not suggest any familiarity with the events. Though thin on detail, the Life shows a strong grasp of the issues, and in particular their place in the canon law tradition, and it is most similar to the reflective works of William of Canterbury and Herbert of Bosham. This Life is also notable for its unusual tendency to allow criticism of Thomas. It was written 1172–73. [10, 55]

Benedict of Peterborough

Benedict was a monk of Christ Church, Canterbury who was present at the murder. He became prior of Canterbury in 1175, abbot of Peterborough in 1177, and died in 1193. He was the first custodian of Thomas's shrine, and his interviews with pilgrims formed the basis of his book of miracles. His Passio of Thomas, written 1173–74, which exists in fragmentary form, is valuable for its eyewitness account of the murder, and description of its aftermath. [52, 54]

William of Canterbury

William became a monk of Canterbury during Thomas's exile, and was ordained as deacon by the archbishop in December 1170. From June 1172 he edited existing miracles and added to them, and his collection was presented to the king in 1174. His Life, which prefaces the miracles, is the closest we have to an official Canterbury Life. Written 1173–74, it is a reflective work, learned, complex and at times pretentious. It reveals access to documentary evidence and a knowledge of canon law. His criticism of King Henry's policy in Ireland has led some to believe that William was of Irish origin. [25, 34, 43, 47, 54]

William Fitzstephen

Along with that of Herbert of Bosham, William Fitzstephen's Life is the most valuable as a work of history and a work of literature. He served as a clerk to both Thomas and Henry, and was present during many of the most dramatic moments in Thomas's life, including his murder. He had a particular interest in London affairs, as illustrated by the famous description of London which opens his book, and he made use of Gilbert Foliot's letter collection. An elegant and erudite writer, he provides a great degree of independent testimony, often with acute eyewitness detail. His account of the Council of Northampton, for example, combines great narrative and rhetorical skill. His description of Thomas's life as chancellor is invaluable, as are many of his reports of affairs in England during the exile. He wrote in 1173–74, by which time he had returned to the service of the king, thereby perhaps explaining the curious absence of any reference to William by the other biographers. His Life survived in two forms: one includes thirty-eight additional passages, many of which reflect badly on the king. [4, 7, 8, 17, 23, 28, 32, 39, 42, 45, 48, 50, 53]

Garnier of Pont-Sainte-Maxence

Garnier's work, in French verse, owes much to Edward Grim but adds some of his own detail and interpretation. Although he never met Thomas, he engaged in extensive research in the Canterbury area after the martyrdom, and interviewed, among others, Thomas's sister. He tells us that an early, inferior, version of the Life was stolen by scribes, but that his revision, completed by late 1174, is superior to all other accounts of Thomas's life. Intriguingly, he refers to an unidentified Life of Thomas written by a woman.[8] [6, 46]

Alan of Tewkesbury

Alan was an Englishman who returned to Canterbury in 1174 after a time as a canon at Benevento. He became prior of Canterbury in 1179, and abbot of Tewkesbury in 1188. He is best known for his work in editing the Becket correspondence, completed in 1176, but less attention has been paid to his Explanatio, a supplement to John of Salisbury's Life with which he prefaced the letter collection. It is especially notable for the description of the conference with the pope at Sens, and while much of the rest is rather unconvincing, it gives us an important insight into which aspects of Thomas's life still required explanation half a decade after his death. [27, 38]

'Roger of Pontigny' (Anonymous I)

Though also highly derivative from Edward Grim, this work, written 1176–77, is superior to its model, especially in terms of the clarity of the narrative. This is especially noticeable in the accounts of the dispute as it emerged in 1163 and early 1164. The author claims to have served Thomas as a clerk at Pontigny, and his identity has been linked to that of a monk called Roger who is known to have served

8 *Garnier* 141 ff.

Thomas during the archbishop's stay at that Cistercian house. Some have cast doubt on this identification, pointing to the author's meagre account of Thomas's stay at Pontigny. A possible explanation is the fact that here, as elsewhere, he is simply following the structure of Grim's life. Still, as long as conclusive proof remains lacking, inverted commas will remain around this author's name. [3, 16, 17, 24, 41]

The Lansdowne Anonymous (Anonymous III)

This is the name given to three distinct fragmentary tracts found in the Lansdowne MS 398 in the British Museum. The most interesting is the third, which provides an account not found elsewhere of the aftermath to Thomas's murder. [56, 57]

Summa Causae inter regem et Thomam

This anonymous work gives an account of the early phases of the dispute between king and archbishop, from the Council at Westminster in October 1163 to Henry's persecution of Thomas's supporters in the early aftermath of the exile. The account of Westminster is one of the most detailed among the Lives. [18]

Herbert of Bosham

Herbert's is the longest, the most complex and perhaps the most rewarding of the Lives. He was Thomas's clerk as chancellor and remained with him when he became archbishop. He was at his master's side throughout the exile and was present at all the major councils and conferences, but, to his great regret, he was sent to France on business just before Thomas's murder. Herbert was on more intimate terms with Thomas than any of the other biographers, and we find many examples of the disciple giving advice, usually very extreme, to the archbishop. He had spent his formative years in Paris where he became an accomplished theologian, and he applied these skills to the story of Thomas's life and death, which he approached in the manner of an exegete. His Life, which was not completed until 1184–86, is self-consciously a 'Gospel according to Herbert', indeed he follows John the Evangelist in describing himself as 'the disciple who wrote these things'. Many have found his theological digressions tedious and irrelevant, but closer inspection shows them to be an integral part of his work. Herbert's Life is an invaluable historical source, but it is also the work of a highly original artist. [9, 12, 15, 21, 26, 29, 31, 33, 36, 37, 40, 44, 49]

The Icelandic Saga

The extant version of the Saga was not written until the fourteenth century, but it is based on earlier sources: a lost Life by Robert of Cricklade, written 1173–74, a Life in French verse by Benet of St Albans, largely derivative of Robert of Cricklade, and an Icelandic translation of the *Quadrilogus*, a composite Life based on twelfth-century biographers. It provides some unique details, for instance that Thomas spoke with a stammer.

The road to Canterbury (?1118–62)

Both medieval and modern commentators have tended to take more interest in Thomas of Canterbury than in Thomas of London. Then and now, more information has been available for the eight years when Thomas was archbishop than for the forty-four or so that preceded them, and those eight years have appeared to hold more for those who sought either proofs of sanctity or material for research. But although the years up to 1162 are usually presented as a prelude to the drama that followed, they contain much of colour and significance, and are essential to an understanding of Thomas's later life. The rise of this London merchant's son to one of the most important positions in the governance of the Angevin Empire is in itself a remarkable story of talent, ambition and patronage, and affords a valuable insight into the changing face of England in the middle of the twelfth century. Many of Thomas's abiding character traits are evident early on, and later events were often shaped by the nature of Thomas's background and training, and his friendship with King Henry. Furthermore, Thomas's early life was controversial: it formed the basis of much subsequent criticism, and led his biographers to develop the notion of a 'conversion' of 1162.

Thomas was born on 21 December, probably in 1118, the son of Gilbert Becket, a prosperous London merchant, and his wife Matilda. Of his youth we know little. His biographers describe it in terms found in many works of hagiography: omens of greatness surrounded his birth [1], his early years were distinguished by divine intervention, and saw the emergence of appropriate virtues [3]. We know that he was educated at the Augustinian priory of Merton, and then at a grammar school in London, possibly St Paul's.[9] Also reported is a

9 *MTB* 3. 14.

spell of study at Paris in the mid–1130s, the days of Abelard, Peter Lombard and Robert of Melun [2], but there is no evidence to suggest that Thomas was a great scholar. He had practical aptitude in abundance, though. His first opportunity to apply these talents came around the age of twenty-one when he entered upon a career as an accountant in the household of a London financier, Osbert Huitdeniers. Two or three years later he took his first steps towards a career in the Church when he was introduced to Archbishop Theobald of Canterbury, apparently made quite an impression, and became his clerk. In this distinguished household, which contained many future bishops, Thomas quickly rose to prominence. He was close to Theobald, and was his only companion when in 1148 the archbishop secretly made his way to the Council of Rheims against the orders of King Stephen. He studied law at Bologna and Auxerre, according to Fitzstephen,[10] and he won many preferments, culminating in October 1154 when he became archdeacon of Canterbury. However, Thomas's ability to make enemies as well as friends was apparent early on. His biographers report how he attracted the hatred of some in Theobald's court, most notably Roger of Pont-l'Evêque, future archbishop of York and arch-enemy of Thomas [3].

Thomas's advancement progressed against a turbulent political background: the 'anarchy' of Stephen's reign, the accession of Henry II and the consolidation of his rule. Stephen's reign (1135–54) saw a reversal in the expansionist and centralising tendencies of Anglo-Norman kingship. The challenge to his crown from Matilda, daughter of Henry I, her husband Geoffrey count of Anjou, and Robert earl of Gloucester, and Stephen's inability to assert his authority, led to civil war and general disorder in England, the loss of the king's continental possessions, and in certain spheres a greater independence from the crown for the nobility and the Church. In the late 1140s the focus of opposition to Stephen shifted to Henry, son of Geoffrey and Matilda, and duke of Normandy from 1149. The death of Stephen's son and heir, Eustace, in 1153 provided an opportunity for the nobles and clergy of the realm to negotiate a peaceful succession, and under the terms of the Treaty of Winchester Stephen was allowed to retain his crown, but was to be succeeded by Henry on his death. Stephen died in 1154 and Henry smoothly acceded to a war-weary kingdom. From the start Henry made clear his intention to restore the kingdom, and royal power, to the position in which it had stood at the death of his grandfather Henry I. Young, energetic and able, he quickly began to reverse the recent decline in royal esteem by destroying illegally-held castles, expelling mercenaries, restoring law and order and beginning the re-establishment of governmental institutions which had lapsed under Stephen. But he also managed to conciliate the most powerful groups within the kingdom.

As an aid to smooth transition he appointed Richard de Lucy, a former administrator in Stephen's government, as royal justiciar, but balanced him with a powerful representative of the nobility, Robert de Beaumont, earl of Leicester, as co-justiciar. And, for his third major appointment he looked to the Church, where he found Thomas.

Thomas was appointed royal chancellor very shortly after Henry's accession, probably at Christmas 1154. The chancellor was one of the most important of the king's servants, being responsible for the royal chapel and writing office, and often acting on the king's behalf. Our best witness to Thomas's chancellorship, William Fitzstephen, provides a detailed account of his duties and way of life [4]. Particularly striking is his description of the chancellor's flamboyant embassy to the French king in 1158 and his role in the siege of Toulouse the following year and subsequent military operations [7]. He also describes the close friendship between the king and his chancellor, sixteen years his senior: 'Never in Christian times', he writes, 'were there two greater friends, more of one mind' [4]. Understandably, this image of Thomas as the king's servant and friend posed problems for those who later sought to present him as the champion of the Church, and provided ammunition for his critics within the Church. As chancellor Thomas was guilty of administering ecclesiastical revenues during vacancies, of imposing a heavy financial burden on the Church for the support of the Toulouse campaign, and in some cases openly supporting the king's authority over that of the Church. Nor did Thomas's extravagant display, his military prowess or his immersion in the ways of the royal court appear to accord with the life of a supposedly saintly prelate. The biographers do not hide Thomas's service to the king, nor the luxury of his life, but claim that behind this worldly exterior a true religious purpose was present. They claim that Thomas worked to restrain the king's more aggressive tendencies towards the Church [5], and in private led a life of chastity and austerity [6]. As many of them put it, while he may have appeared proud and vain on the outside, 'within, all was different'. Through his experience in the secular world, they argue, he developed the skills which he would apply to greater advantage as archbishop, and in the

office of chancellor he laid the foundations of the spiritual purpose
which flourished after his consecration as archbishop.

When Theobald died in April 1161, Thomas was an obvious candidate
to succeed him, but by no means proved an immediate replacement.
Henry had had ample time to decide on a successor during Theobald's
prolonged illness, but he kept the see vacant for a year while Thomas
administered its revenues. The first we read of Thomas's candidacy is
in William Fitzstephen's report of a conversation between the chancellor and the prior of Leicester, who predicts that Thomas will soon
be archbishop [8]. Confirmation apparently came in May 1162 when
the king took him aside and informed him of his intention [9]. Thomas
immediately resisted the honour, citing his unsuitability for the task
and the danger of losing the king's friendship, but eventually capitulated in deference to his duty towards the Church [9, 10]. In medieval
writing it is difficult to find an appointment to high ecclesiastical
office which was not resisted by its recipient, and Thomas's reported
reluctance should not be taken at face value. Still, one can see why
such a proposal might be greeted with trepidation. As a clerk
appointed to a monastic cathedral, a royal courtier appointed to the
highest Church office in the land could not only expect the oppro-
brium of the king, should he fail to follow the royal will, but also the
mistrust of his monastic community and episcopal colleagues. The
accounts of Thomas's election on 23 May suggest that such suspicion
made itself known early on, with Gilbert Foliot, then bishop of Hereford and later bishop of London, openly voicing dissent, while others
muttered their reservations [11]. Equally instructive is Herbert of
Bosham's claim that immediately after the election, Thomas asked
him to monitor not only his behaviour, but what others said about
him [12].

We are told that as soon as Thomas was consecrated as archbishop,
he underwent a dramatic transformation. 'Touched by the hand of God',
he 'put off the old man and put on the new', taking on a new spiritu-
ality, symbolised by his secret adoption of the monastic garb and a
hairshirt, and being imbued with new zeal for ecclesiastical liberty
[13, 14]. The year 1162 is clearly a watershed in Thomas's life, but
the biographers' explanation of the difference in the archbishop's subsequent behaviour in terms of a dramatic conversion has been
received sceptically by modern writers, who have tended to see it as a
hagiographical flourish inconsistent with the evidence. Thomas, they
argue, did not change from Saul to Paul, as his earlier life was never

excessively sinful and his later life not always virtuous.[11] However, a
closer look at what the biographers say suggests that they do not make
such a claim for Thomas: his was not a Pauline conversion, but rather
a catalyst by which he was enabled to achieve more fully the potential
which had always been there. Nor is it an isolated claim: the idea of
ongoing conversion is integrated into the Lives, most notably after
Clarendon, during his stay at Pontigny in exile, and culminating in
his martyrdom.[12] Even if we do not accept the explanation of conversion, it is clear that some change happened. The most widely accepted
interpretation is that Thomas was an actor who capably and enthusi-
astically fitted into whatever role presented itself.[13] Such an interpretation seems fair, but it should not be so surprising that Thomas should
change his approach to the king, to the Church and to his own life. As
Herbert of Bosham points out, even holy men – not only Paul, but
David and Peter – change. Inconsistency is a normal human trait,
even if hagiographers do not often allow it to their subjects. It is just
that perhaps Thomas changed more, and more often, than most.

Conflict with the king (1162–64)

Thomas's establishment as archbishop led to a crisis of unprecedented
severity between the crown and the Church in England. The break-
down of relations was the product of tensions between an acquisitive
and energetic royal power and a confident post-Gregorian Church
which had been emerging for a century, but it was driven by the robust
personalities of Henry and Thomas. Between 1162 and 1164 the conflict took shape primarily as a dispute over jurisdiction, and although the
points of contention during this period came to be complicated and
augmented over the years, they were never properly resolved during
Thomas's lifetime, and remained at the heart of the dispute. Though
partisan, the biographers are excellent witnesses to the emergent dispute. They not only provide vivid eyewitness accounts of many of the
episodes in which the dispute was played out – most notably in William
Fitzstephen's description of the Council of Northampton [23] – but also
reveal an incisive appreciation of the significance of the issues at stake.

11 See, for example, D. Knowles, 'Thomas Becket: a Character Study', in *The Historian
and Character and Other Essays* (Cambridge, 1963), pp. 98–128, esp. p. 100.

12 For a fuller exposition of this argument see M. Staunton, 'Thomas Becket's
Conversion', *Anglo-Norman Studies*, 21 (1999), 193–211.

13 See Z. N. Brooke, *The English Church and the Papacy* (Cambridge, 1931), pp. 193–4.

The dispute took time to emerge. Those biographers – a large majority – who present it as an immediate consequence of Thomas's appointment, pass over his co-operation with the king which marked his first year as archbishop and was found even in his second. Herbert of Bosham, in contrast, lays stress on the early concord so as to make the descent into animosity all the more dramatic [15]. He describes how, on the king's return to England in January 1163, he was so gladdened by his first sight of Thomas as archbishop, that he paid more attention to him than to his own son. In the following months Thomas was often involved in the king's affairs until May when he departed for the papal council at Tours with the king's blessing. Herbert also cites their joint role in the translation of Edward the Confessor and the dedication of Reading Abbey. However, Herbert neglects to mention that the first occurred in October 1163 and the second in April 1164. In fact, the idea of a phase of peace which was then suddenly shattered is as misleading as the picture of a conflict erupting immediately upon Thomas's consecration. The evidence shows that co-operation and contention coexisted from the start until rising contention made further co-operation first difficult and then impossible.

Within weeks of his accession to Canterbury, to the king's surprise, Thomas declared his independence by resigning the office of chancellor. Further proof that he meant to take seriously his duties as archbishop came when he began to reclaim lands and rights which he believed had been unfairly given or taken away from Canterbury [15]. These disputes not only served to make enemies of some powerful nobles, but eventually embroiled their lord, the king. In July 1163 a direct confrontation arose between king and archbishop when Henry attempted to claim for his exchequer the revenues traditionally paid by the Church for the support of his local officials. Thomas refused to accept this new practice and the king resentfully backed down [16]. Around the same time Henry demanded Thomas go back on his excommunication of William of Eynsford, a powerful landholder who had expelled some clerks who had recently been intruded into his parish church, and this time it was the king who prevailed [17]. A case with more far-reaching consequences was that of Philip de Broi, a canon of Bedford who had been accused of killing a certain knight. As a clerk, he was tried by an ecclesiastical court which freed him. When a lay justice attempted to reopen the case, Philip verbally abused him. The justice complained to the king, and Philip was brought before a group of bishops and nobles who imposed a mild sentence for his

insult to the judge, but did not convict him on the charge of murder
[16]. The case of Philip de Broi focused attention on the issue of
'criminal clerks' – the trial and punishment of churchmen guilty of
serious offences. Enraged by this and other cases [17], Henry called
a general council of the Church to be held at Westminster in October
1163.

It was at Westminster that the dispute began to take on a definite
form [18]. Henry first demanded that clerks convicted of serious
crimes be deprived of the Church's protection and handed over to the
secular power. When the bishops, led by Thomas, rejected Henry's
demand, citing the distinctive nature of the clergy, the king adopted a
different approach. He now demanded a general observance of his
royal customs, that is, the rights which he believed his predecessors
had held. After discussion with the bishops, Thomas declared that he
would observe the king's customs, but only 'saving his order', that is,
where they did not conflict with the law of the Church. Henry left the
council in a rage, and a meeting between king and archbishop at
Northampton shortly afterwards did nothing to repair relations [19].
Up to now the bishops had stood firm behind Thomas, but during the
autumn of 1163 Roger of York, Gilbert of London and Hilary of
Chichester began to qualify their support. Finally, after papal pressure,
Thomas agreed to remove the qualification to his observance of the
royal customs at a private meeting with Henry. But the king demanded
this be done publicly, and to this end called a council of the realm to
meet at Clarendon in January 1164. The accounts of this important
episode do not give us a full picture, but the following details may be
made out. Henry demanded a full public acknowledgement of the
customs, to which Thomas and the bishops were eventually persuaded.
Then, to the surprise of the bishops, Henry demanded that the specific
customs of the realm be enunciated and written down in a document
[20], to which the bishops were to affix their seals as sign of recognition. At first Thomas refused, then gave a verbal recognition, but did
not affix his seal [19]. This was the worst of all worlds. By his refusal
to give full assent Thomas had managed to alienate the king, and at
the same time, by failing to stand up for the Church he had lost the
confidence of his episcopal colleagues. This was Thomas's lowest point,
an episode which John of Salisbury would later describe as 'a single
fall'.[14] In penance, Thomas suspended himself from service at the altar
until he received absolution from the pope [21].

14 *LJS* no. 305, pp. 726–7.

After Clarendon, relations between king and archbishop were decidedly cool. At one point, Thomas is said to have come to visit the king at Woodstock only to have the gates slammed in his face. In late summer Thomas tried to flee the country, but bad weather forced his boat back to England [22]. For his biographers this was a sign from God that he had yet to be tried and proven in England. The Council of Northampton in October 1164 [23] was a trial in every sense of the word. It began as a judicial procedure through which the king hoped to humiliate the archbishop, but as it progressed, Thomas succeeded in presenting it as an act of endurance on behalf of Christ and the Church, a battle for righteousness in the mould of the trials of the apostles and the early Christian martyrs. When a knight called John FitzGilbert claimed that he had not received justice in the archbishop's court on a land plea, Thomas was summoned to the king's court, but did not turn up. Consequently he was summoned to a royal council, to be judged by the lay and ecclesiastical magnates on a charge of contempt to the king. Thomas was quickly found guilty, but Henry pressed on, accusing him of embezzlement during his time as chancellor. Thomas replied that he had not been summoned to hear that charge. There followed two days of debate and negotiation, with the clergy passing between king and archbishop. On the sixth day, as threats and tension rose, the archbishop fell ill, but on the next day he rose from his bed for one of the most dramatic days of his life. In the morning he celebrated the Mass of St Stephen, the first Christian martyr, with its introit, 'For princes did also sit and speak against me', and then proceeded to court carrying his cross before him. In the presence of the bishops and nobles he announced that he had appealed to the pope against the bishops, prohibiting them from judging him on any secular charge. The bishops, finding themselves 'between hammer and anvil', unwilling to refuse the king's command that they pronounce judgement, but also unable to go against Thomas's prohibition, in turn appealed to the pope's judgement. The king then excused the bishops from partaking in the judgement but continued to press the lay magnates to give sentence. Thomas, however, refused to hear sentence, and stormed out of the castle to jeers and curses. He and his men hurriedly mounted their horses and hastened to their lodgings. A few hours later Thomas took to flight.

Thomas's biographers lay the blame for the dispute at Henry's door. He, they claim, led astray by bad counsel, embarked upon a 'design against the Church' which would have succeeded in its purpose had Thomas not stood up for ecclesiastical liberties. Henry's insistence on the customs of his grandfather are certainly at the heart of the dispute, but did this constitute a 'design against the Church'? It is important to realise that Henry's policy towards the Church was part of a wider approach to government. In his coronation charter Henry declares, 'For the honour of God and Holy Church, and for the common restoration of my whole realm, I have granted and restored ... to God and Holy Church, to all my earls, barons and vassals, all concessions, gifts, privileges, and free customs, which King Henry my grandfather granted and conceded to them. Likewise all evil customs which he abolished and mitigated, I also grant to be mitigated and abolished in my name and in that of my heirs'. A similar determination to return to the situation that pertained under his grandfather, before the unfortunate interlude of Stephen's reign, may be found in countless other charters of the period. It was also made clear by his early actions in destroying adulterine castles, expelling Flemish mercenaries, and restoring such institutions as the exchequer. But to turn back the clock, Henry needed to be innovative: his purpose may have been conservative, but his method was radical. Over the following years, the extent of Henry's reforming programme became clear in such measures as the establishment of possessory assizes and itinerant justices, the Assizes of Clarendon in 1166 and Northampton in 1176, and the Inquest of the Sheriffs in 1171. The Constitutions of Clarendon are part of the same process, but their implementation proved far more problematic.

The most controversial clauses of the Constitutions deal with two issues: criminous clerks, and contact with the pope. In both of these areas the Church had gained substantial licence during the reign of Stephen, and was unlikely to give up its liberties without a fight. The Church's independence of action towards criminous clerks may have been a product of Stephen's lax rule, but it is doubtful whether any monarch in Latin Christendom could have held back the expansion of papal jurisdiction. The second problem is that Henry's response to these issues was characteristically wide-ranging and inventive. He did not simply demand a broad recognition of his rights concerning the Church, but specified them, and had them written down. The Constitutions are part of a general formalisation of relationships in Anglo-Norman England, standing between Domesday Book and Magna Carta. Herbert of Bosham, for one, quickly realised the novelty and the potential danger of having formerly unwritten customs put down in writing [32], but in doing so Henry was in tune with the prevailing trend. Henry faced a further problem in that he was dealing with someone who saw the Constitutions not in their individual terms, but as part of a general attack upon the Church, and who was prepared to defend his position. Thomas's action in carrying his cross before him at Northampton was a clear declaration of intent. Thomas has been accused of behaving 'as if the Investiture Contest had never been settled'.[15] This is true: he regarded the Church's relationship with the king in a similar way to the reformers of the previous century. But it is also true that while the Investiture Contest had formally ended in compromise, its central issues had never been settled, and instead continued to be played out in different ways over the next centuries, culminating in the Reformation. The Becket dispute emerged along the fault-lines that the Investiture Contest had opened up.

Exile (1164–66)

Thomas's flight and prolonged exile moved the dispute onto a new plane. His action in slipping away from Northampton and making his way across the sea, and Henry's reaction to this, exacerbated the existing crisis. More than this, the archbishop's prolonged absence abroad, and the involvement of other parties, meant that the dispute could never again be a domestic conflict. When Thomas set sail from the port of Eastry in Kent on 30 November 1164, he violated one of the most important of the Constitutions of Clarendon: that a cleric should not leave the realm without the king's permission. In Henry's eyes he had forfeited his position as archbishop: he was now 'Thomas, formerly archbishop of Canterbury'. Thomas and Henry, once so close, did not meet face to face for five years. The exile also served to alienate many among the English clergy, who found themselves without the protection of their leader, and began to regard their absent archbishop as the head of a dangerous and unrepresentative faction. The exile did not only move the participants apart, but also drew other parties into the dispute. Most important in this respect were King Louis VII of France and Pope Alexander III, who found themselves entangled in Thomas's affairs for the next six years.

Thomas's murder made it easier for his biographers to claim that he fled in 1164 because his life was in danger, but this is hard to believe. Had Thomas returned to Canterbury, it is unlikely that he would have faced death, but he might have faced ruin. At the very least, the

15 Warren, p. 514.

essential rapport between archbishop and king had broken down, and there was little prospect of its recovery. This was the reason why Thomas's predecessor Anselm had left England during the reign of William Rufus in 1097, and that is the most likely explanation for Thomas's action in 1164. To flee the country would allow him the opportunity to regroup and win new allies away from the pressures of the English crown, nobility and clergy. For those he left behind, however, it was – as it had been to Anselm's monastic community and episcopal colleagues – an act of cowardice and irresponsibility. Gilbert Foliot said of Thomas's flight, 'The wicked man flees when no one is pursuing'. It appeared that he had abandoned them and the Church to danger, just as the mercenary abandons his flock when he sees the wolf coming. Thomas's biographers were at pains to present it otherwise: as an act which advanced the cause of his Church, and a pilgrimage which continued his spiritual perfection [25].

Hours after the conclusion of the Council of Northampton, Thomas made plans to escape. In the dead of night he slipped away from his lodgings at the monastery of St Andrew accompanied by three loyal companions [24]. He took the least obvious route, first making his way north to Lincoln before doubling back and heading south towards Kent, travelling by night and hiding by day. On 30 November he sailed from Eastry in a small boat and landed at the port of Gravelines in Flanders. From there he continued his furtive progress until he reached the monastery of St Bertin's at St-Omer. There he met Herbert of Bosham, whom Thomas had earlier despatched to Canterbury to retrieve what resources he could find. Meanwhile, the royal party had been quick to respond. Leaving Thomas's property untouched for the moment, Henry sent a distinguished mission to King Louis and Pope Alexander [26].

Louis and Alexander were natural allies of Thomas, but circumstances made any support for him problematic. The main threat to Louis's position came from Henry II. When Louis divorced Eleanor of Aquitaine in 1152, she promptly married Henry, thereby adding extensive southern territories to the lands which Geoffrey of Anjou had amassed in the north-west of France. Henry held his French lands as a vassal of Louis, but he was the far more powerful monarch. Their relationship was a complex one, characterised by uneasy peace, and some co-operation, punctuated by outright conflict. Henry's problems with Thomas were usually an asset to Louis, but at times the archbishop stood in the way of his plans for co-operation with Henry.

Still, Louis was in the main very supportive towards Thomas, and the biographers frequently include eulogies to the French kingdom.

Alexander was in a more difficult position. A distinguished canonist and a reforming pope, he might have been expected to back Thomas, but in the circumstances it is surprising that he supported him so much. A schism emerged after the death of Adrian IV in 1159, when Roland Bandinelli's election as Alexander III was challenged by the election of Octavian of St Cecilia as Victor IV by a party close to Emperor Frederick Barbarossa. Alexander refused to submit his election to imperial judgement and was forced to flee into exile in France, where he depended on the support of both Louis and Henry. His cardinals were in general far more concerned about retaining Henry's favour. Throughout the dispute, Alexander walked a clever middle path, upholding Thomas's claims but limiting his actions, staying amenable to Henry but still applying pressure for a settlement. From 1165 onwards, when he was able to return to Italy, he was tireless in his efforts for peace, and after Thomas's death he succeeded in bringing about a lasting reconciliation. He can be accused of duplicity on occasions, but in the circumstances it was often necessary. Alexander is one of the few people who come out of the dispute with any credit.

During the month of November 1164, both sides approached Louis and Alexander, carefully avoiding each other. The French king rebuffed the royal party, but offered support to the exiles [26]. Henry's envoys were equally unsuccessful in their audience with Alexander at Sens, when the usually eloquent Gilbert of London and Hilary of Chichester stumbled over their words and were humiliated by the pope, a scene which the biographers present as a divinely inspired proof of their mendacity. A few days later, Thomas had an audience at Sens, where he produced the royal customs, and dramatically resigned his office before the pope. Alexander's response was typically even-handed: he restored Thomas to his office, and commended his efforts on behalf of the Church, but also, in an effort to defuse the dispute, sent Thomas to live in simplicity safely out of the way in the Cistercian monastery of Pontigny [27]. Pontigny marked a great change for Thomas. It is depicted as an opportunity for him to make up for lost time, a perfection of the 'conversion' of 1162, and a central part in his 'pilgrimage', which began with his flight from Northampton and culminated in his martyrdom. He who had lived amidst the splendour and activity of the court now turned himself to prayer, learning and acts of asceticism. This period, between late 1164 and spring 1166, is also characterised as a time of preparation for the future, a training-school for the battle ahead [29, 30].

Henry was quick to retaliate against Thomas. When he learned of the failure of his mission to Louis and Alexander, he set about depriving the archbishop and his clerks of their possessions and revenues, which he entrusted to his own men, and he expelled from the country not only Thomas's clerks and supporters but also his relatives, including women and children [28]. For a time, Thomas was powerless to respond to these measures. He was unsuccessful in efforts both to win new support and to arrange for a conference with the king. And, in the summer of 1165, fearful of Henry's contacts with the Imperial party, Alexander restrained Thomas from any action against the king, at least until the following Easter. But, on Easter Sunday, 24 April 1166, the pendulum swung back in Thomas's favour, when Alexander appointed him papal legate within the province of Canterbury, an office which, crucially, conferred the power of ecclesiastical censure. Thomas wasted little time in putting his new power to use. First he sent three letters 'of mounting severity' to the king [31], and then, at Vézelay on 12 June, he pronounced sentence of excommunication against a number of royal officials, and against the bishop of Salisbury, but spared the king [33]. The king responded immediately by constrain-ing his bishops to appeal to the pope against the censures [34]. Then he threatened the Cistercian order with expulsion from his realm should they continue to shelter Thomas. The archbishop took his leave of the monks of Pontigny and made his way to his new home at St Columba's, Sens [35].

The Vézelay censures brought Thomas's critics out into the open. Since the Council of Northampton it had been clear that this was more than a dispute about the royal customs, and the exile gave it new dimensions. Thomas's flight made him the estranged enemy of the king, and his prolonged absence extended the chasm which had already opened up between him and the English Church. Another consequence of the exile was that it affected a range of individuals more profoundly. The seizure of Thomas's property and the expulsion of his kindred brought the message home that this was not just a dispute between king and archbishop over abstract issues. Those, such as the de Broc family entrusted with Canterbury property, now had a stake in keeping the dispute going, as became clear on Thomas's return in 1170. Those censured at Vézelay, and those who felt under threat from similar measures, all became more personally involved. With more people involved, with less to lose than before, opinions became more polarised. Both sides now began to make sophisticated statements of their positions in the polemical letters of 1166. Thomas, in his letters 'of mounting severity' had set out his argument in favour of standing up for the Church at the appropriate time. His critics, Gilbert Foliot in particular, responded, not with a defence of Henry, but with a critique of Thomas's manner of resisting them. The central question was now 'How ought an archbishop to act', and the focus was on Thomas. His time of rest and preparation was very much at an end.

Diplomacy and discord (1167–70)

The period between Thomas's expulsion from Pontigny and his return to Canterbury is the most complex of the whole dispute. First, there was simply so much happening. In each of these years the pope sent a mission to attempt to bring about a reconciliation. These missions progressed against a background of continued excommunications and suspensions by Thomas. Such measures tended to be followed by appeals from those anathemised, the quashing and renewal of the censures, and the suspension and restoration of Thomas's power of excommunication. Through diplomacy and threat, the two parties were repeatedly brought to conferences, and that is apart from the countless low-level negotiations carried out through intermediaries. Even if we had a single, full, detailed narrative, the events would be difficult to disentangle. We have many letters from the period, but the sequence of events is not always easy to follow, not least because of the delay in communication with the pope, who had returned to Italy in 1165. The Lives do not provide an adequate narrative either, though we have excellent testimony to the main events from William Fitz-stephen and Herbert of Bosham. A further problem with this period is that its concerns were not resolved. Much of the reason why this phase of the dispute has attracted less attention than it deserves is that one afternoon in December 1170 imposed a conclusion which all these intensive efforts failed to achieve. This does not make 1167–70 irrelevant: rather, it tells us much about what the various parties wanted, why the dispute proved so intractable, and why it should come to conclude in such a dramatic way. It also allows us to see the dispute at its most mature and complex, before Thomas's murder gave it a spurious simplicity.

Pope Alexander was the driving force behind the activity of this period. His aim was to bring the two sides together through the agency of envoys to negotiate a settlement, and he attempted to enforce such a settlement by threatening censures through Thomas, but frequently suspending his power to allow time for negotiation. Regarding Thomas's power of censure, a pattern quickly developed: Thomas would excommunicate or suspend enemies of the Church; the recipients of these censures would appeal; the pope might confirm the censures; alternatively, he might ask Thomas to suspend them, or he might restrain the archbishop from further action for a fixed term, during which time a reconciliation would be made; as soon as such a deadline passed without a reconciliation being effected, and the restraint on Thomas was lifted, he would renew his earlier censures or issue new ones. Two factors further complicated this situation. First, the distances involved meant that it took a long time for news of censures or appeals against them to reach the pope, and a longer time to hear the pope's reaction. Second, appeals against censures were often made *before* the censures were passed. This form of anticipatory appeal, called the appeal *ad cautelam*,[16] contributed to the convoluted chess-game in which each participant needed to predict the actions of their opponents. The pope bestowed legatine powers on Thomas in the hope that this would bring pressure to bear on the king. It did so, to some degree, but the frequent excommunications also succeeded in bringing more people into the dispute, and complicating the issues further.

From 1166 onwards, each side in the dispute repeatedly sent envoys to plead their case before the pope. Alexander's response was to send missions with full powers, in the hope of bringing about a reconciliation. He sent a separate mission in each of the four years leading up to Thomas's death, and a further mission thereafter. The usual approach was to have one envoy sympathetic to each side, a policy which may have been even-handed, but was hardly likely to ensure success. The first of these missions was that of Cardinals William of Pavia and Otto, who arrived in northern France in the autumn of 1167. They succeeded in arranging the first of many peace conferences, between the castles of Gisors and Trie, on 18 November 1167 [**36**]. In the event, neither side was willing to put much on the table. The cardinals assured Thomas that the king, who was not present, would allow him to return to his see, and the customs could be understood to have

16 The development of this form of appeal is discussed by Morey and Brooke, pp. 162–6.

been abandoned, as long as Thomas did not demand from him a formal renunciation of the Constitutions. The archbishop's party, however, mistrustful of the cardinals, was not prepared to pass over the customs, and they also insisted on the restoration of Canterbury property. The conference broke up, and the cardinals returned to Rome shortly afterwards. The reaction of the English bishops to the failure of the conference was to renew their appeals against the Vézelay censures, which Thomas chose to ignore.

Early in 1168 both sides sent new embassies to the pope. Thomas had been suspended from taking any new offensive action, but in May 1168 Alexander put pressure on Henry by limiting the suspension of Thomas's legation until 5 March 1169. His next mission, consisting of three distinguished monks, Simon, Bernard and Englebert, succeeded in bringing Thomas and Henry face to face for the first time in five years, in the presence of King Louis of France, at the Conference of Montmirail on 6 January 1169 [37]. There Thomas sustained considerable pressure from the 'great and numerous' mediators, to submit himself fully to the royal will in return for a restoration to his see. The stumbling block was Thomas's insistence on qualifying his submission with the words 'Saving God's honour', an echo of his insistence on the phrase 'Saving our order' which had caused deadlock at Westminster in 1163. Thomas's refusal to budge from this proviso infuriated not only Henry, but Louis, who had just secured a peace deal with the king of England [38]. He also alienated many of his own household, including one who mockingly called on him to overtake him with his horse, 'Saving God's honour'.

At the end of February 1169, the pope announced another mission, this time in the form of two officials of his household, Gratian and Vivian. The term of Thomas's suspension lapsed on 5 March, and in April and May he issued new excommunications, most notably that of Gilbert Foliot [39]. These were soon suspended by the pope, but during the summer and autumn of that year, pressure mounted on Henry, as Gratian and Vivian signalled to Thomas that he would be free to renew them if peace were not made by 29 September. As soon as he was able, Thomas renewed the sentences of earlier that year, and added some more. On 18 November at Montmartre, king and archbishop came together once again. Here Henry gave further concessions than ever before: he granted the archbishop's restoration to Canterbury, abandoned all evil customs, at least implicitly, did not demand any submission from Thomas, and promised not to usurp

anything that belonged to the Church. Thomas raised the issue of
financial compensation, but was dissuaded by the French king from
pressing his point. All seemed to be settled, when Thomas asked that
the king bestow the kiss of peace on him as a sign to his followers that
he was returning to England with his blessing, knowing full well that
Henry had taken an oath never to allow him the kiss. Both parties
stood their ground, and the conference broke up in more rancour than
ever before [40]. Thomas reimposed his sentences and threatened
further measures, and the pope launched yet another peace mission.

The coronation of Henry's son as co-king [41] broke the deadlock,
though not in a way that anyone might have expected: it was the
catalyst for peace, but also for murder. Henry's intention was to avoid
the succession disputes which had dogged his predecessors by having
his son, the younger Henry, crowned during his lifetime, a solution
which had brought rewards to the Capetian kings of France, and to
use this as the basis for a division of his territories. On 14 June the
coronation was celebrated by Roger of York, Gilbert of London and
Jocelin of Salisbury, with most of the other English bishops in attendance. The reaction was outrage at the usurpation of the prerogative of
the archbishop of Canterbury. The papal envoys Rotrou of Rouen and
Bernard of Nevers immediately threatened Henry with interdict, and
brought the king to a meeting with Thomas at Fréteval on 22 July
[42]. There, Henry agreed to full restitution to the archbishop and
the Church, and although it does not seem that the kiss of peace was
either demanded or offered, he showed his deference to Thomas by
holding his stirrup as he mounted his horse. However, the peace
quickly proved hollow. The first problem was the failure of the king
and his men to observe the terms in full. While some possessions and
revenues were restored to the archbishop and his men, others were
not. Furthermore, although the king had promised to accompany
Thomas to England, or at least to send the archbishop of Rouen with
him, when Thomas got ready to leave for England, the only escort he
found was the hated John of Oxford whom he had excommunicated at
Vézelay. This related to another failure. The reason Thomas had
wished for the king as his escort, and for the kiss of peace, was so that
a clear signal could be given to the king's men, that he was returning
to Canterbury in full royal favour. The stories of threats to Thomas's
life in the later part of 1170 may be a projection back from the murder,
but it would not be surprising if there was an atmosphere of danger
with Thomas's return imminent. After all, there were many who had
much to lose by the archbishop's reconciliation and return. The final

blow to peace came from Thomas himself. Just before he set sail for
England, he sent before him letters suspending the archbishop of
York and the bishops who had been present at the coronation, and
renewing the excommunication of London and Salisbury. These
letters were to prove to be Thomas's own death warrant.

There is much that is puzzling about this phase in the conflict, not
least why there was no proper resolution. It is not as if efforts were
lacking. The pope was tireless in seeking peace, and he was aided by
King Louis and other distinguished negotiators. For a king who
wanted order and an archbishop who wanted to return to his see, it
might seem that this was the ideal time to seize the peace. But did
they actually want peace? Henry was under great pressure to bring
about a reconciliation, and he seems to have been serious in its pursuit, at least in this period, granting considerable concessions.
Thomas's party was also energetic in negotiations, but the inesca-
pable conclusion is that Thomas himself did not want peace without
victory. Still, it should also be noted that this was not an easy dispute
to resolve. By the late 1160s it had taken on a momentum of its own:
the longer it progressed, the more people and issues came to be swept
along with it, thereby making it more difficult to bring to a conclusion. One cannot say that the only possible solution was Thomas's
death, but it is difficult to see how, after all this, the parties could have
put the conflict behind them.

Martyrdom (1170–74)

Had Thomas died peacefully at an advanced age, he would have been
remembered. His brutal murder at the height of his fame made him
unforgettable. It is only by reading the graphic reports of the murder
and the reactions of those who witnessed it that we can fully appreci-
ate how shocking it was. To the people of Canterbury, the ecclesiastical
capital of one of the most powerful kingdoms in Europe, martyrs
must have seemed a thing of legend, part of more dangerous and less
civilised times. For one of the best-known men in Europe to be
murdered in his own cathedral by agents of the king was unthinkable.
So, while it may be argued that the murder and Thomas's posthumous
acclaim distract attention from the rest of Thomas's life, the extraordinary nature of these events should not be forgotten. The
biographers saw Thomas's murder as the fulfilment of his life – 'consummation' is a word frequently used – and a vindication of his deeds.

It was also seen as a new beginning, for Thomas and his supporters. The Lives are often at their best in describing the murder, its prelude and its glorious aftermath. As one might expect of such profoundly affecting and very public events, they are vividly remembered, but the accounts are also highly coloured by the biographers' search for meaning. Even more than elsewhere, informative detail sits side by side with exegetical reflection.

Thomas's return to England provoked both joy and fear: joy for many of the monks and clergy of his diocese, neglected and oppressed for seven years, and for many of the ordinary people of the locality; fear for those, such as the de Broc family, who had benefited from the dispossession of Thomas and his clerks, for those within the Church who had become enemies of the archbishop, and for the returning exiles themselves. That Thomas was returning to a highly volatile situation is clear from a letter of John of Salisbury to the abbot of St-Rémi, Rheims, written just before the murder, in which he describes 'enemy intrigues', 'fearful persecution', 'the roots of enmity more planted than ever'. Now in Canterbury, he writes, 'we await God's salvation in great danger'.[17] Thomas returned to England, just as he had left it, by trying to throw his enemies off the scent, landing at Sandwich rather than, as expected, at Dover. There he was greeted with great enthusiasm by the local people, but was soon accosted by three senior agents of the king, who demanded the absolution of the censured bishops. Thomas postponed discussions until the next day and travelled to Canterbury, where he was met with great honour. There he had a further meeting with the king's officials, accompanied by clerks of the censured bishops, but again he refused to back down [44]. Thomas's next move was to try to pay his respects to the young king. He made his way to London, where his arrival was greeted with adulation, but shortly after he received the news that the young Henry did not wish to see him, rather, that he should return to his see and not move outside it. Further disturbing signs were evident. News came to Thomas that the de Broc family had been involved in a number of outrages against him: his transport ship laden with wine had been seized, some of his sailors killed and others imprisoned; they had hunted in his park, and stolen some of his dogs; they had cut off the tail of one of Thomas's horses as an insult to the archbishop. Also, they had laid ambushes around the roads leading out of Canterbury, in case the archbishop tried to leave [45].

17 *LJS* no. 304, pp. 714-25.

Meanwhile, the censured prelates had crossed the sea to visit Henry II at Bur-le-Roi in Normandy. Henry had already learned of Thomas's latest censures, and there his famous temper erupted against Thomas, with tragic consequences: here, he said, was a man of lowly birth whom he had raised up, but not only was he ungrateful, he was prepared to kick in the teeth the man who had made him.[18] These words prompted four men, usually described as knights but in fact quite powerful barons, to plot Thomas's destruction [46]. The four, Reginald FitzUrse, Hugh de Morville, William de Tracy and Richard le Bret [47], slipped away from Bur, quickly crossed the sea, and reached Saltwood Castle, the seat of the de Brocs, on 28 December. The king also sent envoys to England, reportedly to arrest the archbishop, but perhaps also to restrain the knights [48]. Whatever the precise purpose of the mission, it was too late. By the afternoon of 29 December, the conspirators had gathered a force and were bearing down on the archbishop's palace.

The biographers present the events of December 1170 as the inevitable and predestined unfolding of Thomas's fate. This is reflected in the liturgical significance which they attach to the events: his return, it is noted, coincided with the season of advent; his entry into Canterbury is described in terms intended to echo Christ's entry into Jerusalem; his murder was on the day after the feast of the Holy Innocents; it was also one of the 'memorable Tuesdays' of his life. Martyrdom is a willingly-undertaken sacrifice, and throughout, Thomas is shown to have known of his death, and to have embraced it. As he left France for the last time, he was warned of the impending danger, but declared his intention to go on [43]. As he entered Canterbury cathedral in triumph, his face was said to appear as if it was on fire [44], a common description of the early Christian martyrs as they enter the amphitheatre. As he entered London, a 'shameless and prattling woman' predicted his death [45]. And as the provocations of the de Brocs and others mounted, Thomas readied himself for death. His last great public act was on Christmas Day, when he ascended the altar and predicted his death to the people, before announcing new anathemas against the enemies of the Church. Then he sent some of his clerks away on business, including Herbert of Bosham, who never ceased to regret missing the martyrdom [49].

Thomas's murder is one of the best documented events of the middle ages. It was witnessed by many people, and at least five of those

18 There is no record of the king saying 'Who will rid me of this turbulent priest?'

present – Edward Grim, John of Salisbury, William of Canterbury, William Fitzstephen and Benedict of Peterborough – wrote reports [51]. There are some discrepancies about details, and there are hagiographical glosses, but there is also a great deal of agreement, and, one suspects, accuracy. Even the rather inelegant, stop–start nature of the narratives suggest truthfulness: if a writer wanted to present a neat, rhetorical account, this was not the way to do it.

In the late afternoon of 29 December, Thomas had finished dining with his household and had withdrawn to an inner room when the knights entered the palace and demanded to see him. Thomas received them coldly, and they addressed him aggressively, accusing him of wanting to dispossess the young king of his crown, and demanding the absolution of the censured prelates. Thomas declared his loyalty to the young king, but asserted that the sentences were not his, but the pope's, to annul. Angered by this response, the knights inveighed against Thomas for not bowing to royal majesty, to which the archbishop responded that no one could escape ecclesiastical censure if they violated the rights of the Church. 'You have spoken in danger of your head', the knights threatened, and they went out to arm themselves. The terrified monks urged the archbishop to flee to the church, but according to the biographers, he was so constant in his wish for martyrdom that he had to be dragged there. They entered the church as the other monks were singing vespers, and were quickly followed by the knights, now fully armed and covered apart from their eyes, causing many to hide themselves in fear. The knights called out to the archbishop, and again demanded that he absolve the censured prelates. When he refused, the knights grabbed him, trying to drag him out of the church, but Thomas fought back. It was at this point that the first blow was struck, probably by FitzUrse, which not only struck the top of the archbishop's head, but also wounded the clerk Edward Grim in the arm. De Tracy, it seems, struck a second and a third blow, prostrating Thomas on the pavement, and he was followed by Le Bret, who struck out so hard that his sword was dashed against the stones. The final indignity was inflicted by Hugh 'Mauclerk' of Horsea, not one of the knights but a clerk in attendance, who put his foot on the neck of the archbishop, as he lay on the ground, and scattered his brains over the floor of the cathedral.

For Thomas's biographers, this was not just a dramatic and terrible event but an echo of Christ's passion and that of other martyrs, and a commentary on Thomas's whole life. The final meal was akin to the

Last Supper; Thomas's constancy in the face of death was like that of
the martyrs of the early Church; like Jesus he asked the murderers to
spare his people; his last words echoed those of Jesus and associated
him with other martyrs; the five blows which killed him paralleled the
five wounds of Christ; and the subsequent plunder of his belongings
recalled the division of Christ's clothes. The murder was the culmina-
tion of Thomas's 'conversion' and 'pilgrimage': whereas once the
appropriate course was to flee, now, he realised, was the time to lay
down his life for the sheep; by warding off his attackers from his
people he proved a true shepherd of the sheep; and though he showed
himself ready to die, he spoke as boldly in resisting the knights'
demands as he had throughout his archiepiscopate in standing up to
the enemies of the Church. When the knights had left, as many of the
biographers note, the pavement of the cathedral was coloured by the
intermingled red of the archbishop's blood and the white of his brains,
the colours of the martyr and the confessor, representing the perfect
fusion of Thomas's violent death and righteous life.

Still, the man who lay dead on the floor of Canterbury Cathedral
had some way to go before he became the wonder-worker who
brought glory on his church. The first reactions to his murder were
not veneration but shock and fear. The man who had endangered
Canterbury during his life now seemed likely to destroy it in death.
Expecting reprisals from the de Broc family, the monks buried the
body of the archbishop hurriedly and with little dignity, and waited
nervously [52]. What happened next was spontaneous, and, as it
happened, unstoppable. The common people of Canterbury, those
who had welcomed his return in such numbers, now began to
attribute miraculous cures and other occurences to the intercession
of their murdered archbishop [53]. As Thomas's supplicants grew
in number and in confidence, and the threat from the de Brocs
receded, the Canterbury monks began to take the lead in fashioning
the cult which came to centre around Thomas's shrine. The turning-
point was Easter 1171 when Thomas was interred in a new shrine.
It soon became host to vast throngs of pilgrims [55], and the reported miracles, recorded by Benedict of Peterborough and William
of Canterbury, came to form the largest miracle collection of any
medieval saint [54]. It soon become clear that Thomas's cult
demanded official recognition. 'It seems wise', wrote John of Salisbury early in 1171, 'to lend aid to God's will, and revere as a martyr,
rejoicing and weeping alike, him whom God deigns to honour as a

martyr.'[19] On 21 February 1173, as miracles continued to be recognised, and pilgrims continued to flock to Canterbury, the pope announced Thomas's canonisation. Even before this, many people began to write about what they had witnessed.

Thomas's cult was at once extraordinary, of its time, and traditional. It was extraordinary in the speed and scale of its success: its rapid acceptance by all social classes, the combination of popular veneration and official recognition, its great geographical spread, and the sheer numbers of miracles and pilgrims. It was characteristic of its time in the fact that the cult grew up within living memory, in the amount of circumstantial evidence which surrounds the subject's life and his posthumous acclaim, and its combination of a local and universal appeal. But Thomas's cult also featured the most traditional form of popular veneration: a martyr worshipped at his tomb. Part of the reason that his cult was so successful was that it featured elements which were not commonly found in new saintly cults of the twelfth century, but it also had a very modern appeal.

Thomas had triumphed in death, but had his cause? Despite what his early biographers say of the victory of the Church through the blood of the martyr, the answer has to be no. We need look no further than Herbert of Bosham's bitter dedication of his Life to Thomas's successors, in which he makes little attempt to disguise his disappointment at the state of affairs as they stood in the mid–1180s. Thomas's death did not bring outright victory to the supporters of ecclesiastical liberty, but nor did Henry and his policy towards the Church survive unscathed. There is no reason to disbelieve the king's reported grief at hearing of Thomas's death, but nor should we assume that his tears were all for Thomas. Henry knew that outrage against him would be followed by more tangible repercussions. Just before the murder, Henry had sent a mission to the pope, but the arrival of two of Thomas's clerks with the shocking news put a sudden end to negotiations. Meanwhile, William of Sens and the French clergy had imposed an interdict on Henry's continental lands. This sentence was confirmed at Easter by the pope, who sent two envoys, Albert and Theodwin, to France to demand Henry's submission. Henry's showed no early signs of accepting guilt, instead writing defiantly to the pope, and crossing to Ireland in the winter of 1171. Since the murder the knights had been lying low in Knaresborough Castle, but in early 1172 it seems that they had agreed to do penance for their crime. They atoned by

19 *LJS* no. 305, pp. 736–7.

taking the cross and fighting in Jerusalem, and according to legend, that is where they died. Henry was finally persuaded to meet the envoys on his return from Ireland, and in May 1172, after some negotiations, they came to an agreement at Avranches. Henry accepted that he shared some guilt for the crime, granted full restoration of Canterbury lands, and agreed to pay for two hundred knights to fight in Jerusalem. His promise to go on crusade himself was later commuted to founding three religious houses. He made a vague renunication of 'evil customs' introduced during his reign, and made an explicit concession regarding appeals to the pope, but it was not until 1176 that he fully settled the issue of criminous clerks in the Church's favour [56].

It may seem that Henry had got off very lightly. He had abandoned the customs, if not explictly, but retained the substantial powers over the Church which had prevailed before 1164. He had been absolved of the murder of his archbishop, and he went on to enjoy the full support of the Church when he faced rebellion from his family. Still, this does not tell the whole story. Henry's submission at Thomas's tomb in 1174 [57] was only the most extreme recognition that the king had to make of Thomas's sanctity – his archbishop's triumph in death would live with him until his own death. For the most powerful king in Europe, who had placed so much importance on his honour, to submit at the tomb of the low-born clerk whom he had raised up from the dust, must have seemed like punishment indeed.

Dissenting voices

Even his biographers accepted that Thomas Becket was a man who divided opinion. Indeed the Lives themselves are full of reported criticism of his actions and his character. Most of the writing we have about Thomas from the twelfth century is in praise of his memory, but there are exceptions. We have letters, written during his life, in which general and specific criticisms are set out. We also have evidence that, despite the murder and his posthumous glory, some remained unconvinced that Thomas deserved the title of saint. Finally, there is evidence that some, while accepting his sanctity, were not prepared to accept that all his actions were praiseworthy.

Though the ones we have are valuable, we do not have many expositions of the case against Thomas. It is unlikely that this is because of posthumous repression: the most vitriolic denunciation of Thomas, Gilbert Foliot's *Multiplicem nobis*, survives in a number of manuscripts and was included in the Canterbury letter collection. There are other more likely explanations. First, for those caught up in the dispute before 1171, individual issues seemed more important than general interpretations. Therefore, letters are more likely to present an argument against, say, Thomas's excommunications, than they are to give a wide-ranging critique of his deeds and character. A related point is that a detailed analysis of the conflict tended to serve the interests of Thomas's party more than that of his critics. For Thomas's supporters, this was a righteous battle between good and evil. As Herbert of Bosham put it, Thomas fought 'against the world on the stage of the world, as a spectacle for men and for angels'. For his opponents, the dispute concerned a minor and unimportant matter which might have been settled if Thomas had been more suited to the job. Thomas's side had the initiative, in much the same way that the Gregorians did over the Henricians the previous century. And of course, when it was possible to review Thomas's life, after 1171, the climate of opinion made it very difficult to voice criticisms.

Thomas's most vocal and eloquent critics came from within the Church. The Lives make frequent reference to them: Roger of York, Hilary of Chichester, and especially, Gilbert of London. But it was not until 1166 that an explicit and coherent case against Thomas, courtesy of Gilbert, came to be formulated. Thomas's action in excommunicating his enemies at Vézelay demanded a response. First, in appealing against them, an argument had to be made, which would influence the pope and galvanise the clergy. Second, argument against further damaging measures needed to be presented to Thomas himself. The flurry of correspondence from 1166 is different from that which had gone before in that while these letters contain certain specific arguments, they are really manifestos. They are not aimed specifically at the recipient but at a broader audience of educated ecclesiastics. In fact some seem to have not even reached their addressee, but were circulated more widely. Their themes combine the personal and political, and show how far, in two years, the dispute had progressed beyond the Constitutions of Clarendon.

In response to Vézelay, Gilbert wrote two letters of appeal in the name of the English clergy. The first, to the pope, expresses outrage at the censures, and praises the moderation of the king. The second, to Thomas [59], is a call for caution, taking as its text the reading,

'Look carefully then how you walk ... for the days are evil'.[20] Thomas was often admonished in these terms. Herbert reports a discussion between Thomas and a group of cardinals at Sens in November 1164 in which caution is urged with reference to this reading. It was also employed by the pope the following summer in urging restraint on the archbishop. This letter, *Quae vestro*, is not merely a piece of advice, however. It includes barbed satirical references to Thomas's life at Pontigny, and implicitly suggests that Thomas is endangering the Church by his poor stewardship. That Thomas's camp regarded it as a serious attack on the archbishop is clear from their response. John of Salisbury pointed to Gilbert as the author, and identified him with Doeg and Achitophel, the evil counsellors of the Old Testament. Thomas followed this up with a general rebuke of the English clergy, and a personal attack on Gilbert. Gilbert responded with the most wide-ranging case against Thomas, and perhaps the finest piece of writing to come out of the dispute, *Multiplicem nobis* [**60**].

Gilbert Foliot was a man of noble birth, a Cluniac monk and a theologian. He was the obvious alternative to Thomas as the successor to Theobald, and much of his resentment towards Thomas must be traced to this. But also, in background, in temperament, and in his manner of action, Gilbert was at odds with Thomas. *Multiplicem nobis* is a response to personal criticism, and in reviewing the dispute it is unashamedly *ad hominem*. His interpretation of Thomas's actions may be summarised as 'He would, wouldn't he?' Thomas's actions, which have brought ruin upon the Church, are the inevitable product of his personal flaws, and his unsuitability for office.

Gilbert begins by reviewing Thomas's promotion. He claims that he bought the office of chancellor, and used his influence in the royal court to become archbishop of Canterbury. His background as a 'pastor of hawks and hounds' and his irregular intrusion into the archiepiscopate through royal pressure, paved the way for the disasters which followed. It was no surprise that he who oppressed the Church as chancellor should fail to defend it as archbishop. Next he turns to the royal customs. Thomas's failure, Gilbert claims, was not that he opposed them, but that he did not oppose them vigorously enough. All the other bishops stood firm, but Thomas abandoned their counsel and capitulated to the king. His criticism of Thomas's behaviour at Northampton is in a similar vein: his fault was not to stand up to the king but to agree to submit to a secular judgement. His subsequent

20 Ephesians 5.15–16.

flight was, in Gilbert's view, an act of cowardice which only served to leave his flock at the mercy of the king. Indeed his flight is used as a metaphor for Thomas's general failings: Thomas not only fled from danger but ran away from the righteous path. The key text here is John 10.11–12: 'The good shepherd lays down his life for the sheep. He who is a mercenary and not a shepherd, whose own the sheep are not, sees the wolf coming and leaves the sheep and flees.' Thomas, the mercenary who became archbishop through the agency of the king, not that of God, could never be expected to defend his flock in a time of danger. He chooses to posture as a martyr while others suffer for his actions. Finally, in an implicit reference to Vézelay, Gilbert claims that Thomas's lack of tact has managed to deny the Church the peace and prosperity which others had almost achieved through more moderate measures.

Gilbert Foliot's central case is that Thomas is to be criticised, not for defending the Church, but because he did not defend it properly. This is an ingenious argument, but it is also a debating ploy, rather than necessarily a full reflection of Gilbert's beliefs. Gilbert was not a royalist, he was a defender of ecclesiastical liberties, but one wonders how far he would have gone in resisting Henry's measures towards the Church. He is guilty of the same disingenuousness as the biographers. For them, such embarrassments as Thomas's life as chancellor, his submission at Clarendon, and his flight from England, could be reconciled as part of a circuitous route to martyrdom. For Gilbert, such episodes made null his frequent, if perhaps incompetent, actions in defence of the Church. Both, in trying to present an internally consistent picture, wilfully fail to represent the complexity of the man.

It has been asked why *Multiplicem nobis* was preserved after Thomas's death.[21] The first reason, I suggest, is that the arguments are likely to have been well known. The second is that, more importantly, the strength of Thomas's cult made its preservation not only possible, but useful. Gilbert left many hostages to fortune, in particular his accusation that Thomas was posturing as a martyr, and his reference to the good shepherd laying down his life for the sheep. *Multiplicem nobis* presented a framework which the biographers, most notably Alan of Tewkesbury and Herbert of Bosham, could use to demonstrate how, in the light of the martyrdom, Thomas's critics had been proved wrong.

21 Morey and Brooke, pp. 167, 169.

The letters must be approached in a different way from the Lives because they are written about different subjects. The letters are strictly contemporary documents; the Lives are retrospective accounts. The letters concern a controversial archbishop at various points in the course of a dispute; the Lives are about an accepted saint and his legend. The atmosphere after 1171 was one in which no criticism could thrive. Gilbert Foliot himself made his submission at Canterbury, and it was the bishop of London who was first to whip Henry's back as he knelt before Thomas's shrine. In the following centuries Thomas's name was invoked in support of English kings, including Henry III, Edward II and Richard II. That is not to say that all dissent was silenced. The defensive tone which pervades many of the Lives, especially the later ones, is testimony to that. But in a situation where an anti-Becket tract was unlikely to receive an audience, all we have is glimpses.

Thomas's sanctity was widely accepted immediately, but the grounds on which it was based proved more problematic. Proof of martyrdom was traditionally based on the penalty, the cause, and the miracles. Herbert of Bosham, naturally, emphasised the cause and denigrated the value of miracles, claiming that they were only for unbelievers. But others, including John of Salisbury, and the pope in his letter of canonisation, stressed Thomas's less controversial talent as a miracle-worker. But even as Thomas was being hailed as the greatest saint of their age, it is clear that some still believed that, as Henry VIII put it in 1538 in suppressing the cult, 'There appareth nothynge in his lyfe and exteriour conversation whereby he should be callyd a sainct'.[22] Caesarius of Heisterbach, writing in the early thirteenth century, reports a debate which occurred in Paris between the renowned theologian Master Peter the Chanter and a certain Master Roger [**61**]. Whereas Peter declared that Thomas was a martyr by virtue of his murder for the liberty of the Church, Roger denounced him as a damnable traitor worthy of death, 'if not such a death'. There is little doubt that this debate occurred only a short time after the murder, and certainly before Thomas's canonisation, but it is still quite remarkable that a view such as Roger's should be advanced publicly in such a place. Caesarius claims that God settled the question by glorifying Thomas with posthumous miracles. It is certainly true that such criticisms of Thomas were soon proved redundant, if not by the power of God, at least by the force of popular veneration.

22 Proclamation of Henry VIII, 16 November 1538, in T. Borenius, *Thomas Becket in Art* (London, 1932), pp. 109–10.

There were others, as William of Newburgh demonstrates [**62**], who could accept Thomas's sanctity but who did not approve of all his actions. William was an Augustinian canon, best known for his *Historia Rerum Anglicarum*, written 1196–98. He was not a royalist, but nor did he always hold conventional views: he showed an unusual tolerance for Jews, and was prepared to criticise Geoffrey of Monmouth's interpretation of English history. But his work is nevertheless striking for criticising Thomas as much as could be expected of anyone in his position, at that time. While acknowledging Thomas's sanctity, and criticising many of Henry's actions, his approval of Thomas's conduct is at best grudging. And he reflects on his approach to Thomas, saying that in some cases one ought to praise the man, but not all his works. The omissions are also interesting: while providing a detailed, if occasionally shaky, narrative, he pays little attention to the more hagiographical arguments in Thomas's favour – the 'conversion' of 1162, the hairshirt, the posthumous miracles.

Modern students of Thomas Becket tend to take a great dislike to him, and the stinging criticisms of Gilbert Foliot are usually preferred to the eulogies of Herbert of Bosham. We do not have a balanced picture of Thomas, partly because far more was written by his supporters than by his detractors, but also because the interpretations of his personality, character and deeds are almost always polarised. Sometimes, however, as with William of Newburgh, we catch a glimpse of how Thomas, even in the twelfth century, did not have to be seen in black and white.

I: THE ROAD TO CANTERBURY (?1118–62)

1. Omens of future greatness (?1118)

These stories are found in most of the Lives and are typical of hagiographical writing. In the same vein is the legend that Thomas's mother was the daughter of a Saracen emir who saved his father from captivity in the Holy Land and followed him to England.[1]

Edward Grim, *MTB* 2. 356–9.

Chosen before the foundation of the world in Christ,[2] Saint Thomas in his propitious birth lit up the capital of the British Isles, London. His father was Gilbert Becket, his mother Matilda.[3] In birth and wealth they were in no way inferior to their fellow citizens, and they far surpassed them in their nobility of habits and in the integrity of their devout lives. It is said that they lived their lives in pursuit of righteousness, without fault or complaint, so that through them like Zachariah and Elizabeth England would rejoice that it had begotten a new John.[4] Nor without reason do I call him John in his way, who resembled John so much in his performance of penance and love, for which he fought to the death, and as a witness to truth did not flinch before the sword. But so the following story will tell. We will resume its sequence a little below, but now let us briefly consider the visions which we believe prefigured the wonderful future of the holy child.

Shortly after his mother conceived, she saw in a vision that the entire River Thames was flowing within her. Filled with womanly fear, she suspected the vision signified some strange trouble, as the common people tend to interpret an overflowing of water. But she heard a contrary explanation, inspired by God, from a wise man, from which she derived much comfort. 'The one who is born to you', he said, 'will rule over many people'. Another, in no way contradicting the former interpretation, added that she was soon to receive a stream of graces,

---

1 *MTB* 2. 451–8.

2 See Ephesians 1.4.

3 Both were Norman by birth. William Fitzstephen claims that Gilbert came from the region of Thierville in Eure (*MTB* 3. 15), but according to the Lambeth Anonymous he came from Rouen. The Anonymous also gives Thomas's mother's name as Roheise and says that she came from Caen (*MTB* 4. 81).

4 i.e. John the Baptist. See Luke 1.

which would be like a river irrigating the land, recalling that gospel saying, 'He who believes in me, out of his heart shall flow rivers of living water'.[5]

In her next vision it appeared to the woman that she had come to Canterbury. And when she, along with the others present, came to enter Christ Church, her womb swelled to such an extent with the boy she was carrying, that she could not get through the doors. The woman was deeply saddened and worried by this vision, thinking it meant that she was unworthy to enter the church, until the third vision dispelled the sorrow of the preceding one.

For when the time to give birth was approaching, it appeared to her that twelve stars of unusual brilliance fell from the sky into her lap. Greatly comforted she tried to figure out what wonderful thing this foretold about her child. But we, aware of what the Lord performed through his servant and the outstanding glory which would await him, believe and declare that in the last judgement he will preside over the world with those twelve elect beacons of heaven.

Again, as the baby was lying in his cot, his mother saw in a dream that he was naked. Angry with the nurse she said, 'Why did you not cover the child?' But the nurse replied, 'He seemed to me very well covered in a folded cloth of precious purple'. The mother and servant made for the cot and attempted to unfold the blanket, so as to cover the child more carefully. But they found the chamber too narrow for this purpose, and the larger hall too, and even the street. Therefore they hurried to Smithfield, which is an open space in the city, hoping to satisfy their wish. When they set to the task, with the width of the place seeming to assure success, a voice thundered from on high, saying, 'Your efforts are in vain. All England is smaller than this purple cloth and cannot contain it'. Whereupon the mother awoke, remembering what she had seen, but entirely unaware of its meaning. However, keen-eyed faith reveals to us that the precious purple cloth signifies the blood of the martyr innocently killed, which covered him in his passion as he lay dead, but is now spread through so many kingdoms and foreign nations, as this vision prefigured ...[6]

And now the candle has been placed upon a candlestick, so that they who enter may see the light.[7] Now in him we see fulfilled what the

5 John 7.39.

6 Grim relates how, on the day of his birth, a fire beginning at Thomas's father's house consumed a large part of the city.

7 See Luke 11.33.

Saviour promised to the elect, 'He who conquers, I will make him a pillar of fire in my temple'.[8] And now, thanks to heavenly providence we have a pillar. Let us fix our gaze on the light. Where he went let us follow, lest our foot stumble on the stone. Because he who walks in the darkness does not know where to go.

2. Thomas as a young man (c. 1138–40)

We are told that Thomas was educated at Merton, an Augustinian priory in Surrey, then at a grammar school in London before studying in Paris. We know little of his study abroad, and his biographers do not tend to emphasise his learning, at least before the 1160s.

Thomas Saga 1. 28–40. Language: Old Icelandic. Translation by Haki Antonson.

When the young Thomas had with humility and true obedience covered all the teaching that he could in his parents' house, he went to school for the purpose of higher study. He became, as much as his age allowed and time permitted, keen of memory and clever in grasping not only learning from books, but all those things which pertain to the heart. Because the Holy Book has so much to teach him, in time he fully and fairly comprehended the seven major liberal arts. Therefore he went to school both in England and in France, particularly in the capital city Paris, which has always had the most famous school as regards both scholars and learning …

At the time when Stephen had become king,[9] the blessed Thomas left school. He was then twenty-two years of age, a slim man of pale countenance and dark hair, with a long nose and regular features.[10] He was gentle of manner and sharp of intellect, and he was easy going and amiable in conversation. He was authoritative in speech, if somewhat stammering. He was so keen in discernment and comprehension that he would always solve difficult questions wisely. His memory was so amazing that whatever he heard of scriptures and legal judgements he was able to cite any time he chose. On account of God's gifts that have been mentioned, wise men could easily see that he was predestined to a great position in God's Church.

8 See Revelations 3.12.

9 1135–54. Thomas would have left school around 1140.

10 William Fitzstephen concurs: 'He was gentle and graceful of countenance, tall in stature, with a prominent and slightly aquiline nose' (*MTB* 3.17). See also the description below, p. 123.

3. Early training (*c.* 1138–54)

In this account 'Roger', developing a technique earlier employed by Edward Grim, presents Thomas's simultaneous outer and inner development, by alternating reports of his advancement in the world with descriptions of his emerging spiritual qualities.

'Roger of Pontigny', *MTB* 4. 3–12.

When the boy reached the age of education, he was taught in literary studies by his mother. Even then at such an age the splendour and grace of his appearance and habits set him apart from those of a similar age. But since it is the worldly that proceeds the spiritual, let us run through his early years, adding nothing in the way of praise or trying to commend anything, but briefly recording the simple truth in sincere and faithful prose. As he grew strong in body he was also enriched by mental intelligence. Such was the power of his intellect and memory that he could easily grasp anything as soon as he heard it, and once he had learned it, he could recall it without difficulty whenever and as often as he wished. Also in figuring out difficult ideas and disentangling perplexing questions he seemed to surpass many important and learned men with the sharpness of his fertile mind. But he also had a remarkable bodily capacity for perceptiveness and subtlety, that we too often witnessed in his later years. Hardly anything could be said in his presence, even if distantly and quietly, that he did not hear, should he choose to lend an ear. Similarly there was nothing that could produce a smell that did not immediately, however remote, either offend his nostrils with its stink, or caress them with its fragrance. And is this not a grace that, even if not yet in the spirit, at least in the body was already working in him to the admiration of many?

In his father's house there lodged a knight called Richer of Laigle,[11] a man who lived a noble and honourable life, but who was nevertheless almost always engaged in hunting with dogs and birds. Thomas, who was still a boy, when free from school for half a year often accompanied him in these pursuits. He enjoyed such occupations very much, and it is thought that this is where he picked up the habit, to which he would devote himself as an adult in later years, whenever he was free to do so. It happened one day that this knight went hunting in his accustomed way, and Thomas followed him on a horse. They came to a crossing over a very rapid river, a small and narrow bridge, just

11 A distinguished Norman knight. See Barlow, pp. 19 and 283 n. 15.

wide enough to cross on foot. There was also a mill not far below, to which this river, its banks running together so as not to let it flow out, turned headlong with great force. The knight, thinking light of the danger in his search for a short cut, crossed the bridge first. Thomas, protected and hooded, suspecting nothing unfortunate, followed directly after. But when he came to the middle of the bridge, the horse's foot suddenly gave way, and the boy along with the horse fell straight into the river. Swept up by the current he was separated from the horse with a violent surge and dragged to the bottom. Now he was approaching the mill, to be ground by its wheel or drowned by the water. But while this was happening, and Thomas seemed on the brink of death, the man who looked after the mill, knowing nothing at all of what was going on, suddenly closed off the water from the mill. The knight then and those who accompanied him followed the boy with loud sympathetic cries from the other bank. Eventually, with the mill now quiet, the man heard the voices and wondered what was the matter. He left the mill, and seeing Thomas in the midst of the current, he quickly stretched out his hand, and dragged him, half dead and hardly breathing, on to land. Who could believe that this happened by chance, and was not the work of divine providence mercifully arranging such a sudden and unexpected rescue for this endangered boy, the future prelate of his Church? Indeed when his mother heard what had happened, she lamented the danger less than she rejoiced for his wonderful and unexpected liberation. And from this she drew hope for the future, that it was not in vain that divine mercy had snatched him from death in this way.

At certain times his venerable mother would weigh him, placing on the scales opposite him bread, meat, clothes, even money, and other things that seemed useful for the poor. She would then distribute these to the needy, hoping in this way to commend her boy to the protection of divine love and the ever blessed Virgin Mary. For in her diligent and unceasing works of piety, she always had a special devotion to the memory of the blessed Virgin. As he would often repeat, she assiduously taught her son to fear the Lord and to endeavour to cherish and venerate the ever blessed Virgin Mary with special devotion, and to invoke her continuously as guide and patron of his life and deeds, and after Christ to commit his hope to her.

But when Thomas reached his twenty-first year, his mother, who alone encouraged his education, died, and as a consequence he became more careless in his studies. Finding his parental home empty and desolate without his mother, he turned to a certain Londoner, a relative of his who was held in great esteem not only by his fellow citizens but also among courtiers.[12] For almost three years he lived with him, showing much evidence of good character to those who knew him. For he hated lechery, buffoonery and greed with such ardour and loathing that he would have made himself hateful to those who indulged in such things, had his extraordinary gentleness and generosity not earned the love of those whom he displeased in this respect. For he did not care about or hold on to anything which he could have had for himself, but instead he distributed everything with unsparing bounty to the use and desire of his friends. Already in such preludes the graces that would later shine in him, contempt of worldly things and concern for the poor, were taking shape. But at the same time, when he happened to be in conversation among his companions, he would use common and somewhat lewd language, so as not to be entirely excluded and considered churlish by such men, when nevertheless his unsullied chastity was admirable. He did this deliberately and deceived many. On the outside, as the wise man advised, he pretended to be the same as others, when in fact within all was different.[13]

At that time the most reverend Theobald, who had been promoted from the monastery of Bec,[14] was presiding over the church of Canterbury with virtue and dignity. He was great and praiseworthy in all things, expert in both secular and ecclesiastical matters. One of his officials had known Thomas well since infancy, as he used to stay in his father's house when business brought him to London. Seeing that he was now a fine youth, as learned in letters as he was prudent and virtuous, he began to persuade Thomas to go with him to the archbishop's court. But Thomas, thinking it more presumptuous than obliging to impose himself uninvited, demurred for the time being. But eventually, with the official's full reassurance, and with fitting and worthy provision, he accompanied him to the court and presented himself to the reverend archbishop.[15] This prudent man inspected him, and at first sight perceiving him to be intelligent of face, received him with favour and honour, and bade him stay with him. From then on

---

12 Osbert Huitdeniers (Eightpence), a financier in the City.

13 See Seneca, *Epistles* 5. This image is employed by many of the biographers to explain not only his outward appearance as chancellor, but also that as archbishop. See below, p. 68.

14 In 1139.

15 William Fitzstephen attributes his introduction to Theobald's household to two brothers from Boulogne, Archdeacon Baldwin and Master Eustace (*MTB* 3. 15).

Thomas was an associate of the court, and in a short time he came to be held in such regard by the archbishop that no one was thought to be closer or more dear to him. Indeed the wise man, quickly recognising the sincerity of Thomas's gentleness and wisdom, would constantly summon him to his councils and frequently entrust his business to him. Finding him prudent in counsel and energetic and faithful in business, he sought to bind Thomas ever closer to himself with chains of affection and intimacy, but not without provoking envy.

For there was a man, as eminent in pontifical familiarity as he was in ecclesiastical dignity, by the name of Roger of Pont-l'Evêque, arch-deacon of Canterbury, who could not bear with equanimity Thomas's favour in court. Nor did he contain this plague of envy within himself, but often let it spill out in insults and taunts, frequently calling Thomas 'Bailhatch's clerk', for that was the name of the man who had accompanied him to court. Nor was this envious malice momentary and transitory, as later events showed.[16] But Thomas, nonetheless, restraining himself in his accustomed manner, won favour before God and men. Meanwhile then, as much as was allowed, he devoted himself to the study of civil law and the sacred canons, so that through this he would be found more learned in debating and deciding matters and extend his knowledge of ecclesiastical matters.[17] A case arose for which Theobald as archbishop of Canterbury arranged to visit the Roman Church.[18] He went on his way, as was fitting, with a fine and extensive retinue, and also took Thomas with him, in whose prudence and fidelity he chiefly trusted. And deservedly so, for on the journey and in the archbishop's dealings Thomas proved himself of great value in many respects. After a safe return, even more certain of Thomas's excellence, and thinking him worthy of more, he first conferred the church of Oxford on him. And later he often sent him to Rome on ecclesiastical business, where he deservedly won praise for his industry.

At that time William, archbishop of York, happily reached the end of his life and his pontifical office, and rested peacefully.[19] The see of

16 Roger, later archbishop of York, became one of Thomas's bitterest enemies, and attracted some of the blame for his murder.

17 He is said to have studied at Bologna and Auxerre (*MTB* 2. 304; 3. 17)

18 The Council of Rheims, March 1148, to which Theobald travelled with Thomas in an unseaworthy ship despite a prohibition by King Stephen. John of Salisbury and Roger of Pont-l'Evêque also attended the council.

19 William FitzHerbert, nephew of King Stephen, died in June 1154. His death may not have been as peaceful as 'Roger' presents it – some supected he had been poisoned.

York being vacant, Theobald, along with all the primates of England, exerted himself by every means to have this Roger, his archdeacon, promoted to that see, and thereby look out for the dignity of the church of Canterbury, his own honour and that of his clerk, and open the way for Thomas's promotion. He was not thwarted in his plan, for when, with the king's consent, Roger was elected and consecrated to the see of York, without delay he assigned the archdeaconry of Canterbury and the provostship of Beverley, along with many other churches, to Thomas.[20]

When Thomas acquired these honours he became no longer content with a private manner of behaviour. Therefore he submitted himself to greater, clearer and more evident proofs of virtue, distributing his revenues mercifully and abundantly for the use and necessity of the poor, and whatever was left, he poured out with wonderful liberality and generosity to anyone else. The archbishop, seeing that he had not been wrong in his judgement of Thomas, rather that he had progressed beyond expectations, was overjoyed at his greatness. But Thomas himself, though he was regarded as great in all things and in every way, nevertheless harboured no insolence, and with his customary reverence and humility obeyed his archbishop completely.

At that time, that is in the year 1154, Henry, son of Geoffrey count of Anjou and the Empress Matilda, succeeded to his grandfather's crown,[21] and England was filled with disturbance and eagerness for new things. And there was no little trepidation in the Church of the realm, on the one hand because of the worrying youth of the king,[22] and on the other because of the well-known antipathy of his courtiers towards the Church's right to liberty. Nor was it mistaken, as the outcome shows. The archbishop of Canterbury, then, as troubled by the present as he was fearful of the future, planned to raise some defence against the evil which was thought imminent. And it seemed to him that if he could introduce Thomas to the king's councils, he could thenceforth provide great calm and peace to the English Church. For he knew him to be magnanimous and prudent, to possess zeal for God and skill, and that he was passionately jealous of ecclesiastical liberty. Therefore the archbishop took into his counsels the bishops Philip of

---

20 Thomas became archdeacon in October 1154 and retained this office through his chancellorship and the early years of the archiepiscopacy until he resigned it to Geoffrey Ridel in March 1163.

21 King Stephen died on 25 October. Henry entered England on 8 December and was crowned on 19 December.

22 He was twenty-one.

Bayeux and Arnulf of Lisieux, on whose advice the king relied in the early days of his accession, and began to raise the subject of Thomas's prudence, energy and loyalty, and his praiseworthy and admirable mildness of manner. And when the bishops gave their approval to what the archbishop desired and urged, Thomas entered the royal court and took on the title and office of chancellor.[23] Thereafter how he played the part of the twin man, the man of the Church and the man of the court, is not easy to explain.

4. Royal Chancellor (1154–62)

For a detailed discussion of Thomas's life as chancellor, see L. B. Radford, *Thomas of London Before His Consecration* (Cambridge, 1894). Most of our information about this period in Thomas's life comes from William Fitz-stephen. His account abounds in classical imagery, but he avoids scriptural references until Thomas's consecration ushers in a flood of them.

William Fitzstephen, *MTB* 3. 17–26.

When Henry II had been consecrated king of England by Archbishop Theobald, through the approval and influence of the archbishop, and the persuasion and effort of the noble Henry bishop of Winchester, Thomas was chosen before all others as the king's chancellor. He was a hardworking man, given to deep thought and enterprising in many great things, and he discharged the duties of obedience and honour with such application, to the praise of God and the benefit of the realm, that it is hard to say whether he was more noble, magnificent and useful to the king in peace or war. The chancellor of England is considered second in rank in the realm only to the king. He holds the other part of the king's seal, with which he seals his own orders. He has responsibility and care of the king's chapel, and maintains whatever vacant archbishoprics, bishoprics, abbacies and baronies fall into the king's hands. He attends all the king's councils to which he does not even require a summons. All documents are sealed by his clerks, the royal seal-keepers, and everything is carried out according to his advice. Also, if by God's grace the merits of his life allow it, he will be made archbishop or a bishop before he dies. That is why the chancellorship cannot be bought.[24]

23 Probably at Henry's Christmas court, 1154.
24 Gilbert Foliot disagrees: see below, p. 225.

During the reign of King Stephen the tempest of war shook the realm of England and everywhere profane hatred vented itself in violent destruction. In almost every third vill those dens of thieves, enemy castles, were built. Native lords were disinherited, and Flemish foreigners and warlike men occupied Kent and many other parts of the realm. Everything had been disturbed by war for so long – almost twenty years – that it seemed impossible to expel the Flemish and restore the kingdom to its former state, its ancient dignity and peace, especially with such a young king. Through the mercy of God, the advice of the chancellor, and the clergy and nobles of the realm, who wanted peace, within three months of the king's coronation, William of Ypres, who had been violently occupying Kent, left the realm in tears. All the Flemish gathered their baggage and arms and headed for the sea. Every castle in England fell, except for the ancient peace-keeping towers and fortifications. The crown of England was restored after its decline. Ancient rights were restored to the disinherited. Brigands came forth from their wooded hiding-places to the vills, and all rejoiced in peace. Swords were beaten into ploughshares, lances into scythes. Thieves too, in fear of the gallows, took up work in the fields or in building. Peace was everywhere. Shields were imported, cabbages were exported. Traders went out safely from their cities and castles, and Jews to demanding creditors.

Through the industry and counsel of the chancellor, through God's disposition, and also thanks to the earls and barons, the noble realm of England was renewed, as if it were a new spring. Holy Church was honoured, with vacant bishoprics and abbacies going without simony to honourable persons. The king, with the aid of the King of kings, prospered in all his doings. The realm of England was enriched, the horn of plenty was filled to the brim. The hills were cultivated, the valleys abounded in corn, the pastures with cattle and the folds with sheep. Chancellor Thomas arranged for the repair of the seat of the realm, the Palace of London,[25] which was then almost in ruins. This great undertaking was completed with remarkable speed between Easter and Whitsun,[26] with so many craftsmen, carpenters and other workmen making such intense movement and noise, that it was almost impossible to hear someone speaking, even if they were next to you.

The chancellor found great favour among the clergy, knights and people. He could have had every vacant parish church in the country

25 Westminster Hall.
26 Either 1155 or 1158.

and the town, for no trustee would have dared deny him, had he asked. But he overcame ambition with such magnanimity that he refused to take the place of poor priests and clerks seeking these positions. Instead, noble in spirit, he sought higher things, namely the provost-ship of Beverley, the count of Eu's donation of the prebends of Hastings, the Tower of London with knight service provided, the castle of Eye with the honour of 140 knights, and the castle of Berkhamstead.

He often played sports, hunting with dogs and birds, his hawks and falcons, and he played chess, 'the war game of stealthy mercenaries',[27] but in a perfunctory manner, not with commitment. The chancellor's house and table were open to the needs of any visitors to the king's court of whatever rank, if they were known to be genuine, or appeared to be. Hardly a day did he dine without earls and barons as guests. He ordered his floors to be covered every day with new straw or hay in the winter, fresh bulrushes or leaves in the summer, so that the multitude of knights, who could not all fit on stalls, could find a clean and pleasant space, and leave their precious clothes and beautiful shirts unsoiled. His house glistened with gold and silver vases, and abounded in precious food and drink, so that if a certain food was known for its rarity, no price would deter his ministers from buying it. Nevertheless he retained the utmost sobriety in these things, so that rich alms were collected from this rich table. And, as I heard from his confessor Robert, venerable canon of Merton, from the time he became chancellor, no lechery polluted him. In this regard the king also laid traps for him day and night, but being God-fearing and predestined by God, Thomas directed the flesh to cleanliness, and kept his loins girded. As a wise man, intent on the government of the realm and on so many public and private cares, such temptations attended him less, since, 'take away leisure and Cupid's bow is broken'.[28] A certain high-born clerk of his, Richard of Ambly, seduced and lay with the wife of a friend of his, after he had persuaded her that her husband, who at that time had been a long time overseas, had died. The chancellor, a pure man, who hated indecency and depravity, banished him from his house and his friendship, and had him imprisoned in fetters in the Tower of London for a long time.

Magnates of the kingdom of England and of neighbouring kingdoms placed their children in the chancellor's service, and he grounded

---

27 Martial, *Epigrams* xiv, 18 (20). Chess was a favoured knightly pursuit, which often involved wagers.

28 Ovid, *Remedia Amoris* 139.

them in honest education and doctrine, and when they had received the belt of knighthood he sent some back with honour to their fathers and family, and retained others. The king himself, his lord, commended his son,[29] the heir to the kingdom, to his training, and the chancellor kept him with him among the many nobles' sons of similar age, and their appropriate attendants, and masters and servants, according to rank. Nevertheless, in the midst of these glories of secular honour he often received discipline in secret, his back stripped for whipping, from Ralph prior of Holy Trinity,[30] when he was in the neighbourhood of London, and from Thomas, presbyter of St Martin's, when he was in the Canterbury area. He was humble in his own eyes, he was humble to the humble, but fierce and violent to the proud, as if it were his nature 'to spare the humble and to tame the proud in war'.[31] Countless nobles and knights gave homage to the chancellor, and he, saving fidelity to the lord king, received and cherished them with extraordinary patronage as his own men. Sometimes he would cross the sea with a fleet of six ships or more, and he would not leave anyone behind who wished to sail with him. When they reached land he would reward his pilots and sailors as they wished. Hardly a day went by when he did not make a gift of horses, birds, clothes, gold or silver wares or money. No wonder it is written, 'Some give freely and always abound, others take from others, and are always lacking'.[32] The chancellor had such a gift for giving, that he found love and favour throughout the Latin world. 'He politely adopted each one according to his age'.[33]

Thanks to the instigation of Almighty God, and the influence of Chancellor Thomas, the lord king did not retain vacant bishoprics and abbacies for long, and thereby use the properties of the Crucified to fill the exchequer (as he later did, but far be it from him to do so any more).[34] Rather, he gave these without delay to honourable persons, obeying God. In addition, on the chancellor's advice the king took to

29 Henry (1155–83), the king's oldest surviving son. He became joint-king in 1170 (see below, pp. 172–4).

30 At Aldgate, London.

31 Virgil, *Aeneid* vi, 854.

32 See Horace, *Odes* III, xxiv, 64, and Proverbs 11.24.

33 Horace, *Epistles* I, vi, 55.

34 When an archbishop, bishop or abbot died, it was customary for the crown to retain the revenues of the church until the office was filled. So, for example, Thomas administered the revenues of Canterbury on the king's behalf for a year after Theobald's death, until he succeeded to the see.

his favour and familiarity the canonical church of Merton, whose inhabitants were worthy of God. And he completed at his own expense the building which had been begun by the head of the house, and enriched it with a perpetual revenue. Sometimes before Easter he would spend three days with the community of monks in penitential vigil. And on Good Friday after night prayers, which are called *tenebrae*,[35] but are actually performed in the light, until the hour of nones, he would visit the poor churches of the neighbouring villages to pray, going on foot, in disguise, with only one attendant to lead the way. Furthermore, on the suggestion of Chancellor Thomas, the king recalled poor Englishmen of good repute, either regular monks or masters of the schools, who were living in France, and set them up in his realm. Master Robert of Melun, for example, he appointed as bishop of Hereford, and William, monk of St Martin-des-Champs as abbot of Ramsey.[36]

In this way on account of these gifts of virtue, his generosity and evidence of merit, which were ingrained in his heart, the chancellor of the realm won great approval from king, clergy, knights and people. When important business had been dealt with, he and the king would play together like young boys of the same age, in the hall, in church, in court and out riding. One such day they were riding together through the streets of London in bitter winter weather. At a distance the king saw an old man approaching, a pauper dressed in flimsy rags, and he said to the chancellor, 'Do you see this man?', to which the chancellor answered, 'I do'. 'How poor, how frail, how naked!', said the king. 'Wouldn't it be a great act of charity to give him a thick and warm cape?' 'It certainly would', replied the chancellor, 'and you, king, have such an eye and a mind to it'. When the pauper approached, the king halted and the chancellor with him. The king addressed him gently, and asked if he would like a new cape, but the poor man, not knowing who they were, thought this a joke. Then the king announced to the chancellor, 'To be sure, this great act of charity will be yours!', and taking hold of his hood, the king tried to pull off his fine new cape of scarlet and grey, while the chancellor struggled to hold on to it. Great disorder and disturbance ensued. The knights and nobles who were following them rushed up wondering what had so suddenly caused a dispute between them, but no one could tell. They were both straining with their hands, so that they seemed about to

35 Literally, 'darkness'.

36 Robert, one of the most distinguished masters of the Parisian schools, and possibly
   a former teacher of Thomas during his brief period of study there, was appointed in
   1163. William, abbot of St Martin-des-Champs in Paris, was appointed in 1161.

fall to the ground. After struggling for a time the chancellor allowed the king to prevail and let him take the cape off him and give it to the pauper. The king then told his attendants what had happened, and all laughed heartily, some offering their capes and cloaks to the chancellor. The poor old man went off with the chancellor's cape, enriched and happy beyond his wildest dreams, giving thanks to God.

The king often dined at the chancellor's house, sometimes for sport, at others times to see for himself what he had heard about his house and table. Sometimes the king came riding on horseback into the house while the chancellor was sitting at table, sometimes with an arrow in hand, coming from a hunt or on his way there. Sometimes he would have a drink and leave when he had met with the chancellor, at other times, leaping over the table, he would sit down and eat. Never in Christian times were there two greater friends, more of one mind.

5. Thomas's difficulties at court (1154–62)

John of Salisbury, *MTB* 2. 304–5.

Right from the start of his chancellorship he carried the burden of so many and such great necessities of various kinds, he was exhausted by so many labours, almost crushed by so many afflictions, assailed by so many traps, exposed to so many snares by the spite of courtiers,[37] that often on certain days, as he was wont to tell his archbishop and friends, he would despair of living, and after his longing for eternal life he wished above all to be freed from the bonds of the court without the brand of infamy. And although the world seemed in all its allurements to flatter and applaud him, he did not forget his condition and burden. On the one hand for the sake of the well-being and honour of the lord king, on the other on behalf of the needs of the church and province every day he was forced to contend as much against the king as against his enemies, and to evade various deceits with various crafts. But he made a special effort to fight incessantly against the beasts of the court, and like Proteus administer business while at the same time being engaged in the struggle. For at almost every breeze, ruin and downfall threatened, unless favour and energy were to save him.

37 John's most famous work, the *Policraticus*, subtitled, *Frivolities of Courtiers and Footprints of Philosophers*, which he dedicated to Thomas, warns against the pitfalls of courtly life.

6. The chancellor's hidden piety (1154–62)

William of Canterbury, in a less detailed version, says that this episode
occurred at Stafford (*MTB*, 1. 6).

Garnier, 288–340. Language: French. Translation by Janet Shirley.

He was deeply humble at heart, yet arrogant in appearance; he was
humble with poor people, proud-looking with the mighty, a lamb
inwardly but outwardly a leopard. Early or late, he never delayed in
serving and pleasing the king. But whatever he was outwardly, there
was not a scrap of falsity in him: he kept all his inmost self for God.
Perhaps he may have been proud and given to vanities, as far as
worldly cares go and in outward appearance, yet he was chaste in
body and healthy in soul. Although he was fully occupied in the king's
service, yet as much as he could be, he was Holy Church's right hand.
At this time Henry II, lord of England, was in Staffordshire; he was in
love with a lady, the most elegant in all the empire, as I have heard,
Avice of Stafford. But she could see that the king's affection was
already dwindling, his passion was beginning to cool, and this grieved
her, as she loved him dearly. Thomas the chancellor was then at
Stoke-on-Trent, and this lady often sent messengers to him; the man
in whose house he was staying (a light-minded fellow) thought this
suspicious (it was Vivian the clerk with whom he was staying). One
night when Thomas's bed was all carefully made, with a silken cover
and expensive fine sheets, this man thought that he was in bed with
the lady; he was sure that she had come there. When he supposed that
the baron[38] was asleep and had had all his enjoyment of the lady, he
took a lantern, wanting to know for certain if Thomas was betraying
the king, and went to the place where the bed was. He found it empty,
and was astonished. None of the sheets had been disturbed; it was just
as it had been arranged late that evening. Then he imagined that
Thomas had gone to the lady, and he held the candle up higher to
make sure – there lay wise Thomas on the floor before the bed. He had
a cloak over him, partly covering him, leaving his legs and feet bare.
He had worn himself out with praying and had lain down on the floor
exhausted and was now fast asleep, because he had watched so long.
The more Thomas climbed in the secular world, the more humble he
was at heart, whatever he appeared to be. Many times and in many
places he did wrong on the king's behalf, but he used to make amends
privately to God at night; and that is why God has built so greatly on

38 *Il ber*, i.e. Thomas.

this good foundation. No member of his household, clerk or companion, chamberlain or servant, seneschal or serving-lad, ever had grounds for suggesting that St Thomas was ever guilty of this kind of offence.

7. The chancellor in diplomacy and war (1158–61)

As well as informing us about Thomas's more worldly pursuits in the service of the king, this section illustrates Henry's complex relationship with King Louis VII of France (1137–80).[39] Thomas's embassy to the French king was in 1158, the siege of Toulouse in 1159, and the campaign in La Marche in 1161. William Fitzstephen, *MTB* 3. 29–31, 33–5.

At one point the king of England, after discussions with his chancellor and certain other magnates of the realm, decided to ask the king of France to have his daughter Margaret joined in marriage to his son Henry.[40] This indeed is the great covenant of realms and great men – 'This, I take it, is how to make friends, and to keep them when made'.[41] Who but the chancellor would be sent to make such a petition to such a prince? He was chosen and assented. The chancellor then, giving heed to the business, to the persons involved and his own office, and measuring himself for such a great mission – as the poem says, 'Take the measure of your undertaking; he equips himself as to a wedding who is sent to arrange a future wedding'[42] – he prepared to display and lavish the opulence of England's luxury, so that before all men and in all things the person of the sender might be honoured in the one sent, and the person of the one sent in himself. He had about two hundred of his household on horseback with him, knights, clerks, stewards, servants, esquires and sons of noblemen serving him in arms, all arranged in order. All these and all their attendants were adorned in glistening new festive clothes. Indeed he had twenty-four changes of clothing, 'fleeces of wool dyed again and again in purples of Tyre',[43] many garments of silk, almost all to be given away and left overseas, and elegance of every kind, of gris and of foreign pelts, of cloths and tapestries, like those which adorn the floor and bed of a

39 See above, p. 21.

40 This was decided at a conference on the River Epte in August 1158. Henry was three years old, Margaret even younger. Margaret's dowry was to be the strategically important Norman Vexin. They were married on 2 November 1160.

41 Horace, *Satires* I, iii, 54.

42 Unidentified.

43 Horace, *Epodes* xii, 21.

bishop. He had dogs and birds of all kinds with him, as kings and nobles have. He also had in his retinue eight wagons, each drawn by five horses, in frame and strength like war-horses. To each horse was assigned a strong youth, dressed in a new tunic, walking beside the wagon, and each wagon had a post-horse and a guard of its own. Two wagons carried just ale, made by boiling away water from the tissue of corn, kept in iron-bound barrels. This was to be given to the French, who admire this type of liquid concoction, a healthy drink indeed, refined, the colour of wine, but better tasting. The chancellor's chapel had its own wagon, as did the chamber, bursary and kitchen. Others carried various kinds of food and drink, others cushions, sacks with night-gowns, bags and baggage. He had twelve cart-horses and eight cases which contained the chancellor's furnishings: gold and silver, vessels, cups, bowls, goblets, casks, jugs, basins, salt cellars, spoons, dishes and fruit-bowls. Other of the chancellor's chests and packing-cases contained money, more than enough for his everyday expenses and gifts, and also clothes, books, and suchlike. One cart-horse, walking before the others, carried the sacred vessels of the chapel, and the ornaments and books of the altar. Each of his cart-horses had a groom, equipped as was fitting. Also each wagon had chained to it, either above or below, a great, strong and fierce dog, which looked a match for a bear or lion. And on top of each horse was either a long-tailed monkey or 'an ape, man's imitator'.[44] When they entered the French villages and towns, first came the foot servants, 'born to consume earth's fruits',[45] about two-hundred and fifty of them, in troops of six or ten or more, some singing in their own tongue in the custom of their country. There followed at some distance braces of hounds and greyhounds on leashes and chains, with their keepers and followers. After a little the iron-bound wagons, covered with great hides of animals sewn together, clattered over the paving stones. At a little distance there followed the cart-horses, ridden by grooms, with their knees placed on the horses' haunches. Some of the French would come out of their houses to see what the approaching din was about, and to whom this retinue belonged. When they were told that it was the chancellor of the king of England on a mission to the king of France, they said, 'If this is how the chancellor proceeds, how great must the king be!'
[...][46]

44 Claudian, *In Eutropium* i, 303.
45 Horace, *Epistles* I, ii, 27.
46 Fitzstephen goes on to discuss, in similar style, Thomas's manner of living in Paris.

In the army that laid siege to Toulouse,[47] where all England, Normandy, Aquitaine, Anjou, Brittany and Scotland released their military strength and power of war to aid the king of England, the chancellor had a select force of 700 knights from his own household.[48] And indeed, so great was the English army, that if his advice had been followed, they would have attacked and captured the city of Toulouse, and the king of France, who in partiality to his sister the Countess Constance had admitted himself to the city,[49] but improvidently without an army and strong force. But the king, led astray by vain regard and reverence to the counsel of others, refused to attack the city in which his lord the king of France was installed, while the chancellor argued on the contrary that in standing as an enemy against him there, in violation of agreed treaties,[50] the king of France had abdicated his position as lord. Not much later, when it had been summoned and assembled, the French army entered the city, and the king of England with the king of Scotland and all his army, retreated without achieving their objective. Nevertheless, he captured first the city of Cahors and many castles in the vicinity of Toulouse, which had belonged to the count of Toulouse and his suffragans, or which the count had earlier taken away from the patrons of the king of England. When the king of England withdrew and the other earls excused themselves, the chancellor along with his household, and Henry of Essex, constable and baron of the king, remained to protect all these castles. And later the chancellor himself put on hauberk and helmet and with his men took by force three heavily fortified castles, which seemed impregnable. He also crossed the Garonne with his troop of soldiers in pursuit of the enemy, and when all this province had been confirmed in obedience to the king, he returned in favour and honour.

After a little[51] in the war between the king of France and his lord the king of England in La Marche, at the common frontier of their lands

47 Henry claimed Toulouse as duke of Aquitaine, just as King Louis had when he was married to Eleanor. The unsuccesful siege which lasted from mid-summer to mid-autumn 1159 came back to haunt the archbishop. At Northampton in 1164 Thomas was asked to repay the money lent to him during the campaign (see below, p. 103), and Gilbert Foliot later criticised his role in taxing the church to fund the adventure (see below, pp. 226–7).

48 As his tenant-in-chief, the archbishop of Canterbury owed military service to the king.

49 Constance, widow of Eustace, King Stephen's heir, was now married to the count of Toulouse.

50 A reference to the marriage alliance mentioned above.

51 1161.

between Gisors and Trie and Courcelles, the chancellor, besides 700 knights of his own household had another 1,200 cavalry and 4,000 infantry paid to serve for 40 days. And to every knight was given three shillings to take care of horses and shield-bearers, and all these knights sat at the chancellor's table. He, although he was a clerk, fought on a spurred horse set at a gallop with lance lowered, with a strong French knight from that region, Engelram of Trie, and succeeded in knocking him off his horse and claiming his charger. And in all the army of the king of England the chancellor's knights were always first, always the most daring, always performed excellently, as he himself taught, led, and urged them on, sounding the advance and sounding the retreat on the war-trumpets peculiar to his army, but well known to everyone in the battle. Hence he, even as an enemy and conqueror of the king of France, who ravaged the land with fire and sword, found great favour with the French king and all the French magnates, on the basis of his outstanding merits of faith and remarkable nobility, which favour the king showed him later at an opportune time. For virtue may be praised even in an enemy.

8. Thomas's promotion is predicted (?1161–62)

Thomas's appointment as archbishop did not happen quickly. Theobald died on 18 April 1161, Thomas was elected on 23 May 1162 and consecrated on 3 June 1162.

William Fitzstephen, *MTB* 3. 25–6.

Once the chancellor was taken gravely ill at St Gervase, Rouen. Two kings together came to see him, his lord the king of England and the king of France.[52] After at time he began to recover, and one day he was sitting playing chess, wearing a cape with long sleeves. Asketil, prior of Leicester, came to visit him on his way back from the king's court which at that time was in Gascony. Addressing him frankly, with a bold familiarity, he said, 'Why are you wearing a cape with long sleeves? This dress is more fitting to a falconer, but you are an ecclesiastic with one person but many dignities – archdeacon of Canterbury, dean of Hastings, provost of Beverley, canon of this place and that, proctor to the archbishopric[53] and, as is the repeated rumour in court, a future archbishop'. To this last statement the archbishop said,

---

52 Probably after the truce following the Vexin campaign, June 1161.
53 All preferments granted by Archbishop Theobald.

'Truly I know three poor priests in England, any of whom I would choose for promotion to the archiepiscopate before me. For if I happened to be promoted, inevitably I would either lose the king's favour or (far be it!) neglect the lord God's service, for I know my lord king "inside out"'.[54] And that is how it later turned out.

9. Henry informs Thomas of his design (1161–62)

Herbert of Bosham, *MTB* 3. 180–1.

These things being so, while our Thomas with the utmost royal favour and glory far outshone others in court, and was already administering the most important matters, the oft-mentioned archbishop of Canterbury, Father Theobald, now an old man and full of days, went the appointed way of all flesh.[55] He had been a man of evident sanctity and religion, who had been a chariot and horseman for our Thomas,[56] when he had ruled the church of Canterbury with energy and prudence for twenty-two years. As soon as the king and courtiers heard of this, all immediately began to speculate, some whispering, others openly asserting that the chancellor would be the late archbishop's successor, and the people proclaimed this too. The king concealed his intention entirely, except that the archiepiscopacy, as is the custom for vacant bishoprics and abbacies, was handed over to the care and custody of the chancellor. The chancellor, however, who from certain signs and conjectures already had an idea of the king's intention, nevertheless held his peace, just like the king, and considered the matter in silence. The king was then overseas outside the realm, and the chancellor with him. On account of the frequent attacks of the Welsh[57] and certain other affairs of the realm, the king arranged to send the chancellor to England, none other of his men being adequate to such a great charge. Aware of the outline of his mission for some days now, on the point of his departure the chancellor came to court at the castle of Falaise in Normandy, to pay his respects to the king before he set out. The king called him aside and told him privately, 'You do not

54 Persius, *Satires* iii, 30.

55 18 April 1161.

56 See 2 Kings 2.12, Elisha's words when Elijah is taken up to heaven and he is designated as his successor. Later said of Elisha himself, 2 Kings 13.4.

57 Rhys of Deheubarth was attacking Norman lands in Wales at this time, and in 1162 seized the royal castle at Llandovery.

fully know the reason for your mission'. And he added, 'It is my wish
that you be archbishop of Canterbury'. To whom the chancellor,
looking down and pointing with a smile at the florid clothes he was
wearing said, 'How religious, how saintly a man you wish to appoint
to such a holy see and above such a renowned and holy community of
monks! I know most certainly that if by God's arrangement it happened thus, very quickly you would turn your heart and favour away
from me, which is now great between us, and replace it with the most
savage hatred. I know indeed that you would demand much, and even
now you presume a great deal in ecclesiastical matters, which I would
not be able to tolerate with equanimity. And so the envious would
take advantage of the opportunity, and as soon as favour is extinguished they would stir up endless hatred between us'.

10. Thomas's reluctance is overcome (spring 1162)

The Lambeth Anonymous, *MTB* 4. 85–88.

As a man experienced in many things and accustomed to appraise the
future, ⌈Thomas⌉ foresaw and considered clearly enough the danger
of such a duty. No doubt he could see that this lofty position was
equally an honour and a burden, for as the head of the entire Church
of the realm, every ecclesiastical transgression would fall upon his
head. He could also see how he would have to give up accustomed
luxuries and put off the old man entirely,[58] if he wished to advance on
the appropriate path of service. He knew too, that if he were to cool in
the rigour of his ecclesiastical correction he would provoke the
reproach of men and disappointment among the common people, but
if he were to proceed in this regard as he ought, he would invite
widespread resentment. Eventually he would lose either his beloved
lord the king, or God. For he would not deserve to reign with God, if
he submitted to the king's manoeuvres, nor could he rejoice with the
king, if he put the laws of God's saints first. He foresaw this without
any doubt, and turning it over again and again in his mind, anxious
and fearful, dreading the scale of his elevation he fled in the spirit.[59]
For while the king persevered, he tried to decline it, excusing himself,
not passing over or hiding from him how promotion would end up
depriving him of God's favour or his. But the more he resisted, the

---

58 See Ephesians 4.20–4, Colossians 3.9.
59 See Augustine, *Contra Gaudentium* 1. 17.

more forcefully the king blazed up in favour of his desire, so highly did he rate his remarkable integrity, so much confidence did he have in his loyalty and devotion towards him. Certainly the king was a man whom one must obey, or risk proscription and hatred.

But also at this time Henry of Pisa, cardinal-priest of the Roman Church, was performing the office of legate in Normandy.[60] Thomas listened to his advice and agreed that he ought not refuse a gift so insistently offered on behalf of Christ's Church, nor spurn so honourable an opportunity, through which, unburdened from human obligations, he could be free from now on to God's work. When the clergy of England eventually gathered to appoint a metropolitan, it was reported that the demands of the mother Church and the suffragan bishops in this regard had been met. And although as tends to happen in such situations, certain rivals[61] sighed with no little regret, yet nothing was openly advanced to hamper or delay the undertaking. When such people were unable to prevent the election, Thomas cast his thoughts on the Lord,[62] and justly thinking His decree to be that which human zeal had urged, he decided it was better to put himself in God's hands, committing and submitting himself entirely to His mercy …[63]

So, putting himself in danger on the Church's behalf, he did not reject this prize, but with the clergy pleading and the king urging he accepted, albeit unwillingly. It was as if one of the seraphim had flown to him, and touched his lips with a burning coal which he had taken with tongs from the altar, and to God, seeking who to send, he answered, 'Here I am, send me'.[64] He decided that from now on he would not be silent before the people of unclean lips,[65] would not be quiet, and if he were unable to do so with the aid of love's privilege, at least by force of reason he would work to achieve the liberation of the Church before the king.

---

60 Cardinal-priest of St Nereus and St Achilles, Henry was one of the pope's legates in France, along with William of Pavia.

61 Presumably a reference to Gilbert Foliot.

62 See Psalm 55.22.

63 See Ecclesiasticus 2.22. At this point the Anonymous reviews the policy which Thomas adopted towards the Church as chancellor, how he tolerated some outrages but also attempted to rein in the king's ambition towards the Church's liberties.

64 See Isaiah 6.6.

65 See Isaiah 6.5.

11. Election as archbishop (May 1162)

Edward Grim, *MTB* 2. 365–6.

Meanwhile Archbishop Theobald came to the end of his worldly life, and the see was empty of a prelate. The king, then, thinking that the chancellor would follow his desire in all things, as before, and obey his orders, bestowed the office of archbishop on him. But the plan was delayed a little, until consent was secured from the community,[66] which was long accustomed to have a free voice in the election of a pontiff. For if it cried out against it, no one in the kingdom could intrude anyone of his own authority. So he sent three bishops to Canterbury,[67] and with them Richard de Lucy, a noble and the justiciar of the realm, to gain the community's approval. He also sent the chancellor to England on various errands, and especially to gain the fealty and subjection of all to his son, then to be crowned and sworn in as king.[68] The bishops crossed the sea and came to Canterbury where they greeted the community in the king's name. In the chapter before all, Richard, a man of great eloquence, pleaded the cause for which he had been sent in the chapter, before all. 'This', he said, 'the king orders you, since this Church has been too long deprived of a pontiff, to the serious danger of the flock. You know it to be his wish that you enjoy free election of the archbishop just as before. All the same, may such a person be provided who is equal to such a burden, worthy of the honour and pleasing to the king'.[69] To which the prior said, 'May the Lord Creator of all things, who established the Church through the shedding of His own blood, deign to provide a pastor acceptable to you, profitable to us, a model of virtue and an example of righteousness to his whole church. And thanks be to the king for not depriving us of this dignity, which we have had for so long'. As their common response, the envoys added, 'When you are all inclined to comply with royal mandates, it is well advised that you choose someone who would freely protect the cause of your church, and who would have influence with royal majesty in all things. For if a

---

66 The monastic community of Christ Church Canterbury.

67 Hilary of Chichester, Bartholomew of Exeter and Walter of Rochester.

68 This did not happen until 14 June 1170, with momentous consequences: see below, pp. 172–4.

69 Though the monks of Christ Church were entitled to elect their archbishop, the king's wish tended to play a very important role.

candidate is chosen who does not please the king, you will find schism and discord with such a pastor providing disturbance not refuge, when you have before you no few who would be pleasing to the king if chosen'. Driven then to sounder counsel, with the envoys present, they proceeded with the election, and after invoking the Holy Spirit, through whom rulers perceive what is correct, the chancellor was chosen as pastor and patron, according to the wish and acclamation of all, no doubt divinely inspired.[70] The king's envoys approved the election, asserting that the king would freely give his consent, and that there was no one more suitable or virtuous for this honour in the realm.

What else? Counsel was solemnly taken in London,[71] the chancellor was chosen by the clergy and people, and the election was confirmed, and was pleasing to all. Only the bishop of London[72] cried out against it, but with the throng crying, 'the voice of God and not man', he became silent and put a finger to his mouth. The election was presented to the king's son, yet to be crowned. He consented, and he was thankful. But the bishop of Winchester, a prudent man of great age, addressed the gathering in these words, and especially those to whom the king had committed his duties in this matter. 'This man', he said, 'whom by common consent we have chosen as patron, when he was chancellor and foremost in the country, held in his hand the king's treasures and the revenues of the realm, and undertook many tasks as demanded. But lest in the future he be open to exaction or false accusation, as if he had spent his lord's wealth more according to his own wish than to the advantage of the country we receive him free and absolved from all charge. For it does not seem right for Holy Church to appoint a father or patron who is shown to be a slave to money, and who is liable to the necessity of human servitude'. To which the servants of the king said, 'from the mouth of the king we cry out that he is free from all accusation and exaction now and

---

70 Herbert of Bosham reports the opposition of some who argued that 'the archbishop, plucked not from the church but the court, would freely rage against the Church's belongings. And besides that, it would be incongruous, and against all divine law, for a man chained by the military belt rather than the monastic office, a follower and pastor of hounds and hawks, to be established as pastor of the sheep' (*MTB* 3. 182). The Lambeth Anonymous also reports critical voices (*MTB* 4. 85).

71 A council of senior clergy, nobles and royal officials chaired by Bishop Henry of Winchester was held on 23 May 1162.

72 The see of London was in fact vacant. Grim has in mind Gilbert Foliot, then bishop of Hereford, who transferred to London a year later.

forever'.[73] And thus iniquity closed its mouth for the moment, and the false accuser was silent, seeing that it had failed in its cherished hope.

12. From election to consecration (May–June 1162)

Herbert of Bosham, *MTB* 3. 185–6, 187–9.

Our Thomas then, now no longer chancellor of the court but elect of the Church, and absolved from all obligations to the court, soon, like a man awaking from a deep sleep, considered in his heart what he had been for a long time, and how he ought to be from now on. For a long time in court, like a man suffering from lethargy, as it seemed, he was forgetful of himself, but now returning to himself he meditated in his heart. And out of this meditation his heart grew warm, and soon began to kindle to a flame. In this way the new man,[74] thought to have been extinct, was nourished and strengthened, and little by little began to grow, but did not yet raise its head. Nevertheless, as we have already said, this new man in his discreet caution was hidden in the habit of the old man, rather than oppressed by the old, unless one considers such concealment to be oppression. But now, at the beginning of his transformation the new man hungered to be revealed, and would let himself be hidden no longer.

Our elect, just as he was born in London, was also elected there. Soon after the election he set out for the metropolitan see of Canterbury with a large and numerous retinue. On the journey, without turning into a field, rather remaining on the path, he sent for the disciple who wrote these things,[75] and told him privately of a vision he had received the previous night in which a certain venerable person had stood by him and offered him ten talents. The disciple turned his mind a little to its interpretation, but hesitated to draw a conclusion about the dream. However, when it turned out to be fulfilled of Thomas, as had not then been thought, this evangelical servant, without any hesitation or mystery, understood it most clearly as signifying the man who

73 The biographers' reports differ as to the nature of this absolution. William of Canterbury claims he was absolved from all secular business (*MTB* 1. 9), Fitzstephen, from any secular judicial proceedings (*MTB* 3. 36); Garnier, from rendering of accounts (Garnier, 514–30), Herbert, from obligations to the royal court (*MTB* 3. 185), 'Roger', from every imaginable claim against him (*MTB* 4. 17–18). The various reports are discussed by Barlow, pp. 71–2.

74 See Colossians 3.9.

75 John the Evangelist's description of himself, eg. 21.24.

received five talents by lot, and gained a further five by investment.[76] Still speaking in private to the disciple as they went along the road, he quickly added, 'This I desire, this I instruct you, that whatever men say about me, you tell me boldly and in private. And if I fail in any of my work, as I say, I enjoin you to tell me freely and confidently, but secretly. For many things may be said about me from now on which are not said to me, which to a great extent is also true of others, especially the rich – many here and there speak about them in public, but few or none to them. Likewise, also point out any transgressions that you see and judge to be so'. And at the end of his talk he added, 'Certainly four eyes see more circumspectly and clearly than two' ...[77]

So we all travelled from London, where he had been elected, to Canterbury, where as metropolitan see, following custom and canonical provision, the consecration of the metropolitan was to be performed. Already almost the whole of the realm thronged to this consecration, on account of reverence for the one to be consecrated. The clergy went according to their duty, but so did the great and noble of the realm, so that they might show their esteem and obedience to the king, whom the business pleased so much, and also to the elect, who had advanced from the court. Therefore in that sacramental time, in those days of extraordinary and wonderful anointing, in the week of Pentecost,[78] on the Saturday of the week, time and order, as soon became clear, being in harmony with the sacraments, the archdeacon and elect of the Church was ordained priest, and the next day, the day of the Lord, was consecrated archbishop.[79] But when he had been ordained priest, it was soon debated among the pontiffs which of the provincial bishops ought to have the main hand in the consecration. The episcopal seat of London, to which it was recognised to pertain, then being vacant, the bishop of Winchester, who took the place of London when he was absent or no longer there, claimed that it belonged to him in every way. But the bishop of Rochester, on the contrary, contended that it was his and no other's, because from the foundation of his church by special and peculiar right he was chaplain to the archbishop. But nevertheless, because of certain things which here I pass over, saving the right of the church of Rochester in this particular,

76 See Matthew 25.14 ff.

77 Herbert reflects on Thomas's prudence in employing this policy.

78 It was on the feast of Pentecost that the disciples were first filled with the Holy Spirit (Acts 2.1–4).

79 2 and 3 June 1162. Thomas, though a clerk and archdeacon, had not been priested.

by the consent of the venerable man of Rochester, so distinguished in generosity and holiness, the consecration of the archbishop was handed over to Henry bishop of Winchester, and on the next day, the day of the Lord in the week of Pentecost, very festively and magnificently, as was appropriate to such a great future archbishop, it was consummated. In addition to the almost countless crowd of great men and nobles of the realm, most notably the illustrious Henry, still a boy,[80] the king's son and heir, fourteen co-provincial bishops were present at the consecration, fifteen including the consecrated archbishop, if I am not mistaken. And so our elect was consecrated archbishop, he being then around 44 years of age.[81]

So envoys were immediately sent to Alexander III of happy memory, pontiff of the Holy See, who again on account of the schism, which was then troubling the Roman Church, had taken himself to Montpellier and there had stayed for some time.[82] Those who were sent, then, religious men, lettered and honourable, as is proper urgently and energetically asked for that symbol of metropolitans which is called the pallium.[83] Because of favour towards them and especially because of favour towards the one to whose use this was being sought, they received the pallium quickly and easily from the apostolic see, and in short they returned with it joyfully and safely. And so our Thomas with the greatest devotion received the pallium and was made archbishop.

13. Change of life (1162)

Thomas's wearing of the hairshirt and monastic garb was apparently hidden from all except his confessor. See below, no. 52.

William of Canterbury, *MTB* 1.10–11.

When he had been consecrated, so that along with the sacrament the essence of the sacrament should follow, he set out to renew the old

80 He was seven years of age.

81 It was customary for the newly-consecrated archbishop to have a copy of the gospels held above his head and for him to point at random to a passage which would act as his 'prognostic', a foreshadowing of his term in office. Gilbert Foliot tells us that Thomas's prognostic was Christ's condemnation of the fig-tree, '"May no fruit ever come from you again!" And the fig-tree withered at once' (Matthew 21.19. See below, p. 227). Not surprisingly, none of the biographers mentions this.

82 See above, p. 22.

83 A type of stole which an archbishop or bishop received from the pope as a symbol of office.

man. And giving his thoughts to hows high he had climbed, how previously as a courtier he had neglected himself, he exerted himself to make up for lost time. So, as if transformed into another man,[84] he became more restrained, more watchful, more frequent in prayer, more attentive in preaching; and thinking true progress of renewal should begin from himself, and that in order to rule over others properly he should first learn to preside over himself, he subjected his body to servitude, teaching it to be subservient, and taught the spirit to rule.

And having put on the monastic habit with the hairshirt, the spiritual man, which nevertheless under the seemliness of his clothes he hid from the eyes of men, he filled with merits. And few being aware, he served as a soldier under the breastplate of faith,[85] happy because in threefold dress he performed the functions of a threefold person; on the outside he showed the clerk, beneath he hid the monk and within he suffered the hardships of the desert without being in the desert; happy because on the outside he deceived the world, beneath he conformed to his brothers, and within he subdued the illicit stirrings of the flesh; happy because on the outside he exposed the canon, beneath he hid the hermit, and within he satisfied the Lord's mandate. For he heard from a certain monk of Canterbury, most holy in his way of life, to whom the Lord spoke in a vision, that if he should put on the monk, he would earn the Lord's favour and aid in his business.

14. Thomas as archbishop (1162)

This description of Thomas's life influenced many of the other biographers. Herbert of Bosham takes a different, 'day in the life' approach in which at great length he describes, for example, Thomas's ministrations to the poor, celebration of the divine office, his duties as judge and conduct at table (*MTB* 3. 198–238).

John of Salisbury, *MTB* 2. 306–8.

Upon his consecration he immediately put off the old man,[86] and put on the hairshirt and the monk, crucifying the flesh with its passions and desires.[87] Going over the fact that he had taken on the office of

84 See Ephesians 4.20–4; Colossians 3.9.
85 See 1 Thessalonians 5.8.
86 See Ephesians 4.20–4.
87 See Galatians 5.24.

teacher and pastor, he fulfilled the duty of preaching, and whatever
time he could withdraw from pressing business he almost always gave
to prayer and reading. He prayed alone until he was filled with the
miracle of tears, and was so caught up in the office of the altar that it
was as if he beheld Christ's passion before him in the flesh. He performed the divine sacrament with great reverence in order to inform
the faith and morals of those who witnessed. He spurned all gifts and
completely expelled the filth of avarice from his house. He was also
prudent in counsel, and a scrupulous and disciplined judge in the
consideration of cases, thorough in questioning, prompt in response,
impartial in justice, and entirely free from bribery, in every way a
most upright administrator of the law. Beneath the seemliness of his
dress he studiously concealed the soldier of Christ, lest its merits be
diminished by vainglory, and following the decree of the wise man, he
conformed on the outside to the people, while within almost everything was different.[88] He would not approach the palace table unless
paupers were first admitted, and for this purpose he wished the table
to be more lavishly and plentifully enriched, so that from what
remained beggars might be consoled more fully and thankfully. A
pauper begging from house to house never left his door empty-handed.
Through his men he carefully enquired into the homes of the sick and
disabled, and he visited them with gifts, supporting many of them
with food and clothes daily. Since his predecessor Theobald of pious
memory was accustomed to double the established alms of his own
predecessors, Thomas, in an act of pious rivalry, decided to double
even his doubling. So as to observe this religious work, he set aside a
tithe from everything which he received by whatever right. Every day
in his private cell on bended knees he would wash the feet of thirty
paupers in memory of Christ, and after a full meal would lavish four
silver coins on each of them. And on the few occasions when he was
prevented from doing so in person, he arranged most diligently that it
be carried out through a proxy. He entertained religious men with
such reverence that it seemed that in them he was paying homage to
the Divine Presence or to angels. He was so effective in exercising
hospitality and other generous works that his resources appeared as if
they were the common property of all. And however much his home,
according to normal custom, was ennobled by precious utensils and
various instruments of show, nevertheless on God's behalf he condemned riches and all worldly goods as dung, using transitory things

88 See Seneca, *Epistles* 5.

more for necessity than savouring the voluptuous enjoyments of desire. In food and drink he held to the mean of temperance, lest by absolutely abstaining he be accused of fanaticism, or by consuming too much he be charged with over-indulgence. Avoiding almost equally then the mark of the offender and the hypocrite, he observed the best kind of fast, keeping a measured sobriety. And even in precious clothes he was a pauper in spirit, with a happy face he maintained a contrite heart, at a lavish table he opted for penury, often with a stomach more refreshed than full, and sometimes more empty than refreshed.

Always remaining sober then, he conformed to those dwelling with him, following the apostle, who by the most beneficial disposition was made all things to all men,[89] to the profit of all. He freed the poor from the powerful, as he who was in fact given by the Lord as a father of paupers and consoler of the deserving. He freely condemned the vices of powerful men, knowing that where there is the Spirit of the Lord, there is freedom. Still, as a prudent man he would consider the character of men whom he criticised or advised, so as not to give holy things to dogs or cast pearls before swine.[90] And as he was instructed by the heavenly unction,[91] whether he spoke to the lettered or un-lettered, he appeared wonderful in his eloquent and erudite way, and his preaching was pleasing and effective as much from the weight of the argument as purity of words. After a meal and sleep when it was necessary, he would, without consideration of the time, begin afresh on business or scriptures or praiseworthy conversations, avoiding leisure with the utmost effort, lest his enemies see him, and mock his downfall.[92] What he could deduct from nightly sleep without grave damage to the body, he devoted to tears and prayers, and holy medita-tions, pursuing chastity in the body, observing purity in heart, modesty in speech and righteousness in action, so that those whom he was meant to teach by word, he might affect more powerfully by the example of his holiness. He struck out indefatigably against heretics and schismatics, and could never be induced to communicate with excommunicates, and whoever was an enemy of sound doctrine, he did not doubt would be an enemy to him in Christ. Also being ardent in zeal for justice, he exerted himself to protect what was his, oblivious to gifts and inducements.

89 See 1 Corinthians 9.22.
90 See Matthew 7.6.
91 I.e. by the oil of anointing which he received in his consecration.
92 See Lamentations 1.7.

II: CONFLICT WITH THE KING (1162–64)

15. Initial harmony (1162–64)

Herbert's account is unusual in emphasising a period of harmony before the friendship between Thomas and Henry was shattered.[1] While it is a welcome antidote to the biographers who describe an immediate eruption of conflict upon Thomas's elevation to Canterbury, Herbert's version is also guilty of distortion. He passes over the danger to the relationship between archbishop and king caused by Thomas's claiming of royal castles and his antagonising of the king's tenants-in-chief. The description of the council of Tours is highly selective, ignoring the involvement of other English bishops, Thomas's quarrels with York, and his failed attempt to have Anselm canonised. His most serious distortion is in putting together the dedication of Reading Abbey and the translation of Edward the Confessor as an example of concord: the translation probably occurred on the first day of the Council of Westminster, 13 October 1163, when disputes had already arisen between the archbishop and the king, and the dedication of Reading Abbey took place on 19 April 1164, between the Council of Clarendon and the Council of Northampton, when the conflict had already become very bitter.

Herbert of Bosham, *MTB* 3. 250–5, 260.

And now Thomas, who up to this had sailed in the harbour of the church, began to set out into the secular sea and deal with secular matters – something that is often necessary for a pontiff, but never pleasant for a wise one. He raised the issue of estates which certain magnates of the realm, great and powerful men, had taken from his church[2] because of either the impotence or negligence of his predecessors. He asked for the return of some, but took back without question many where there seemed to be obvious injury. The latter, those commonly called fee-farms,[3] the archbishop recalled to his own dominion immediately upon his entrance to the archiepiscopacy as if they belonged to his own estate. He expelled those called fee-farmers without the inquiry of any fiscal judge. He was called to answer and refused to plead concerning these lands which were known to belong to his estate, even if they had been alienated on whatever unjust claim. And

---

1 The Lambeth Anonymous also allows for this period, but describes it in less depth (*MTB* 4. 92–5)

2 I.e. Canterbury.

3 Lands, usually with heritable status, rented for a fixed sum. Presumably Thomas thought the rent too low.

so he held and managed these estates according to his will until he was banished and, proscribed for justice' sake, he lost these and others. Moreover with great urgency he demanded that fief which was said to belong to William of Ros, a fief, if I am not mistaken, of seven knights' fees, which had been confiscated soon after the death of Archbishop Theobald. But the archbishop limited himself to raising the question of the fief until the king, who was then outside the realm, returned. But as it happened, because of other things that came up, he did not address the issue when the king next returned, but put it off. The archbishop also had a serious clash with the earl of Clare, when he demanded the earl do him homage for Tonbridge Castle and all the land belonging to it, and in particular for everything within a league of the castle, commonly called the bailiwick, or in Latin *bannum leugae*. The earl offered homage, but refused to state explicitly the basis upon which he did so, as the archbishop had wished.[4] The archbishop also called for the custody of Rochester Castle to be returned,[5] which he also claimed by right of his church, producing to this end a public instrument, a charter of William of blessed memory, illustrious former king of England, who had acquired the realm forcefully on the battlefield through the strength of his hand.[6] When he put forward these and similar questions, and recalled some estates and asked for others back, the archbishop was quickly faced with many disputes, quarrels and adversaries. However all were hidden because of fear of the king, for they were aware and respectful of the extraordinary royal favour in which, as we have shown above, the archbishop was still held, and on this account they were quite afraid to offend the archbishop. Nevertheless, some who either felt they had been injured or feared injury made their way to the king who was still outside the realm. In pleading their case some made known what had happened to them, and others outlined the injury which would befall them through the archbishop, unless royal clemency directed itself to justice. And hoping perhaps in some way to undermine the king's constant favour towards the archbishop, they added that too much royal favour would make the archbishop arrogant. But the king, who loved him in deed and truth was in no way moved by these pleas, and refused to listen.

---

4 William of Ros and Roger of Clare, earl of Hereford, were tenants-in-chief of the king, the latter a particularly powerful one.

5 Rochester he claimed from the king, along with the royal castles of Saltwood and Hythe.

6 I.e. William I.

And because he was on the point of crossing the sea, he put off the petitioners until his arrival in England.

After a little, the king was, according to right and custom, announced to have landed at the southern port of Southampton. He landed in the first year of the archbishop's consecration, shortly after Christmas Day, if I am not mistaken.[7] The archbishop who, in the company of that distinguished boy, Henry the king's son and heir, had awaited his arrival for many days, immediately came to meet him. And when the archbishop was admitted to the king's lodgings with the king's son Henry, the king and all his men came running to him, and there was great joy and celebration throughout the whole court. The king and archbishop threw themselves into mutual kisses and embraces, each trying to outdo the other in giving honour. So much so that it seemed that the king was not effusive enough towards his son, being entirely effusive towards the archbishop, and spread himself out into joy, now for the first time seeing his Thomas, once of the court, as archbishop. For he was especially and above all filled with joy because he had already privately heard so many great things about the sanctity of the archbishop who had been plucked from his court. But shortly after they had exchanged joyful greetings, the archbishop, out of consideration for the king's weariness and exhaustion after his sea journey, left and returned to his lodgings. The next day, however, they met and set out together, with no attendants, just the two of them, speaking frankly together in private, and complimenting each other. But when they had spent a few days in this manner, the archbishop, along with his charge, the king's son, took his leave of the king in the highest favour. But the aforesaid plaintiffs,[8] seeing and hearing these things, made themselves scarce and dropped their petitions.

Then after a little, Pope Alexander III of happy memory convened a council throughout the entire Catholic Church[9] – for there was at that time a schism in the Roman Church. Therefore our archbishop, who

---

7 He arrived in late January 1163.

8 See above, p. 71.

9 See R. Somerville, *Pope Alexander III and the Council of Tours (1163)* (Berkeley, 1977). The main purpose of the council was, like that of the Council of Montpellier in May 1162, to assert Alexander III's authority over the antipope (see above, p. 22). During the council Thomas clashed with Roger of York over seating arrangements. He also tried to secure the canonisation of his predecessor Anselm, but the pope deferred all petitions because there were too many. After 1170, the question of Anselm's canonisation was rapidly overshadowed by the success of Thomas's cult.

was great in all things, prepared himself with great splendour to cross
the sea. The king, whom he loved as a lord and more than a man,
visited him, and the archbishop's charge[10] was restored to his father.
After some days spent in pleasant and intimate conversation, he said
goodbye to the king and awaited a favourable wind on the Kent coast
in one of his own villages, called Romney. When after a few days such
a wind was provided, he set sail and landed safely in Flanders, in the
port of Gravelines, with great and magnificent splendour. Soon Philip
count of Flanders and Vermandois came to him there, and on the next
day the magnates and nobles of the land hastened to him, eagerly
showing him full honour and offering whatever they could. He then
travelled through Normandy and Maine, all in the dominion of the
illustrious king of the England, through cities, towns and villages,
received with as much honour as if it were the king himself.
Approaching Tours, he entered the city, if I am not mistaken, on the
third day before the celebration of the council. Hearing of the arrival
of the archbishop of Canterbury the whole city was immediately
roused, and all went out to meet him, not only the citizens and locals,
but also the ecclesiastical persons who had now almost all assembled
for the council, archbishops and bishops of diverse nations. And one
ought not omit that, contrary to the custom of the Roman Church, the
lord fathers and rectors of the Church, all the cardinals, came out to
meet him well before he reached the city, except for two who
remained with the lord pope, lest in such a crowded throng he be left
without company. So great was the crowd of followers, as the
archbishop entered the palace to meet the lord pope, that the pope,
out of necessity lest he be crushed, left the chamber in which he had
been, and entered the palace. As if impelled by the spirit of prophecy,
the pope, who seldom got up for anyone, came to meet the archbishop,
and hastened to show him reverence. Indeed this whole meeting,
honorific and prophetic, like another Presentation of the Lord in the
person of the Lord's anointed, seems like a foretelling of the future.
This we fully see today, when people come to visit him from the
whole Christian world, from east and west, through many difficulties,
and a greater number adore him. So the lord pope then received him
most pleasantly, and more pleasant was it for him, who for a long
time had wished to see the archbishop, and had heard so much good
about him. And having consideration for his journey, as it seemed, he
dismissed him, saying, 'Go and rest father. Rest is needed after

10 I.e. the young Henry.

labour'. So then we[11] withdrew and resorted to our lodgings in the king's castle nearby.

Early the next day you would have seen a great crowd converging on these quarters, as those who had heard of Thomas's greatness now beheld it. So, day after day, ecclesiastics of diverse realms flocked to him, seeking and offering favour and friendship. Besides nobles and potentates of the land who repeatedly came and returned to us, also in particular royal justices, knowing the archbishop to be high in the king's favour, were constantly present around us, either performing service or ready to do so. And what is even greater, the Roman Church honoured our archbishop before all others as it were with the honour and respect due to primogeniture, as if he were the first-born of the many gathered there. But when the council had already been proceeding for a number of days, and at his petition some privileges of the archbishop's church had been renewed, the pope dismissed him and all of us who were with him with a kiss of peace, secure in apostolic blessing and favour. And indeed crossing the sea to England with a gentle breeze, we returned speedily in joy and prosperity, now in the second year of the archbishop's consecration. And, according to custom and right, he was received by the king in all happiness and enthusiasm as if a father by his son ...[12]

After a little the archbishop called together many co-provincial bishops and magnificently dedicated that noble and royal abbey of Reading, in which Henry of divine memory, formerly king of England, and grandfather of our illustrious king Henry II, himself its founder, rests in a glorious mausoleum.[13] This was done at the king's wish and in his presence. And in the same year[14] in London, at the equally famous and royal abbey of Westminster, he raised from the dust the body of the glorious and truly saintly Edward, as a very distinguished and precious vessel of perfect continence.[15] And on account of the many outstanding merits of his royal life he solemnly elevated it and placed it among the bodies of the saints, likewise at the wish of the king and

11 Herbert accompanied Thomas to Tours.

12 Here Herbert describes how Thomas encouraged the king to fill vacant sees.

13 The dedication of Reading Abbey, which became something of an Angevin shrine, took place on 19 April 1164, and was one of the last acts of co-operation between Thomas and Henry.

14 Probably 13 October 1163.

15 The cult of King Edward the Confessor (1042–66) was vigorously promoted by Henry, who was a kinsman through his great-grandmother Margaret of Scotland. This translation probably took place on 13 October 1163.

in his presence. And, as we have said, the heart and mind of the illustrious king and holy pontiff were as one in God, and through this kingship and priesthood converged in the greatest peace and tranquillity, through the power of the God of peace and love.

But alas and truly alas, nothing in life lasts forever, nothing stays the same, but according to the saying of the wise and most experienced man, 'For everything there is a season, and a time for every matter under heaven: a time to weep, and a time to laugh, a time to love and a time to hate, a time for war and a time for peace: for everything there is a season'.[16] Great certainly the reputations and beloved bonds of such a great king and such a great pontiff. Indeed it would have been difficult to find in any other country in the world such a great king and so great a pontiff, and such harmony between such great men. Great indeed the harmony, but brief the duration.

16. Beginning of the troubles (summer 1163)

The biographers tend to identify the root of the conflict in Henry's project, inspired by evil counsellors, to limit the Church's rights, combined with Thomas's new zeal for ecclesiastical liberty. Most point to the Council of Woodstock as the first major clash between the king and archbishop when Henry attempted to levy the Danegeld in the form of 'sheriff's aid'. The case of Philip de Broi discussed here is the most celebrated case of 'criminous clerks' – those clerks accused of a serious felony whom Henry believed were receiving unduly lenient treatment in ecclesiastical courts.

'Roger of Pontigny', *MTB* 4. 22–5.

It happened at that time in certain crowded gathering that Thomas delivered a sermon to the clergy and people in the presence of the king. His sermon concerned the kingdom of Christ the Lord, which is the Church, and the worldly kingdom, and the powers of each realm, priestly and royal, and also the two swords, the spiritual and the material.[17] And

---

16 See Ecclesiastes 3.1; 4.8.

17 '[The disciples] said "Look, Lord, here are two swords". And he said to them, "It is enough"' (Luke 22.38). In the eleventh century this became one of the most commonly used images of temporal and spiritual power. It was expounded by Gottschalk of Aachen and Peter Damian and later by Bernard of Clairvaux and was the source of much discussion in the continental schools of the twelfth century. See Smalley, pp. 26–8; I. S. Robinson, *Authority and Resistance in the Investiture Controversy* (Manchester, 1978), pp. 135–9. Herbert of Bosham reports how Thomas pointed to the distinct order of clergy in these terms at the Council of Westminter, October 1163: 'Holy church, the mother of all, both secular and priestly, has two

as on this occasion he discussed much about ecclesiastical and secular power in a wonderful way – for he was very eloquent – the king took note of each of his words, and recognising that he rated ecclesiastical dignity far above any secular title, he did not receive his sermon with a placid spirit. For he sensed from his words how distant the archbishop was from his own position: that the Church owned nothing and could do nothing unless he granted it. How that which had already lurked in the heart of the king from then on came out in the open, how the venerable archbishop opposed himself as a wall for the house of the Lord,[18] and with what constancy he came to interpose himself to royal fury in order to protect ecclesiastical liberty, the following will tell. For whenever tyrants occupied the kingdom, they destroyed ecclesiastical liberties completely. This king Henry, following in their footsteps, usurped for himself the entirety of ecclesiastical management and organisation. For he conferred bishoprics and abbacies on whomsoever he wished, and now at his order and decree he drew priests and clerks to secular judgement, as if they were no different from the common people.

The first occasion then, whereby the archbishop's intention and constancy became known was like this. It was the custom in these parts that the king, for the greater security and custody of the kingdom, would appoint one of his vassals as sheriff[19] in each county of the realm. And the counts and barons were accustomed to arrange a payment from their men to this sheriff, the king's official, of two shillings a year from each measure of their land, which they call by the ancestral name of hides, seeing that these officers protect them by their service and favour from facing exaction and false charges. Realising that these two shillings from each hide, if put together, would amount to a huge sum – for there are many thousands of hides – the king wished to attach it to his own use and revenues. On this account the bishops and nobles of the realm were called together at Woodstock,[20] and the king began to outline his plan to include this money in his revenues. And when this speech was met with universal

---

kings, two laws, two jurisdictions and two types of punishment: two kings, Christ the King of Heaven and the worldly king; two laws, human and divine; two jurisdictions, priestly and lay; two types of punishment, spiritual and worldly. "Behold there are two swords". "It is sufficient", said the Lord' (*MTB* 3. 268).

18 See Ezekiel 13.5.

19 The principal royal official in each locality.

20 1 July 1163.

silence, the archbishop alone answered, with great frankness but enough mildness, 'Lord, it does not become your excellence to deflect something that belongs to another to your use, especially when these two shillings are conferred on your ministers not out of necessity or duty, but rather as a favour. For if your sheriffs conduct themselves peacefully and respectfully towards our men, we will indeed give freely. But if they do not we will not, nor can we be forced by law'. To this the king in a fury said, 'By the eyes of God, they will be enrolled immediately', referring to those rolls in which a record of royal revenues are kept,[21] 'but you yourself well ought to assent to my wish in this regard'. Then the archbishop said, 'By the eyes by which you swear, never while I am living will they be given from my land'. Sensing then that the archbishop was clearly opposed to him, the king was greatly displeased.

Not much later another bitter conflict arose between them on account of a certain canon called Philip de Broi,[22] whom certain people had accused of killing a knight. He had given adequate answer to the king on this homicide charge, and when his adversaries had failed in the case, he purged himself to prove his innocence more clearly. But a certain Simon FitzPeter, whom the king had appointed as judge in the region of Bedford, where the same Philip lived, tried to reopen the case. Philip, however, refused to answer again to a charge which had already been concluded and terminated by judicial procedure, certainly before a lay justice. Furthermore, he indignantly rebuffed this Simon, injuring him with many insults and calumnies.

The king being then in London, Simon came to him and told him all that Philip had done to him. Hearing these things the king flew into a rage, and swore fearfully in his accustomed way by the eyes of God, that he would regard the abuse thrown at his knight as if Philip had thrown it at himself. So, without delay he ordered him to be judged. But the archbishop, who was present and heard this said, 'By no means will it be so, for laymen cannot be the judges of clerks. If a clerk offends in some way he ought to be corrected in the ecclesiastical court. So, if the king or his knight complains of any offence to himself let him come or send his men to Canterbury, and there he will receive

21 The pipe rolls, in which accounts of the exchequer were kept.

22 This is the most celebrated case of a 'criminous clerk'. On this issue, see C. Duggan, *Canon Law in Medieval England* (Variorum Reprints, London 1982), especially 'The Becket Dispute and the Criminous Clerks' (first published in *Bulletin of the Institute of Historical Research*, 35 (1962), 1–28).

full justice on ecclesiastical authority'. The king was enraged and said much, but nevertheless, though unwilling, he sent certain bishops and nobles to Canterbury on the day appointed by the archbishop, who urgently assailed Philip with the old charge of homicide. And when it was judged that a terminated case ought not be repeated in an ecclesiastical court, he was finally charged on the insults made to the king's knight. And since Philip would not deign to deny it, for he was a great man from a great family, his adversaries burst out in public, saying, 'We demand judgement on the evident injury which has not been denied'. And even when Philip offered himself for voluntary satisfaction, it was still demanded that he be judged. Therefore Philip was sentenced to place his benefice in the king's hands for two years, and the king during this time would do as he wished with his revenues. But he also offered himself naked before the knight, to make satisfaction, following the custom of the land. When those who had been sent returned and reported on what had been done, the king answered that his honour had been injured and denied. But when the bishops said that they had judged justly, except they had for the sake of peace and the king's honour oppressed Philip more than he deserved, the king became angrier and said, 'By the eyes of God, you will swear to me that you will pronounce true judgement'.

17. Early disputes (summer 1163)

William Fitzstephen, *MTB* 3. 43, 45–6.

The archbishop granted the church of Eynsford to a certain clerk called Lawrence. For it was his right not only to fill vacant churches on the estates of the monks of Canterbury but on those of the arch-bishop's barons. The lord of the estate, William of Eynsford, objected, and expelled Lawrence's men, so the archbishop excommunicated him. The king immediately wrote to the archbishop that he should absolve him. The archbishop answered that it was not the king's place to order the absolution or excommunication of anyone. The king claimed that it was his royal right that none of his tenants-in-chief[23] was to be excommunicated without his consultation. Eventually, to allay the king, who was now furious with him, and would only communicate with him through envoys, the archbishop absolved William. And the

23 Those who held their lands or offices directly from the king, i.e the senior nobility and royal officialdom.

king, being at Windsor said, 'I give him no thanks for it now' ...[24]

An early dissension between the king and holy Thomas arose over a certain clerk in the district of Worcester who was said to have lain with the daughter of a certain distinguished man, and on her account to have killed her father. The king wished this clerk to be examined and judged by a proceeding of the secular court. The archbishop resisted, and arranged that the clerk be kept in the bishop's custody, so as not to be handed over to royal justice. Another dispute arose over a clerk who stole a silver cup from the church of his archbishop, St Mary-le-Bow in Cheapside, London. When he was arrested the king wished him to be judged in a secular court. But the archbishop had him stripped of his order by the Church court, and also had him branded to placate the king.

18. The Council of Westminster (October 1163)

Summa Causae Inter Regem et Thomam, MTB 4. 201–5.

Henry, noble king of England, duke of Normandy and Aquitaine and count of Anjou, came to London on 1 October 1163,[25] as did Thomas archbishop of Canterbury, Roger archbishop of York, and all the bishops of England. The sole and entire purpose of the council was that the metropolitan of Canterbury be solemnly designated as primate of all England, to which only the archbishop of York objected.[26] When, lo and behold, to everyone's surprise the king of England began to propose certain rather harsh measures.

First he bitterly complained of unruly archdeacons,[27] who turned the wrongs of others into profit for themselves, who exacted payment for sins, and used it to cultivate their own excessive luxury, without

---

24 Here William describes a case dating from Theobald's time regarding exactions by archdeacons and rural deans.

25 This date has been challenged on the basis that the conference is more likely to have begun with the translation of Edward the Confessor, which seems to have occurred on 13 October: see *Councils and Synods*, pp. 849–50.

26 This claim is not corroborated by the other sources, and is probably a reflection of Canterbury bias. It refers to the 'primacy dispute' between Canterbury and York, a matter of heated debate since the late eleventh century. Canterbury claimed a position of supremacy over the entire English Church, while York claimed equal status to Canterbury.

27 Bishops' deputies and representatives. They tended to have a reputation for corruption.

rendering the correction due to sinners. And he said that archdeacons should not summon anyone on any charge, however great the suspicion, without the knowledge of his official. And soon turning to another subject he said, 'I am very concerned with peace, and greatly distressed on its behalf, which in my kingdom is disturbed by the wickedness of clerks who perpetrate rapine and theft and often murder. Therefore I seek and desire that by your consent, lord of Canterbury, and that of your fellow bishops, clerks caught in evil-doing or who confess to it be convicted in the ecclesiastical court, and then be transferred immediately to the magistrates of my court, so that stripped of ecclesiastical protection they receive physical punishment. I also desire and seek that you consent to my officials being present as the clerk is stripped of ecclesiastical orders, so that they can take hold of him immediately, and not allow him an opportunity to flee physical punishment'.

The archbishop of Canterbury, when he was unable to obtain a respite until the next morning for an answer to this request, withdrew in conclave with his fellow bishops. Soon various arguments were advanced. The bishops said that according to secular law discharged clerks should be transferred to the court, and after this spiritual penalty should receive physical punishment. Having a greater dignity on account of their order, they should be judged more harshly for their offence, and being judged more harshly, they should be punished more severely. 'No wonder then', they said, 'if punishment to the body should follow the deprivation of their order'. This they proved not only with reference to laws, but also with authoritative examples. They pointed to the Levites of the Old Testament, who when convicted of a very serious offence were punished with death, or for a lesser crime lost a limb.

But the lord of Canterbury, being consistent with the holy canons, argued the contrary, asserting that it would be altogether unjust and contrary to the canons and to God, if to punish one crime, someone submit to two judgements. '"For God does not judge twice for the same thing".[28] For what the Church judges', he said, 'is either just or unjust. You will not grant that it is unjust, therefore it is just. And when a judgement is not an absolution, it is a condemnation. If then the accused is condemned, and stripped of his office, one ought not initiate another trial to condemn the same sin. Also, we must be aware that our consent does not allow the oppression and destruction of the

28 Jerome's commentary on Nahum 1.9.

Church's liberty, for which, by the example of our Most High Priest,[29] we are bound by our office to fight to the death. You have not yet resisted to the point of shedding your blood.'[30]

The bishops replied that the destruction of the Church's liberty would bring no danger to the Church. 'But', they said, 'it is better that it perish than that we all perish. Let us do therefore what the king requires. Otherwise no refuge will remain to us, and no one will care for us.[31] But if we give our consent to the king we will enjoy the sanctuary of the lord as our inheritance, and sleep secure in our ecclesiastical possessions. We must make allowances for the evil of these times'.[32] So said the bishops, as if the evil of the times were not enough without the added evil of the bishops.

In response the lord of Canterbury, inflamed by zeal for the house of God said, 'I see that you console yourself for your inertia under the guise of patience, and suffocate the liberty of Christ's bride under the pretext of management. Who put a spell on you, foolish bishops? Do you think you can cover up your manifest iniquity by calling it prudent management? What do you call management, that is destructive to the whole Church? Let things be called by their names, do not pervert things and words. I certainly agree with what you say, that we must make many allowances for the evil of the times, but that does not mean that sins should be heaped on sins. God is capable of improving the Church's condition without worsening ours. Is God unable to help the Church except through the crimes of the Church's teachers? I think you are feeling sorry for Christ's weaknesses, as if he were unable to lift up his bride,[33] unless aided by our judgement. In fact God is testing you. Let me ask, when ought bishops to offer themselves to danger, in tranquillity or in danger? You would certainly be ashamed to say that it is in tranquillity. Then it must be, that when the Church is threatened, the pastor of the Church ought to oppose himself to the danger. For it is just as worthy for us in our time to spill our blood for the liberty of the Church, as it was for the bishops of old to found the Church of Christ in their blood. And I affirm, with God as my witness, that it is not safe for us to retreat from this principle that we received from our saintly fathers. Nor

29 I.e. Christ.
30 Hebrews 12.4.
31 See Psalm 142.5.
32 See Ephesians 5.16.
33 I.e. the Church.

ought we to expose anyone to death, when we are not allowed to be present in a judgement involving bloodshed'.

These words were speedily reported to the king. Hearing that so many of the Church which he knew to be not columns but reeds, that swayed and quivered in the wind, were not about to submit to his will in every way – and certainly they would have given in to threats, had they not seen the archbishop's constancy so clearly – he realised that he could not achieve what he wished with this formula. Therefore, quickly turning to another, he asked if they would obey his royal customs in every respect. But the archbishop of Canterbury, when he had received counsel, said, 'Yes, in every way – saving in all respects our order'. Then the king asked the same of each in turn, and all replied in the same way. And when he continued to press, asking again and again if the archbishop of Canterbury would promise to observe his customs entirely, absolutely and without adding the exception of his order, he was unable to obtain what he wanted from the vicar of Christ. Therefore the king was greatly troubled, and all Jerusalem with him,[34] and in this heated mood he left London without notice, with all his business unfinished, and lawsuits left hanging.

You would have seen then disquiet among the laity, commotion among the clergy. The bishops, worried and fearful, pursued the king when he left, afraid that they would hear they had lost all their possessions if they did not find the king first. Soon they procured a secret meeting with the king, and disregarding all mention of God and their order, they gave their assent to his petition so freely that it seemed that they had conceded before they had even been asked. So much so that those who were thought most knowledgeable among them we found most eager to oppress the Church's liberty. Meanwhile the archbishop of Canterbury sat alone, looking right and left; no one took notice of him.[35] He sought solace in his brothers, but they shrank from him, and no longer walked with him. Finally, recognising the peace of sinners, and that danger was threatening him on all sides, he said, 'I have said that by no means would I obey the royal customs of an earthly king, unless in every way saving my order. On this account I incurred the offence of the king, on this account my brothers abandoned me, on this account I offended the whole world. What of

---

34 See Matthew 2.3: 'When Herod the king had heard [the wise men's report of Jesus' birth] he was troubled, and all Jerusalem with him.' The biographers make a number of similarly sly identifications of Henry with Herod and other tyrants.
35 See Psalm 142.4.

it? Whether the world likes it or not, in negotiating with a mortal man I will never, God willing, be forgetful of my God and my order. Far be it from me, that through fear or favour of any mortal I am found to have disparaged God. If an angel came down from the sky and gave me such advice I would curse it.'[36]

19. Thomas is persuaded to submit to the royal customs (winter 1163–64)

The day after the council of Westminster Henry demanded back the castles he had granted Thomas during his chancellorship, and removed his son Henry from Thomas's care. Pressure was brought to bear on Thomas from the English clergy and nobility and from a papal mission, until he agreed to accept the royal customs at Clarendon in January 1164.

'Roger of Pontigny', *MTB* 4. 27–37.

Frustrated in his purpose for the time being, soon after when he was staying at Northampton the king summoned the archbishop. He wanted to tempt him, to see if there was some way to turn him around and bend him to his will. The archbishop approached the town and announced his arrival to the king who, with whatever cunning, sent some men to meet him, who told him, 'The king is staying in town with many men, and you have come with no less a multitude. The place is not big enough to hold you both. Therefore the king commands you to wait here for him, and he will come and speak to you'. The archbishop then turned into a field, and the king arrived immediately without delay. The archbishop approached him, taking care to meet him first with the due honour of greeting. But because the horses on which they sat were so frisky, neighing and rearing up, they were unable to approach each other, so eventually when they had changed horses the two stood together, apart from the others.

Then the king addressed the archbishop in this way: 'Did I not raise you from a humble and poor rank to the highest peak of honour and distinction? And this did not seem enough to me, unless I also made you father of the realm, and even exalted you over myself. How is it then that so many favours, and such signs of my love for you, well known to all, could so suddenly be banished from your mind, so that not only do you turn out to be ungrateful, but even hostile to me in every way?' 'Far be it, my lord', said the archbishop. 'I am not

36 See Galatians 1.8.

unmindful of your favours, which in fact not simply you, but all-bestowing God, deigned to confer on me through you. For this reason far be it that I appear ungrateful or in any way hostile to your wish, provided that it agrees with God's will. For your dignity knows how much loyalty I have shown you, from whom I expected such great temporal reward. How much more necessary is it that we perform faithful and sincere service to Almighty God, from whom we receive temporal benefits and hope for eternal ones. Yes, you are my lord, but He is my Lord and yours, and to neglect His will so that I comply with yours would not be good for you or me. For in his terrible tribunal we will both be judged as servants of one Lord, neither of us will be able to answer for the other, but each of us will, without excuses, receive according to his deeds. For worldly lords ought to be obeyed, but not against God, as St Peter said, "We must obey God more than men".'[37]

To this the king said, 'I do not want a sermon from you. Were you not the son of one of my villeins?' The archbishop answered, 'True, I was not "sprung from royal ancestors",[38] nor was St Peter prince of the apostles, to whom the Lord deigned to confer the keys of the kingdom of heaven and command of the entire Church.' 'Yes', said the king, 'but he died for his Lord'. But the venerable archbishop answered, 'I too will die for my Lord when the time comes.' 'You adhere and rely too much on your manner of ascent', said the king. 'I have confidence and trust in the Lord', replied the archbishop, 'because cursed is he who puts his trust in man.[39] Nevertheless, whatever you say and I answer, I am prepared now, just as before, to serve your honour and pleasure, saving my order. But on those things which bear on your honour and the well-being of your soul, you ought to have consulted me, whom so often you have found productive and useful in counsel, rather than those who, under the pretext of your honour, without provocation lit the flame of envy, and strive to exact revenge on me, who has done them no injury. You will not deny, I believe, my faith to you before I reached holy orders. How much more ought you to think me faithful to you in every way now that I have been raised to the priesthood?' The archbishop concluded with many salutary words full of love and faith, but nevertheless the king forcefully insisted that that phrase, 'saving your order', be entirely

37 Acts 5.29.

38 Horace, *Odes* I. i.

39 Jeremiah 17.5.

omitted. But as he could not obtain this, while the archbishop persisted resolutely in his purpose, they withdrew from each other.

At the same time, Arnulf bishop of Lisieux, who had offended the king,[40] crossed the sea and came to him, seeking to appease him by whatever means possible. He spoke to him in an entirely flattering and pleasing way, and was not even afraid to counsel him against the archbishop. For he said to the king, 'The present dispute between you and the archbishop is a difficult one and cannot be ended easily. For it is impossible to subject the archbishop to your will as long as his suffragans are of the same purpose and share his viewpoint. So, if you are unable to tear all of them away from him, at least try in some way to attach some of them to yourself. When you have done that, the remainder will not find it easy to stand firm. For, with the bishops on your side, if the archbishop chooses to persist stubbornly in his purpose, not only will he be unsuccessful, but with the bishops taking care of it he will incur sentence of suspension.' The king then, following this counsel, summoned to Gloucester those he believed were the more pliable of the bishops, Roger of York and the bishop of Lincoln,[41] and worked on them until they were prepared to confirm his customs, promising that he would demand nothing from them that would go against their order. So these two submitted, vowing to do as he wished, and not much later the king attached Hilary of Chichester to his party.

When this had been done the same Hilary visited the archbishop at Teynham, and began to urge him, because he could not convince him, to devote himself to the king as he wished, asserting that this would benefit him greatly in every way. For he was very learned, and spoke with polished and persuasive words. But the archbishop, who sought not his own but the things of Jesus Christ said, 'Far be it that I buy back the favour of an earthly king through such commerce, offering him the Church which the king of heaven purchased with his own blood. You, along with Lincoln[42] and York – let's hope not with impunity – may have made ecclesiastical laws something to buy and

40 This may be a reference to Henry's anger at Arnulf's enthusiastic championing of Alexander III in the papal schism before he had decided between the candidates. On the loss of Arnulf's favour before the king, see F. Barlow, *The Letters of Arnulf of Lisieux* (Camden Society, 3rd series, lxi, London, 1939), pp. xxix–xxxii.

41 This should probably read London (*Londoniensem*) rather than Lincoln (*Linconiensem*): Gilbert Foliot rather than Robert de Chesney.

42 See n. 41 above.

sell, or rather worthless as far as you are concerned, promising the king that you will observe his customs, which everyone knows to be contrary to the canons of the holy fathers. Nevertheless, whatever you may have done, or others might do, you will never have me as an ally in such appalling presumption.' To this Hilary said, 'I ask you, what is this evil that is so great and appalling that you alone see and understand it, and no one else? The king asked us to defer to him in this phrase, and honour him, and he promised us that he would never use this concession to seek anything from us that would have consequences for our order. Is this, I ask you, so great an evil, so enormous a presumption, to honour one's lord?' 'It is not evil', said the archbishop, 'but good, to honour one's lord, as long as God is not dishonoured, and Holy Church is not disturbed or endangered. For this you most certainly will discover, that the king exacts from you whatever you promised him, but you cannot force him to stick to his promises.'

At the same time Pope Alexander, who was residing in France,[43] sent a Cistercian abbot called Philip of Aumône, a man of great renown and authority, to restore peace, if possible, between the king and the archbishop. The abbot came to England and joined up with Robert of Melun, bishop of Hereford, and John count of Vendôme. They came to the archbishop at Harrow,[44] and Philip presented him with a letter from the pope, and letters from certain cardinals, in which the archbishop was urged to show himself moderate and flexible to the will of the king. Indeed he was reminded in these letters that due to schism the Church's standing was troubled and overcast. And he was warned to be very much on his guard lest the tempest, which had taken hold of the Church's head, should also be spread through the limbs, because then there would be no rest. Therefore in the meantime dispensation would be necessary, it not being expedient at present for rulers of the Church to exercise due severity. Instead much dissimulation was necessary, and some things ought to be tolerated for the time being. These letters contained much in this manner. And together the bishop, abbot and count added verbally that the king had ensured them in the word of truth that he would never demand anything from the archbishop contrary to his order and wish. The king, they said, had been dogged in his purpose because it would have seemed shameful to him to be defeated by the archbishop, without persuading him to even think fit to honour him verbally. So

43 See above, p. 22.
44 The archbishop's manor.

these men begged and urged and insisted in every way that the archbishop come with them to the king, and that he indulge his wish with
the simple word alone, omitting that phrase, 'Saving our order'. When
this was done, he and the English Church would gain the king's full
peace and favour, and the reference which had been made to the
customs of the realm would be completely forgotten forever. For this
abbot of Aumône was of such reputation and fame that he easily
inspired faith. Hence the archbishop, swayed by the advice of the lord
pope and the cardinals and the words of this abbot and the others who
came with him, and trusting in their promises, set out along with
them to the king.

Finding the king at Woodstock,[45] the venerable archbishop spoke to
him with great mildness, proposing as an example to him those
saintly kings of the realm, who were not only made acceptable to God
by their faith and piety, but in some cases were even made glorious by
the crown of martyrdom.[46] He urged and begged with humble entreaty
that he also follow their examples and footsteps, and, when he had
destroyed and condemned forever the abuses of tyrants, that he strive
to associate himself with the merits and company of saintly kings.
'And lest', he said, 'I should seem to interpose any obstacle to your
goodwill, if the Lord has thought fit to inspire it in you, know that I
will observe the customs of the realm in good faith, and from now on,
as is right and just, I will in all respects be compliant to you in good'.
Then the king said to him, 'Everyone knows how stubborn you showed
yourself by using that phrase and how much you offended my honour
by your defiance. Therefore, as you refused to honour me as was
fitting, what is known by all to have been detracted from my honour
in this regard must be corrected and acknowledged before all. Send
your messengers, therefore, and call together the bishops and abbots
and all others who are most eminent in ecclesiastical honours. And I
on my side will call all the nobles of the realm so that this wording
may be acknowledged in the presence and hearing of all to my honour.'

When then all gathered at Clarendon at the appointed time,[47] the king
began vigorously to demand that the aforesaid pledge regarding the

---

45 Grim and Garnier also place this meeting at Woodstock, but the more reliable
   witnesses Gilbert Foliot and Herbert of Bosham place it at Oxford nearby. Both
   were royal residences.

46 Presumably a reference to Edward the Martyr, king 975-79.

47 Late January 1164. In the royal chronicles it is dated 13 January by Gervase of
   Canterbury, and 25 January by Ralf of Diss (see below, p. 107 n. 116). The
   Constitutions of Clarendon are dated 30 January.

observation of the customs be given by the archbishop. The archbishop then realised that the situation was far from the impression
given to him by the abbot of Aumône, and that the king was in no
way to be restrained from his evil plan; instead that he would press on
with all his might to firmly establish and confirm these hateful
customs. Therefore he chose to give the king an opportunity for
calumny against him alone, rather than put the Church's cause
entirely in danger. So he dissimulated and hid himself as much as he
could, so as not to make any recognition or concession there. When
the king heard of this, he was beside himself with rage, and resolved
to employ no longer counsel but the sword, threatening that soon he
would be another Saul to the priests of the Lord[48] unless his will was
satisfied immediately and without delay. The king's indignation was
quickly made known, throwing everyone and everything into turmoil.
Royal attendants ran this way and that, showing more aggressive
expressions than usual, as if already preparing themselves for an
outrage. Everyone there was filled with horror and dread, and no
wonder, for the anger of the king is like a roaring lion.[49] All the while
the priests of the Lord stood like a flock prepared for sacrifice,
terrified and distraught. The archbishop alone retained a merry and
happy appearance, and he consoled them, saying that such was fitting
for true priests of the Church. But those of the clergy present who
were of a less evident reputation and name dispersed hither and
thither, stealing themselves away from the danger which they now
feared was imminent.

For there were then among the bishops two, Jocelin of Salisbury and
Roger of Norwich,[50] whom the king detested for different reasons.
For Norwich, who was a close relative of the king, although he was
young in age, was nevertheless a devout man jealous of ecclesiastical
liberties, and had incurred the king's wrath by freely rebuking him for
his transgressions. Salisbury had earned his hatred for other reasons.[51]
These two came to the archbishop with wavering voice to ask that he

48 Saul was an Old Testament king who had his priests killed: see 1 Samuel 22.

49 See Proverbs 20.2.

50 This is surely Roger of Worcester, the king's cousin, aged around thirty at this
time, and known to rebuke the king for his treatment of the archbishop (see *MTB*
3. 104–6), rather than the elderly William of Norwich. Clarendon occurred
between his election in March 1163 and his consecration in August 1164.

51 There are many references in the sources to the king's displeasure towards Jocelin
de Bohun, but no explanations. See D. Knowles, *The Episcopal Colleagues of Thomas
Becket* (Cambridge, 1951), p. 21 n. 1.

have pity on them, saying that unless that very day he made full peace with the king, even if others were spared, they would not be, indeed they would be killed. But the archbishop, meeting their timidity and faintheartedness with gentle consolation, remained immovable in his opinion. At the same time two of the greatest and most noble lords of the realm, William[52] of Leicester and Reginald of Cornwall, the king's uncle, came to him, warning and resolutely asking how much he pitied his people and those who had come with him, saying that the king was very angry and agitated, and that he had already drawn the sword, ready to avenge the contempt to him. 'We', they said, 'who are friendly and faithful to you, pray that you have pity, because unless you fully satisfy the king today, we will inevitably have to carry out an unprecedented outrage by our own hands.' 'It would not be great or unprecedented', said the archbishop, 'for us to die for ecclesiastical laws, since an innumerable crowd of saints has taught us this by word and example. May God's will be done.'

Then when these withdrew rebuffed, two Templars came to him, themselves in their way also of great renown and reputation. One was Richard of Hastings, master of the Templars of the whole kingdom, the other called Hostes,[53] no less well-regarded in court. These two stood before the archbishop and said to him with sighs and groans, 'Lord, why are you so inexorable in the cause of Holy Church, which today will undoubtedly suffer grave and unprecedented danger unless the king's wish is satisfied? For we know most certainly that the king is planning neither fraud nor deceit against you, but to him it seems too harsh and unbearable, if he is seen to be defeated by you regarding this formula. For this reason we entreat you in every way, and advise and counsel you in good faith to satisfy the king verbally, and you will never again hear mention of these customs which you recoil from and detest so much. But as soon as you honour the king in the hearing of all, just verbally, all indignation and enmity will be wiped away and full peace between you and him will be restored. This we faithfully promise you in the word of truth, and we give ourselves as vouch-safers and guardians in this business, and may our souls be liable to eternal damnation if the king requires anything from you from now on against your will or that of your order.'

Moved by their tears and their words uttered with such affirmation, and seeing the king and his men ready to carry out outrage and

52 This should read Robert.
53 Of St-Omer.

slaughter, the archbishop spoke first with the bishops about these things which he had heard, and then at one with them he came to the king and spoke to him thus: 'My lord king, if controversy had arisen between us over your law you would have immediately found me to have conceded to your will straight away and without contradiction. But now when a serious debate full of danger to both of us is aired regarding ecclesiastical business, for the time being committed to us, it ought not to appear remarkable or unseemly if I am somewhat more scrupulous in God's cause, knowing that I will have to hand in an account of my stewardship to Him who does not spare the sinner.[54] But now, having better hope on account of your prudence and mildness, I freely consent to your demands, and I declare that I will keep the customs of the realm in good faith.'

Hardly had the words left the pontiff's mouth than the king answered in a loud voice, 'You all hear what my archbishop has conceded to me of his own accord. It remains now that the bishops, by his order, do the same'. The archbishop said, 'I wish that they satisfy your honour just as I did'. Then the bishops rose and gave their assent, all except Jocelin of Salisbury who remaining seated asked the archbishop if he should do the same. The archbishop said that he should and he gave his assent. Shaking his head the king showed his disapproval of the bishop of Salisbury, who had always been conspicuously hostile to him. The archbishop, however much he thought the controversy over, following what he had heard from the Templars, still awaited the outcome of the matter anxiously and hesitantly, as if it hung in the balance.

And so the king said, 'I believe all have heard that the archbishop and bishops have conceded to me that the laws and customs of my realm will from now on be firmly held and observed. Therefore so that no further contention or contradiction arise between us, let the more prudent and senior nobles rise and go outside with my clerks to recollect the laws and customs of my grandfather King Henry. And when they have been carefully written down, let them be brought quickly to me.' Without delay it was done as he had ordered, and when the customs were recorded and brought forward the king ordered them to be read. When they had been read the king again said, 'See, these are the customs which have been conceded to me. Therefore, lest a disputed point arise from now on in relation to these, or perhaps new pleas emerge, we desire that the archbishop affix his seal to them.' To this the archbishop said, 'By Almighty God, never while I am living

54 See Luke 16.2; Job 9.28.

will my seal be put to these.' Then the clerks and officials of the king turned themselves to another contrivance. At the king's bidding they quickly drew up a chirograph,[55] divided it through the middle according to custom, and gave one part to the archbishop. The archbishop said, 'This I accept, not as consent or approval, but as precaution and defence of the Church, so that by this evidence we may know what is to be done against us. For once we have understood the snares and traps concealed for us, God willing we will be more cautious.'[56] Having said this he got up, enraged, and left.

20. The Constitutions of Clarendon (January 1164)

The Constitutions survive in a form which indicates which were condemned or tolerated by the pope. The contentious clauses concerned royal and ecclesiastical jurisdiction (1, 2, 3, 7, 9, 15), relations with the pope (4, 8), excommunication (5, 6, 10) and vacancies (12). See the commentary in *Councils and Synods*, pp. 855–77.

Councils and Synods, 877–83; *MTB* 1. 18–33.

In the year from the incarnation of our Lord 1164, the fourth of Alexander's pontificate, the tenth of the most illustrious king of England Henry II, in the presence of the said king, was made the record and acknowledgement of a certain portion of the customs, liberties and privileges of his ancestors, that is of King Henry I and of others, which ought to be observed and maintained in his kingdom. And because of the disagreements and conflicts which had arisen between the clergy and the justices of the lord king and the barons of the realm regarding the customs and privileges of the realm, this recording or acknowledgment was made in the presence of the archbishops, bishops and clergy, and the earls and barons and nobles of the kingdom. And these customs were recognised by the archbishops and bishops and earls and barons and by the most eminent and senior men of the realm. Archbishops Thomas of Canterbury and Roger of York, Bishops Gilbert of London, Henry of Winchester, Nigel of Ely,

---

55 A charter divided into two or more parts and given to the individual parties as testimony to the agreement.

56 It is clear that Thomas accepted his part of the chirograph, and almost certainly as an act of approval, whatever his subsequent rejection of the customs. The suggestion that Thomas was merely doing so as a precaution is an attempt on the part of 'Roger' to lessen the damage of this most embarrassing episode in Thomas's career.

William of Norwich, Robert of Lincoln, Hilary of Chichester, Jocelin
of Salisbury, Richard of Chester, Bartholomew of Exeter, Robert of
Hereford, David of St David's and Roger bishop elect of Worcester
gave their consent and in the word of truth resolutely promised aloud
that they were to be kept and observed to the lord king and his heirs
in good faith and without evil intent. These were present: Robert earl
of Leicester, Reginald earl of Cornwall, Conan count of Brittany, John
count of Eu, Earl Roger de Clare,[57] Earl Geoffrey de Mandeville,[58]
Hugh earl of Chester, William earl of Arundel,[59] Earl Patrick,[60] Earl
William de Ferrières,[61] Richard de Lucy, Reginald of Saint-Valéry,
Roger Bigod, Reginald of Warenne, Richer of Laigle, William of Briouze,
Richard de Camville, Nigel de Moubrai, Simon de Beauchamp, Hum-
phrey de Bohun, Matthew of Hereford, Walter of Mayenne, Manasser
Biset the steward, William Malet, William de Courci, Robert of Dun-
stanville, Jocelin de Balliol, William de Lanvalis, William de Chesney,
Geoffrey de Vere, William of Hastings, Hugh de Morville,[62] Alan de
Neville, Simon fitzPeter, William Maudit the chamberlain, John
Maudit, John the Marshal, Peter de Mara and many other magnates
and nobles of the realm, clergy and lay.

A certain part of the recognised customs of the realm is contained in
the present document. These are its points.

Here begin the customs which are called ancestral.

1. (This the Holy Roman Church under Pope Alexander III con-
    demned)
    If a dispute should arise between laymen, or between clergy and lay,
    or between clergy concerning advowson[63] and presentation to
    churches, let it be tried and concluded in the court of the lord king.

2. (Tolerated)
    Churches in the fief of the lord king[64] may not be given in perpe-
    tuity without his agreement and consent.

57 Of Hereford.
58 Of Essex.
59 William of Aubigny.
60 Of Salisbury.
61 Of Derby.
62 One of Thomas's murderers.
63 The patronage of an ecclesiastical office or benefice.
64 Churches which are held as a direct grant from the king.

3. (Condemned)

    Clerks charged and accused of any offence, when summoned by
    the king's justice, shall come to his court to answer there
    concerning what seems to the king's court ought to be answered
    there, and in the ecclesiastical court for what seems ought to be
    answered there, but in such a way that the justice of the king
    sends men into the court of Holy Church to see in what way it is
    tried there. And if the clerk should be convicted or confesses, the
    Church ought no longer protect him.[65]

4. (Condemned)

    Archbishops, bishops and beneficed clergy may not leave the
    realm without the king's licence. And if they shall leave, if it
    pleases the king, they shall give security that neither in going nor
    in staying nor in returning shall they promote evil or damage to
    the lord king or the realm.[66]

5. (Condemned)

    Excommunicates ought not give a surety for good conduct nor
    offer an oath, but only a surety and pledge to adhere to the judge-
    ment of the Church in order to be absolved.[67]

6. (Tolerated)

    Laymen ought not to be accused except by certified and lawful

---

65 This, the most controversial of the Constitutions, is also the most complex and
   ambiguous. 'The intention, wrapped in decent obscurity, seems to be this: anyone
   accused of a criminal offence shall appear before the appropriate secular tribunal,
   but if he is there able to establish that he is a member of the clergy, the case shall
   be referred for trial to the ecclesiastical court; a royal officer will, however,
   accompany the accused to his trial and take charge of him when the church has
   found him guilty and "withdrawn her protection". The unexpressed implication, of
   course, is that the former clerk would be held for punishment as a layman': Warren,
   p. 481. 'From the royal side the constitution seems to incorporate four ideas: that
   royal courts should have jurisdiction, which was Henry's original and general
   claim; that what was done in ecclesiastical courts should be subject to surveillance
   by the royal court; that in so far as there was a powerful counterclaim by the
   church, this should be met by accepting the possibility that both secular and
   church courts had jurisdiction over aspects of such cases; and that convicted clerks
   should be handed over to the royal court for punishment': *Councils and Synods*, pp.
   860-1.

66 It was accepted practice for prominent churchmen to ask the king's licence to leave
   the kingdom, but the pope objected to any lay restrictions on the clergy's move-
   ments. Thomas violated this constitution when he attempted unsuccessfully to flee
   to the Continent, probably in early autumn 1164, and again in October 1164 when
   he succeeded in doing so.

67 That excommunicates should only give a pledge to observe the judgement of the
   Church, and not be required to promise to future good behaviour.

accusers and witnesses in the presence of the bishop, but in such a way that the archdeacon does not lose his right or anything that belongs to him from this. And if the accused are such that no one wishes or dares to make a charge against them, let the sheriff act when called by the archbishop, and let twelve lawful men of the neighbourhood swear that according to their conscience they will make known the truth.

7. (Condemned)
No tenant-in-chief of the king, or any of his ministers of his demesne shall be excommunicated, nor shall the lands of any of them be placed under interdict, unless first the king is approached if he is in the realm, or his justiciar if he is outside, so that he do right concerning him, and so that what belongs to the royal court is concluded there, and what pertains to the ecclesiastical court be sent there and dealt with there.[68]

8. (Condemned)
Appeals, if they should arise, ought to proceed from archdeacon to bishop, and from bishop to archbishop. And if the archbishop fails to do justice, it ought finally reach the lord king, so that by his order the dispute shall be concluded in the archbishop's court, in such a way that it ought not proceed further without the assent of the lord king.[69]

9. (Condemned)
If a dispute should arise between a clerk and a layman, or between a layman and a clerk, over any holding which the clerk wishes to appropriate to free alms,[70] but the layman to lay fee,[71] it will be resolved by the declaration of twelve lawful men through the consideration of the chief royal justice, whether the holding belongs to free alms or lay fee. And if it is declared that it belongs to free alms, the plea will be held in the ecclesiastical court. But if it belongs to lay fee, unless both appeal to the same bishop or baron, the plea

---

68 This addresses the issue raised by the case of William of Eynsford (see above, pp. 78–9).

69 This sought to regulate appeals to the pope, probably an impossible task considering the expansion of papal jurisdiction over the previous decades. The frequent appeals by Thomas, Gilbert Foliot and others over the following years made a mockery of it, and it was dropped by Henry at Avranches in 1172.

70 *Frankalmoign* tenure, by which churches held land, not for any of the usual feudal obligations, but for spiritual service, e.g. prayers for the donor.

71 The normal lay tenure, by which the tenant rendered rent, military service, etc.

will be heard in the royal court. But if both appeal concerning this fief to the same bishop or baron, the plea will be held in his court, in such a way that he who was first in possession will not lose possession on account of the declaration, until according to the plea the matter as been settled.[72]

10. (Condemned)

If anyone from a city or town or borough or demesne manor of the lord king is summoned by an archdeacon or bishop upon any offence and hence ought to answer to him, and according to their summons refuses to give satisfaction, it is quite lawful to place him under interdict, but he ought not be excommunicated before the chief minister of the lord king of the town has been approached so that he may order him to give satisfaction. And if the king's minister fails to do this he will be at the mercy of the lord king, and then the bishop will be able to punish the accused by ecclesiastical justice.[73]

11. (Tolerated)

Archbishops, bishops and all beneficed clergy of the realm who are tenants-in-chief of the king, hold their possessions from the lord king by barony, and are answerable for them to the king's justices and officials and they should respect and observe all rights and customs. And like other barons they ought to be present at the judgements of the lord king's court with the barons, except in cases concerning mutilation or death.[74]

12. (Condemned)

When an archbishopric or bishopric or an abbey or priory of the royal demesne is vacant, it ought to remain in the king's hand and he ought to receive all revenues and duties from it as his demesne. And when the time has come to take thought for the church, the lord king ought to commission the principal beneficed clergy of the church, and the election ought to be held in the chapel of the lord king, by the assent of the lord king and the counsel of the clergy of the realm, which he shall call to do this. And there the elect shall perform homage and fealty to the lord king, as liege lord, for his life and limbs and his earthly honour, saving his order, before he is consecrated.

72 This established the assize *Utrum*, a standardised procedure by which a sworn inquest would decide by which form of tenure the land was held.

73 This, like clause 7, is intended to regulate excommunication.

74 As, for example, when the bishops were prevailed upon to judge Thomas at Northampton (below, pp. 102–3, 113).

13. (Tolerated)

If any of the magnates of the realm should prevent an archbishop or bishop or archdeacon from showing justice to himself or his men, the lord king ought to bring him to justice. And if by chance any-one should dispossess the lord king of his right, the archbishops and bishops and archdeacons ought to bring him to justice, so that he make satisfaction to the lord king.

14. (Tolerated)

No church or churchyard ought to retain against the king's justice anyone's chattels if they have been forfeited to the king, because they belong to the king, whether they are found in churches or not.

15. (Condemned)

Pleas regarding debts, whether agreed with or without an oath, belong to the king's justice.[75]

16. (Tolerated)

Sons of villeins ought not to be ordained except with the consent of the lord on whose land they are recognised to have been born.

The record of these royal customs and privileges was made by the aforesaid archbishops, bishops, earls, barons, nobles and elders of the realm at Clarendon, on the fourth day before the Purification of the Blessed Virgin Mary,[76] in the presence of the lord Henry the king's son, and his father the lord king.

There are also many other great customs and privileges of the Holy Mother Church, and the lord king, and the barons of the realm, which are not contained in this document. May they be safe for Holy Church and the lord king and his heirs and the barons of the realm, and may they be observed undamaged forever.

21. Thomas laments his compliance (January 1164)

After his capitulation at Clarendon, Thomas, in penance, suspended himself from saying Mass until he gained absolution from the pope. Meanwhile Henry began to enforce observance of his customs, and attempted, unsuccessfully, to win the pope's approval for them.

Herbert of Bosham, *MTB* 3. 289–92.

75 Church courts claimed jurisdiction in cases of oaths and perjury.
76 29 January 1164.

But on the road [from Clarendon] the archbishop seemed unusually disquieted and gloomy, for once not speaking to anyone on the way, nor anyone to him. He called no one, no one approached him, but alone and apart he rode along the way, alone on the road in thought. We, the companions of the journey, quickly noticed this. We conferred and offered consolation, already suspecting a little what the matter was. But eventually the disciple who wrote these things presumed to approach him and said, 'Lord, why do you wear such an uncharacteristically sad expression? Why do you not show that face that you wore yesterday and the day before, and why do you not confer or discuss with your men on the road as you usually do?'

The archbishop replied, 'No wonder I now seem like that when the English Church which my predecessors, as the world knows, ruled so prudently among so many dangers, should through my sins be delivered into slavery. In the midst of its enemies they fought so bravely on its behalf, and triumphed so successfully, and some of them resisted boldly and faithfully even unto death. But now, alas, because of me, the lady who stands before me[77] seems fit for slavery. Would that I had died before any eye had seen me.[78] And indeed it is fitting that the Church should suffer these things through me, and in my time, because I was raised to this office not, like my predecessors, from the church but from the court. Not from the cloister, not from any place of religion, not from the company of the Saviour, but rather from the retinue of Caesar, proud and vain, from a keeper of hawks I was made shepherd of the sheep. From a patron of actors and a follower of hounds, I was made pastor of so many souls. I know not who put me as guardian of the vines,[79] I who did not watch over but neglected myself. My previous life was certainly far removed from the well-being of the Church, and now these are my works. So also I clearly see myself worthy to be abandoned by God and removed from the holy seat in which I was placed'. Then as sorrow bore down on him in this way, an outpouring of water fell from his eyes, so that amidst continuous tears and frequent sobs, he was forced to cut his speech short before its completion …[80]

So the disciple having pity, addressed his master thus, repressing tears and sobs as much as he could:[81] 'Lord, it is written that "in

77 I.e the Church.
78 Job 10.18.
79 See Song of Songs 1.5.
80 There is a break here in the manuscript.
81 This reported speech seems to be influenced by Augustine, *Ennarationes in Psalmos* l, 3.

everything God works for good with those who love him, who are called according to his purpose".[82] So much indeed that if they stray and deviate along a twisted and roundabout road and life, and wander in trackless wastes,[83] this same trackless route may be to them a certain shortcut to the path of health, to the true fatherland, because they stray in this way with God, their leader and guide, wonderfully directing them. So also our wonderful God leads his saints down a marvellous path, so marvellous that for them that digression may be a road to safety, a road home. Be confident, therefore, my lord, that if you fell, with God's support you will rise up stronger; if you collapsed under the pressure of another you will rise up more cautious; if you fell by your own force, more humble. So also the leader of the apostles, the model of pastors, Peter, taking it for granted that he would die rather than deny his Master, first denied Him at the question of a serving-girl, but later led before kings and rulers did not cease in his righteousness, from presumption made more learned and humble, from apostasy more faithful, from denial more constant. Thus the all-knowing Spirit of wisdom is able to extract good from evil, like a violet from dry land, a rose from the thorn, honey from the rock, and oil from the hardest stone …[84]

Therefore all that remains is, if as you say you fell disgracefully, rise up bravely and fittingly, and shake yourself out, if you are the son of the shaken-out,[85] or rather because you are, and act boldly and let your heart be comforted. Do not let sorrow devour you, instead let righteousness rise: act boldly, I say, and take comfort, and from now on be cautious, brave and strong. And know for certain that God will be with you, a strong helper, as he is read to have been with David king and prophet, who was first an adulterer and traitor, and, as we have already said, with the leader of the apostles, first an apostate, and with that holy and apostolic sinner,[86] and finally with that outstanding teacher of peoples, first and before all persecutor of the Church.

---

82 Romans 8.28.

83 See Psalm 108.40.

84 Herbert expands on this theme, and assures Thomas that his life had not been consistent with this fall.

85 See Psalm 127.5. This image, one of Herbert's favourite, is particularly obscure. Augustine suggests that the 'shaken-out' are the prophets, and their sons the apostles (*Ennarrationes in Psalmos* cxxvi, 10), but later writers identify the 'shaken-out' with the apostles themselves. See J. C. Robertson, *Becket: a Biography* (London, 1859), pp. 336–7.

86 *Peccatrix*: the woman who was a sinner. See Luke 7.37–50.

Indeed you were also, as it seemed then and was said, once Saul. If now you wish to be Paul, having wiped away the scales from your eyes, clearly by this action may your Jesus show you how much you ought to suffer for His name.'[87]

This exhortation seemed to soothe a little the melancholy described above, the archbishop having more regard indeed to the love and faith of the speaker than to the quality of his words. And just then it was reported that that bishop, whose persuasion and urging caused that phrase 'saving our order' to be suppressed,[88] was following us. And the archbishop, turning to the disciple who had just before spoken to him and was still with him, said, 'Get thee behind me, Satan'.[89]

22. Thomas attempts to flee (August–September 1164)

Herbert of Bosham reports that some time after the Council of Clarendon, Thomas came to Woodstock to speak to the king, but had the gates shut in his face. He also says that Thomas tried twice to flee the country.[90] Such an act was, of course, contrary to Clause 4 of the Constitutions of Clarendon (see above, p. 93).

Edward Grim, *MTB* 2. 389–90.

Considering that almost all the bishops by unanimous agreement had conspired against him, and that the indignation of the king could not be placated by any means, and in all this no sign of peace was apparent, the holy archbishop decided to withdraw his presence to suit the occasion. That is, so that by removing the person who was believed to have fuelled the disturbance, because he would not tolerate royal usurpations, the king would at least take pity on the desolate Church. He also settled on another reason to leave the land, that by the authority and aid of the lord pope, whom he planned to visit, he might somehow assist the oppressed flock. So, taking a few with him he boarded a ship, and at first indeed the winds blew favourably. When now they sailed out to the open sea, the sailors spoke to each other saying, 'What are we doing, transporting an enemy of the king from the realm? We have acted foolishly. We and all our families will be disinherited by perpetual proscription'. To the archbishop they also

87 See Acts 9.18, 16.
88 Hilary of Chichester.
89 Mark 8.33.
90 *MTB* 3. 293.

spoke and asserted that in such a wind no one could land as he ordered. He very placidly answered, 'If it is true that the winds are against our objective, let God's will be done, and keep to the port which God assigns', and immediately they were carried back to England. But the holy man later recognised and confessed to his men that it had not been God's wish that he cross then, since as yet the painful battle and the trials through which he would pass so that he appear more proven were still before him, as indeed it turned out. The king then, hearing that the archbishop had boarded the ship, remained sad and anxious, until he heard of his return, for he greatly feared that by his going to the lord pope the kingdom would be placed under interdict.

23. The Council of Northampton (6–12 October 1164)

John FitzGilbert the Marshal, a distinguished knight, claimed that he had not received justice in the archbishop's court on a land plea. Thomas was summoned to answer to this charge in the king's court on 14 September 1164, but neither appeared in court nor offered an adequate excuse. He was then summoned to answer at a royal council at Northampton. The case of John the Marshal was dealt with quickly and the council was transformed into a titanic contest between king and archbishop. Henry attempted to use the council as an opportunity to humiliate the archbishop by having him charged with embezzlement during his time as chancellor. Thomas's response was to characterise himself as a martyr who was suffering trial not for himself, but for Christ and the Church. In the middle were the bishops, unwilling to offend the king or condemn their archbishop. The king and archbishop did not meet. The king remained in an upper room, the archbishop and his party below, and the bishops and magnates passed up and down between them. William Fitzstephen's eyewitness account is one of the most celebrated passages from the Lives.

William Fitzstephen, *MTB* 3. 49–68.

Some time later the king announced another council to be held at Northampton on Tuesday 6 October, and when the day came we made our way there. The archbishop did not see the king that day because the latter had been hunting with hawks around the rivers and streams and came late to Northampton.[91] The next morning,[92] after Mass and hours, the archbishop came to court at the king's castle. First he was admitted to a chamber where he sat waiting for the king,

---

91 He also found his lodgings occupied by royal squires under William de Courcy, seneschal of Normandy, and was forced to take himself to the priory of St Andrew nearby.

92 Wednesday 7 October.

who was hearing Mass. When he arrived the archbishop rose with reverence and showed a constant and placid expression, ready to receive the customary English honour of a kiss, if the king were to offer it. But he was not welcomed with a kiss.

The archbishop first took up the subject of William de Courcy, who had occupied one his holdings. He asked the king to order William to return it to him, and the king gave the order. Next he said that he had come in response to the royal summons to answer the accusation John the Marshal[93] had made against him. For John had laid claim to a certain piece of land in the archiepiscopal estate of Pagham, and when a number of days had been set aside to deal with this case, he came to the archbishop's court with a royal writ. When he was unsuccessful there, being supported by no right, he, according to the law, pointed to a failing of the Church court. But he swore upon a troper,[94] which he took out from under his cloak, and the justices of the archbishop's court protested that he ought not have brought that book or any like it for that purpose. Returning to the king, he purchased letters of summons for the archbishop to answer to him in the king's court on 14 September. But the archbishop did not come on that day, and instead sent four knights with letters from him and the sheriff of Kent, witnessing to the injury done by John and the inadequacy of his proof. What next? The king, incensed because the archbishop did not come in person to answer his summons and argue his case if he wished, treated his envoys badly, angrily abusing them with threats for answering the king's summons with a false, empty and useless excuse, and even after they had given sureties he would hardly let them go. On the insistence of the said John he fixed another day – the first day of the council – to hear the same case, and sent letters to the sheriff of Kent to summon the archbishop.[95] For he did not wish then, or for a long time before, to write to him, because he was unwilling to greet him. Nor did the archbishop have any other solemn letters directed to him as a summons, as was the ancient custom. The archbishop, as I say, said that he had come at the king's command to answer the case of John. The king said that John was on his service in London, but would come the next day, and then he would investigate the case. For John was in London with the treasurers and other

93 John FitzGilbert.

94 A service-book, rather than the Bible, as if to avoid the charge of perjury.

95 This was an insult to an archbishop, who was accustomed to receiving a personal summons from the king.

receivers of royal revenues and public money at the quadrangular
table which is commonly called the Exchequer on account of its chequered counters, but is also the table of the king with its blanched
coins where the pleas of the crown are heard.[96] That day nothing
more was done between the king and the archbishop. Instead the king
told him to go to his lodgings and return for his case the next day,
and he did so.

The next day,[97] with all the bishops, earls and barons of England, and
many of Normandy, except for the bishop of Rochester,[98] who had not
yet arrived, and one other, the archbishop was accused of contempt of
the crown, because, as described above, he did not come to answer the
case of John on the king's summons, nor did he give an adequate
excuse. The archbishop was given no heed when he cited in rebuttal
the injury done by John, and his own jurisdiction over the case, and
the integrity of his court. The king demanded judgement, and none of
the archbishop's arguments were given any time. It seemed to all that
because of reverence to royal majesty, and the obligation of liege
homage, which the archbishop owed the king as his lord, and on
account of the faith and obedience to his earthly honour to which he
had sworn, he had little defence or excuse. For when summoned by
the king he had not come, nor did he plead through his envoys
infirmity of body or necessary Church business which could not be
postponed. So they said that he should be condemned to forfeit all his
goods at the king's mercy.

There was a dispute between the bishops and barons about pronouncing sentence, each trying to pass it on to the other one and excuse
themselves. The barons said, 'You bishops ought to pronounce sentence. This does not concern us. We are laymen, you are ecclesiastics
like him, his fellow priests and fellow bishops.' To this one of the
bishops replied, 'No, this is your duty, not ours, for this is a secular
judgement, not an ecclesiastical one. We sit here not as bishops but as
barons. Here we are barons just like you. In vain does your argument
rely on our status, because if you take note of our ordination, you
should also take note of the archbishop's. For because we are bishops

96 The name Exchequer (*Scaccarium*) derives from the word for chessboard. Computa-
   tion was done with counters on a chequered board, an adaptation of the abacus.
   Blanching was a process by which the purity of coinage was tested. A random
   sample of the payment to the exchequer was tested for silver content and a supple-
   mentary payment was exacted to cover any deficiency. See Warren, pp. 266–75.

97 Thursday, 8 October.

98 Walter.

we cannot judge our archbishop and lord.' What next? On hearing this argument the king was infuriated, and put an end to it, and on his command the bishop of Winchester,[99] though unwilling, finally pronounced sentence. The archbishop, because it was not lawful to go against the sentence or decree of the English king's court, on the bishops' advice held his peace. As is customary, the court granted him bail to satisfy and honour the king. All the bishops stood surety for him except for Gilbert of London, who refused when asked, thereby making him stand out.

Later the same day, the archbishop was called to answer for £300 he had received as custodian of the castles of Eye and Berkhamsted. The archbishop said (though not in formal pleading, as he had already refused to answer on a charge to which he had not been summoned) that he had used this money and more to repair the Palace of London[100] and these castles, as was plain to see. The king refused to allow it, because this had been done through the archbishop. He demanded judgement. The archbishop, for the king's sake, agreed to return this money, because he did not want some question of money to be the cause of bad feeling between them, and he separately pledged laymen to give sureties, the earl of Gloucester and William of Eynsford and a certain third person, his vassals. After that, at the end of the day, they dispersed.

On the third day, Friday 9 October, the archbishop was sued through intermediaries for a loan of 500 marks incurred in the expedition to Toulouse[101] and another 500 marks borrowed on the king's guarantee from a certain Jew. He was also cited for a lawsuit of wardship concerning all the revenues of the archbishopric when vacant, and other bishoprics and abbacies vacant during his chancellorship, and was ordered to account for all these to the king. The archbishop replied that he had neither been prepared nor summoned for this. If he should be charged on this, at the place and time, he would do what was right to his lord king. The king demanded sureties from him as a precaution, but he said he should consult his suffragans and clerks on this matter. The king did not give way. He withdrew, and from that day forward no barons or knights came to his lodgings, as they understood the mind of the king.

99 Henry.

100 I.e. Westminster.

101 See above, p. 57.

On the fourth day[102] all the clergy came to the lord archbishop's lodgings, where he held discussion and took counsel separately with the
bishops and abbots. On the advice of the man who had ordained him,
the noble Henry bishop of Winchester, who promised him considerable aid, they tried to placate the king with money. He offered the
king 2000 marks but he refused. There were some among the clergy
who said to the archbishop that on account of the office he had
assumed he ought to protect the Church of God, and take account of
his person and dignity. They said that he should honour the king in
all respects, but saving reverence to God and ecclesiastical honour,
and ought to fear nothing, since no blame or shame could be imputed
to him. He had been handed over to the church of Canterbury free
from the chancellorship and all secular complaints of the king, just as
no vacant abbey would receive a monk from another house as their
abbot elect unless handed over immune from all obedience to his
abbot. Others, more inclined to the secret ear and mind of the king
were of a very different opinion, saying, 'The lord king is very angry
with him. From certain signs we can interpret the king's wish to be
that the lord archbishop should in everything, and especially by
resigning the archiepiscopacy, throw himself entirely on the mercy of
the king.' Among these Hilary of Chichester, who was sympathetic to
the king's party, said to him, 'If only you could be not archbishop but
just Thomas'. And on another occasion he said, 'Every plant which
my heavenly father has not planted will be rooted up',[103] implying that
the declared wish of the king had prompted his election. Later during
the exile the archbishop said to someone about Hilary, 'and he among
the brothers took the place of Judas'. And later, before the archbishop's reconciliation and recall, as if struck by God, he died.[104] The
same bishop of Chichester, on his own behalf and on that of some
others of his accomplices added, 'Because of a chancellor's intimacy and
familiarity with the king, you know him better than we do. Undoubtedly you will prevail over him more easily, whether you oppose him
or yield. As his chancellor, in peace and war, you did your duty
properly and worthily, winning praise if not without envy. Those who
envied you then now inflame the king against you. Who could
sponsor you for such a great reckoning or so uncertain a sum? It is
reported that the king said that both of you could no longer remain in

102 Saturday, 10 October.
103 Matthew 15.13.
104 16 July 1169.

England with him as king and you as archbishop. It is safer to abandon all to his mercy lest perhaps – God forbid – he charge you with extortion of his money in your time as his chancellor and receiver of revenue, and detain you without sureties or treat you with violence, thereby bringing sorrow to the Church and shame to the realm'. Another said, 'Far be it that he should consider himself and the safety of his body in this way, and dishonour the church of Canterbury which elected him. None of his predecessors did so, though they suffered persecution in their time. Besides, he could perhaps surrender the archiepiscopal lands, estates and suchlike into the king's hands to suit the moment, saving the right of the Church, but by no means could he surrender his office.' In this way those consulted were divided between different views, some saying one thing, others otherwise.[105]

The fifth day,[106] which was Sunday, was devoted entirely to counsels. There was hardly time to catch one's breath. The archbishop did not leave his lodgings.

On the sixth day,[107] he was detained by an apparently sudden weakness and he could not go to court. His loins trembled with cold and pain and warm pillows had to be applied repeatedly.[108] When the king heard this he sent all his earls and many barons to seek an answer from the archbishop, now that he had taken counsel, whether or not he would give sureties for the revenues received from the vacant churches during his time as chancellor, and stand judgement on the matter in his court. The archbishop answered through the bishops that, health permitting, he would come to court the next day and do as he should.

The next morning he celebrated the Mass, 'For princes did also sit and speak against me'[109] before the altar of St Stephen, the first martyr. Spies immediately informed the king of the Mass, malignly suggesting that the archbishop had celebrated the Mass for himself, as if another

105 Alan of Tewkesbury, not an eyewitness, gives a detailed but unconvincing report of discussions: *MTB* 2. 326–29.

106 Sunday, 11 October.

107 Monday, 12 October.

108 D. Knowles suggests that Thomas was suffering from renal colic, *Episcopal Colleagues*, pp. 167–8. It is likely that fear of the king also had much to do with it.

109 Psalm 118.23, the *introit* to the Mass of Stephen, the first Christian martyr, whose feast day is 26 December. It may be significant that this, 13 October, was the first anniversary of the translation of Edward the Confessor (see below, pp. 74–5). Thomas would have been expected to say a Mass commemorating Henry's ancestor. See J. O'Reilly, 'The Double Martyrdom of Thomas Becket: Hagiography or History?', *Studies in Medieval and Renaissance History*, 7 (1985), 218–35.

Stephen, the first martyr, against the king and the enemies persecuting him.

Later he went to court. On the way he said to Alexander his cross-bearer[110] who preceded him, 'It would have been better if I had come in my vestments'. For he had proposed to enter the king's presence barefoot, vested and carrying the cross to plead to him on behalf of the peace of the Church. But some of his clerks dissuaded him from this plan, nor did they think that he should carry his cross. When he had dismounted from his horse to enter the hall of the castle, he took his cross, which Alexander the Welshman had been carrying before him in his hands. The aforementioned Gilbert of London met him at the door of the hall, and Hugh de Nonant, a certain archdeacon of Lisieux, who had come with the archbishop and was from his household said, 'My lord bishop of London, why do you allow him to carry his cross?' The bishop replied, 'My good man, he was always a fool and always will be'. All stopped to allow him to pass. He went into the chamber and sat in his accustomed place, the bishops sitting near him, the bishop of London next to him. Everyone present was astonished, and all eyes turned to him. The bishop of London urged him to give the cross to one of his clerks, saying that he looked as if he was ready to disturb the whole realm. 'You hold the cross in your hands', he said. 'If the king were now to put on his sword, then we would see a king well adorned and an archbishop well adorned!' The archbishop said, 'If it were possible I would hold it in my hands at all times. But now I know what I am doing, to preserve the peace of God and of my own person and of the English Church. Say as you like, if you were in my place you would feel differently. But if, as you say, the lord king were now to put on his sword, that would certainly not be a sign of peace.' Perhaps the archbishop remembered how tense the situation had been at Clarendon when the messengers of the king came to him with tears in their eyes.

All the bishops were summoned to the king and remained within for a long time. Among them was Roger, archbishop of York, who had come to court last so as to enter more conspicuously, and not appear to be part of the king's counsel. He also had his cross carried before him, though he was outside his province, like 'javelin threatening javelin'.[111] He had in fact been forbidden by the lord pope by letter to

---

110 Alexander Llewelyn, one of those closest to Thomas and accustomed at times to upbraiding him for his conduct.

111 Lucan, *Pharsalia*, I, 7.

carry his cross before him in the province of Canterbury, but when he received this prohibition he lodged an appeal claiming a false allegation by the archbishop of Canterbury, so he assumed himself safe. No wonder if sorrow and groaning and contrition of heart troubled the archbishop, for he had heard that on that day he would either be imprisoned on some sentence or other, or if he escaped that he would be attacked and killed by a conspiracy of evil men against him, as if without the king's knowledge. Meanwhile in the silence Herbert, his master in the holy page,[112] said privately to the archbishop, 'Lord, if it should happen that they lay impious hands on you, you can immediately lay a sentence of excommunication upon them, so that their spirit may be saved in the day of the Lord'.[113] To whom William Fitzstephen, who was sitting at the archbishop's feet, said a little more loudly so that the archbishop could hear, 'Far be it from him. Not so did God's holy apostles and martyrs do when they were captured and lifted up. Rather, if this should happen, he ought to pray for them and forgive them and possess his soul in patience. If then it happen that he suffer for the cause of justice and the liberty of the Church, by the Lord's fulfilment, his spirit will be at rest, his memory blessed. If he pronounces sentence against them it will seem to all that from anger and impatience he had done whatever he could to avenge himself. And without doubt he would be acting against the canons. As the blessed Gregory wrote to Archbishop Januarius, "You do not show yourself to think of the heavens, but you show yourself to have a worldly way of life, when to avenge your own injury, which is prohibited by the holy law, you pass sentence of anathema"'.[114] John Planeta,[115] hearing this, struggled to hold tears from bursting forth. Similarly Ralf of Diss,[116] archdeacon of the church of London, was very tearful there that day. Hearing these words the archbishop considered in his heart. After a little, the same William Fitzstephen wished to speak to the archbishop, but was prevented from doing so by a royal marshal who stood beside him with his rod, saying that no one was to speak to him.

112 I.e. his teacher in the interpretation of the Bible.

113 1 Corinthians 5.5.

114 Gregory, *Epistles* ii, 49; Gratian, *Decretum*, De Pen. II, c. xxiii, q. 4, c. 27.

115 One of Thomas's clerks, known as 'The Cantor', and described as a pupil of Peter Abelard.

116 Or 'Diceto', the writer of *Ymagines Historiarum* and *Abbreviationes Chronicorum*: see C. and A. Duggan, 'Ralf de Diceto, Henry II and Becket', in *Authority and Power: Studies on Medieval Law and Government in Honour of Walter Ullmann*, eds B. Tierney and P. Linehan (Cambridge, 1980), pp. 59–81, repr. Charles Duggan, *Canon Law in Medieval England* (Variorum Reprints, 1982).

After an interval he turned to the archbishop and by raising his eyes
and moving his lips he signalled to him to look at the image of the
cross and the Crucified which he was holding as an example, and
remain in prayer. The archbishop understood this sign well, and did
so, and was comforted in the Lord. Indeed, after many years, when he
was an exile in France at St Benoît-sur-Loire,[117] the archbishop reminded the same William, who was on his way to the pope, of this, among
other evidences of his struggles.

But, Christian king, what do you do? By reason of seigneurial right
and property, in your lay court do you make the son judge the father,
the subject judge the archbishop, the sheep the shepherd, when in a
lay court not the lowest clerk is held liable? You say no, it is a king
judging a baron.[118] To which I say it is more significant that you are
a Christian, that you are God's sheep, that you are God's adopted son,
than that you are a king. And in that it is more important that he is
archbishop, that he is the vicar of Jesus Christ, than that he is your
baron. Be aware of your ranks. Less is his property than his position,
but the greater prevails over the lesser, the worthy over the unworthy. Therefore rank ought to be stronger and more effective than
seigneurial right and property, so that he be exempt from your court
and not be held liable there. And, if you look deeper into this property
of his, it is not his but the Church's. It was secular: given to God it
was made ecclesiastical. Secularity was absorbed in it by a claim of
divine right. Hence the secular court has no right to hold the archbishop liable. Therefore neither by reason of his person, nor by reason
of what he possessed, may he be judged in the royal court. Judgement
of the archbishop is reserved to the pope alone; of the pope, to God
alone. If what you had against him could not be mitigated by the
intervention of agreement and charity, you ought to have referred it
to the pope. Called to be judged by him he would answer to our
legates, bishops and clerks, or alternatively you could arrange to have
sent to your realm legates of the lord pope with full judicial powers.

The bishop of Hereford, Master Robert of Melun,[119] who for more
than four years taught dialectic and the holy page at Paris, one day in
a certain gathering of many bishops and clerks proposed a tearful
question. 'If it should happen', he said, '(which far be it), that the lord
archbishop in this cause for the liberty of the Church is killed, would

117 A Benedictine monastery at Fleury. This meeting probably occurred in 1168.
118 See above, p. 95 n. 74.
119 On his career and his influence on the Becket dispute see Smalley, pp. 51–8.

we consider him a martyr? To die for the mother faith is to be a martyr.' To which someone answered, 'Undoubtedly if (which far be it), it turns out thus, it would be said that he had taken on the most glorious crown of the martyr. Not only faith is the cause of the martyr, for there are many causes – truth, the liberty of the Church, love of country or neighbours – each a sufficient cause, since God is in the cause. St John the Baptist did not discuss a point of faith with Herod or Herodias, but died for truth because he said "It is not right for you to have the wife of your brother".[120] Similarly also Thomas said "It is not lawful for you, king, to press this Church into servitude, so that ecclesiastical men, the ordained of God, be held subject to your customs, which are contrary to the canons". Again, seven brothers, their mother looking on and urging that they stand bravely, suffered various kinds of martyrdom, since they would not go against the mandate of God and the observances of their fathers concerning the eating of pig's flesh.[121] Also the blessed Archbishop Lanfranc consulted the holy Anselm, then abbot, about whether St Elphege[122] ought to be considered among God's martyrs, setting out how he had been killed by foreign enemies who had come to England by sea, because he refused to hand over the gold which they had imposed as tribute on the sons and men of the church of Canterbury. The blessed Anselm said, "In this he ought to be held special, who did not wish for the sake of the defence or prolongation of his life that his sons and neighbours be harassed in the payment of gold, which his enemies had exacted. He died indeed for the liberty and freedom of his neighbours. No one has greater love than to lay down his life for his friends. And the distinction of innocence, unsurpassed by any battle, makes the martyr".[123] For this reason too Abel is said to be the first to be crowned a martyr. Truly that was a wise statement of the pagans: "A bitter fate pursues the Romans, the crime of a brother's murder: ever since blameless Remus' blood was spilt upon the ground to be a curse to posterity".'[124]

120 Mark 6.18.

121 See 2 Maccabees 7.

122 Archbishop of Canterbury 1005–12, he was captured by Danes who demanded a huge ransom. When he refused to pay, and instructed his people to do likewise, his captors killed him.

123 This is a loose rendition of Eadmer, *Vita Anselmi* i. 30.

124 Horace, *Epodes* 7. The references to fratricide, in the cases of Abel and Remus, may be an allusion to the role of Thomas's brother bishops, who judged him at Northampton, and later played a role in his death.

Good God, how many of the clerks and knights who stood there, put forward true and splendid speeches on the contempt of the world, while the archbishop stood alone there holding the cross, and all his suffragan bishops and earls and barons had been called forth to the king, and removed from him. One man said, 'O deceptive world! Like a tranquil sea, however calm it may appear on the surface, it nevertheless conceals tempests within.' Another said, 'It is a world of ups and downs.[125] Love of the Lord is not to be sold. O worldly honours! Even those hoped for are to be feared!'

Speaking with the king within, the bishops said, among other things, that when that day they had come to the archbishop, he accused them of evil transactions because recently they, along with the barons, had treated him in a hostile manner, and judged him more severely than was just and in an unprecedented way. For one absence, which they said was a default to the king, he ought not have been judged insolent, nor ought he have been condemned to the mercy of the king on penalty of all his moveable goods. In this way the church of Canterbury could soon be destroyed, if the king mercilessly wished to harden his heart against him, and the bishops and barons themselves could suffer a similarly harmful judgement in a similar case. But it had been established that in every county one sum of money was to be paid by those condemned to financial forfeiture at the king's mercy. So, in London it was fixed at 100s. But in Kent, which being near to the sea has to fend off pirates from the English coast, and lays claim to the first blow in battles against a foreign enemy, because it has a greater burden, has also greater liberty and there 40s. is fixed as a fine for those condemned in this way. And he, having his domicile and see in Kent, should at least be judged and fined by the same law of Kent. The bishops added that on that same day, within ten days of the sentence being passed, he had appealed against them to the lord pope and he prohibited them on the pope's authority henceforth to judge him on a secular charge relating to the time before he became archbishop. The king enraged sent his earls and many of his barons to the archbishop, asking him if he was responsible for this appeal and prohibition, especially since he was his liegeman, and bound to him both by common oath and the special stipulation in word of truth at Clarendon, that he would keep his royal dignities in good faith, without deceit and lawfully. Among the customs was one, that the bishops sit in all his judgements, except those involving bloodshed.

125 Terence, *The Eunuch* 2. 2, 44.

The king also asked him if he would provide guarantees for bail, and in his court stand judgement on rendering the accounts of the chancellorship. In response, looking at the image of the Crucified, firm in mind and countenance, and remaining seated, so as to preserve his dignity as archbishop, he gave a speech like this, calmly and evenly, without halting in one word.[126]

'Men and brothers, earls and barons of my lord king', he said, 'indeed I am bound to our liege lord the king by homage, fealty and oath, but the priestly oath has justice and equity more especially as its companions. By a submission both devoted and owed, I am bound on account of obedience to God to discharge honour and faith to the lord king, saving obedience to God, and ecclesiastical dignity, and the honour of my ecclesiastical person. I decline this suit, as I received a summons neither to render account, nor for any other suit, apart from that of John,[127] nor am I held liable to answer or hear sentence in any other case here. I admit and remember the many official duties and dignities I received from the king, in which I faithfully devoted myself to him on both sides of the sea. And when, with pleasure, I spent all my own revenues in his service, I found myself heavily indebted to creditors. When then I was, by divine permission and the lord king's favour, archbishop-elect and due to be consecrated, I was released by the king immune before the consecration, and given free to the church of Canterbury, quit and exempt from all secular claims of the king.[128] But now in anger he denies this, which many of you, and all the ecclesiastics of the realm, well know to be true. And you who know the truth of this, I pray, beseech and entreat, that you put this forward to the lord king, against whom it is not safe to call witnesses, even if were lawful. Nor is it necessary, for I will not litigate. After the consecration, I set out to perfect the honour and duty I had taken on

126 Thomas is said to have had a stammer (see above, p. 42). Nevertheless he is often reported as speaking with great eloquence at crucial moments during public confrontations, and his eloquence, divinely inspired, is favourably contrasted with the worldly eloquence of his adversaries. This convention, commonly found in medieval writing, is based on Christ's instruction to the apostles, 'Beware of men; for they will deliver you up to councils, and flog you in their synagogues, and you will be dragged before governors and kings for my sake, to bear testimony before them and the Gentiles. When they deliver you up, do not be anxious how you are to speak or what you are to say; for what you are to say will be given to you in that hour; for it is not you who speak, but the spirit of the Father speaking through you' (Matthew 10.17-20). See M. Staunton, 'Trial and Inspiration in the Lives of Anselm and Thomas Becket', in *Anselm: Aosta, Bec and Canterbury*, eds D. Luscombe and G. R. Evans (Sheffield, 1996), pp. 310-22.

127 See above, pp. 100-3.

with all my might, and in some way to bring benefit to the Church of
God, over which I had been placed. In which matter if I am not allowed
to make progress, if I am unable to be of use, being buffeted by adversity, I do not impute this to the lord king, or to anyone else, but
principally to my sins. God is able to increase favour to whomsoever
he wishes whenever he wishes.

'As regards rendering accounts, I cannot give sureties. I have already
obliged all my bishops and helpful friends, nor ought I be compelled
to this, since this has not been assigned to me judicially. Nor am I
involved in a case concerning accounts, since I was not called to that
case, nor did I receive a summons to any other suit except that of John
the Marshal. As regards the prohibition and appeal objected against
by the bishops today, I recall indeed that I said to my fellow bishops
that for one absence, and no defiance, they have condemned me with
unjust severity, and contrary to long-established custom and prece-
dent. Hence I have appealed against them, forbidding them to judge
me again on a secular complaint relating to the time before I became
archbishop, while the appeal is pending, and I still appeal. And I place
my person and the Canterbury church under the protection of God
and the lord pope.'

He finished. Some of the nobles returned to the king in silence, weighing and examining his words. Others said, 'Behold the blasphemy of
prohibition that we have heard from his mouth'.[129] Others of the barons
and the attendants of the royal party, turning their heads and looking
at him askance, spoke among themselves quite clearly so that he could
hear. 'King William', they said, 'who conquered England knew how to
control his clerks. He arrested his own brother Odo, bishop of Bayeux,
who rebelled against him.[130] He threw Stigand archbishop of Canterbury into a murky pit and condemned him to perpetual imprison-
ment.[131] Indeed the father of our lord king, Geoffrey count of Anjou,
who also subjected Normandy to himself by force, had eunuchs made
of Arnulf elect of Séez and many of his clerks, and had the genitals of
the castrated brought before him in a basin, because without the
duke's consent to his election to the church of Séez he behaved as if he

128 See above, p. 64 n. 73.
129 See Matthew 26.65 (the High Priest's condemnation of Jesus).
130 Odo, William I's half-brother, bishop of Bayeux and earl of Kent was arrested for
    offending William, supposedly for aspiring to the papacy. It seems he was kept in
    prison until William's death in 1187.
131 Stigand was deposed in 1070.

had got assent and acted as if elected.'[132]

When the king received the archbishop's response, he pressed the bishops, ordering and entreating by the homage and fidelity owing and sworn to him, to pass sentence along with the barons. They began to excuse themselves on account of the prohibition which the archbishop had interposed. The king was not satisfied, asserting that this simple prohibition did not hold against what had been done and sworn at Clarendon. On their part the bishops insisted that the archbishop could bring his power to bear upon them, and oppress them if they did not observe his appeal and prohibition and for the good of the king and the realm they wished and were bound to acquiesce in his prohibition. When the king was eventually persuaded, the bishops took counsel and went in to the archbishop. Robert of Lincoln was crying and some others could hardly contain their tears. Then the bishop of Chichester spoke thus: 'Lord archbishop, saving your grace, we have great reason to complain about you. You have greatly offended us, your bishops. By this prohibition you have put us in a tight corner, as if you had placed us between the hammer and the anvil. We are snared in the bonds of disobedience if we do not comply, snared by the customs and offence to the king if we do. For recently when we were called to Clarendon by the king to discuss the observance of the royal customs, and gathered together with you, lest we hesitate, he showed us those customs in writing. Eventually we swore assent and promised to observe them – you in the first place, and we as your suffragans later, at your command. When in addition the lord king demanded an oath of guarantee and the impression of our seals, we said that our priestly oath, which we had given to him in the word of truth, that we would observe these his royal principles in good faith, without guile, and lawfully, ought to suffice for him. The lord king was persuaded and agreed. You now compel us to go against this, forbidding us to sit in judgement, as has been demanded of us.[133] From this grievance, and lest you add to our injury, we appeal to the lord pope, and on this account we fulfil obedience to your prohibition.'

The archbishop answered, 'What you say, I hear, and God willing I will submit to your appeal. But nothing was conceded by me, or you

---

132 This occurred in 1144 when the cathedral chapter of Séez went ahead with Arnulf's election without seeking the customary licence from the count. Geoffrey later repented and had his agents responsible for these mutilated punished. See *The Letters of Arnulf of Lisieux*, ed. F. Barlow (London 1939), pp. xxxiv–v.

133 See Clause 11 of the Constitutions, above, p. 95.

through me, at Clarendon, except saving ecclesiastical honour. As you yourselves say, we retained there three reservations, "In good faith, without guile and lawfully", through which the dignities of our churches, which we have from papal law, are saved. For what is against the faith due to the Church and the laws of God, cannot be observed in good faith and legitimately. Nor is it a dignity of a Christian king, when ecclesiastical liberty, which he swore to defend, perishes. Furthermore, those which you call royal dignities, the lord king sent in writing to the lord pope for confirmation, and he returned them more condemned than approved. He gave us an example in teaching, so that we also do thus, ready with the Roman Church to accept what he accepts and reject what he rejects. Besides, if we lapsed at Clarendon (for the flesh is weak), we ought to regain our spirit, and in the strength of the Holy Spirit rise up against the ancient enemy, who tries to make the one who stands also fall, and prevent the one who falls from getting up again. If under a guarantee in the word of truth there we conceded there or swore unjustly, you know that by no law are we obliged to that which was unlawfully sworn'.

The bishops returned to the king, and excused by his permission from judging the archbishop, they sat apart from the earls and barons. Nonetheless the king demanded sentence on the archbishop from the earls and barons. Certain sheriffs and barons of the second rank, old men, were called to join them in passing sentence. After some delay the nobles returned to the archbishop. Robert earl of Leicester, who surpassed the others in age and character, tried to impose the pronouncing of sentence on certain others, but when they refused he began to recall blow-by-blow the business at Clarendon. And the less than hilarious Hilary of Chichester, as if manifest lèse-majesté had been done to the king, and a transgression of the promise made there in the word of truth, said to the archbishop that he must hear his sentence. But the archbishop would put up with no more, and said, 'What is it that you wish to do? Have you come to judge me? You ought not. Judgement is a sentence given after a trial. Today I said nothing as part of a trial. To no suit was I called, except to that of John, who has not gone to trial with me. On this you cannot judge me. I am your father; you are nobles of the palace, lay potentates, secular persons. I will not hear your judgement'. The nobles withdrew. After an interval the archbishop rose, and carrying his cross approached the door, which all day had been securely locked, but opened to him as if of its own accord. A slanderer following him said that he was leaving as a perjurer to the king, another that he was withdrawing as a traitor and carried the sentence of the lord king with him. In the hall full of men he stumbled over a bundle of firewood not seeing it, but he did not fall. He came to the gate, where the horses were. When he had got on his, master Herbert, who could not get on his own horse as quickly on account of the pressure of crowds, rode with him to their lodgings at the monastery of St Andrews. O what a martyrdom in spirit he bore that day! But he returned more happily from the council, because he was held worthy there to suffer insult for Jesus' name.

III: EXILE (1164–66)

24. The flight from Northampton (October 1166)

'Roger of Pontigny', *MTB* 4. 52–4.

As the blessed man came out of the town, the common people, who had been waiting for the outcome of the council greeted him with joy and humbly begged for his blessing. As he showered blessing left and right he was delayed for a time by the crowd but eventually reached the monastery where he was staying.[1] Then he immediately prostrated himself in prayer before the altar, and spent a long time tearfully praying. As soon as he rose from prayer, he asked whether it was time for nones yet, but hearing that the hour had already passed, he sang nones and vespers together, and ordered his table to be placed there. And because hardly ten remained from his great retinue – for the rest had fled in fear and terror – he ordered in their place the monks' refectory to be filled by the poor, and plenty of food to be put before them.[2] Then he joined his men who were sitting at table rather morosely, and showed himself light-hearted and affable towards them. And while still sitting at table he ordered his bed to be brought into the church, and a quiet place to be prepared for him there. So his bed was brought down into the church in full view and there they prepared a place to sleep behind the great altar. And by his arrangement a servant was put there who prevented anyone from approaching, saying that the archbishop, exhausted by the day's work, should not be disturbed. But when the man of the Lord rose from the table he withdrew with a few men to a more secret place where they carefully discussed what could most appropriately be done for the cause of the Church of God in this moment of pressing need. For he was certain that if he lingered until the following day he would be captured and imprisoned. In this way the king would be regarded as committing a less serious crime if, detained in prison custody the archbishop happened to be butchered, seemingly without the king's knowledge. And however much the holy man was prepared to die for ecclesiastical liberty, nevertheless, lest the Church's cause should die with him, he resolved, certainly not to evade death, but to defer it for a time.

1 St Andrew's.

2 An echo of the parable of the rich man, Luke 14.16–24.

Day turned into night, for the meal had continued into twilight, and the man of God summoned two lay brethren whom he had with him in his retinue, Robert de Cave and Scaiman, and a very prompt and loyal personal servant called Roger of Bray. He privately intimated to these three alone how he had planned his departure, advising them to prepare themselves without delay. Also, as an important precaution, so that no suspicion should fall on his men as a result of his departure, he decided not to take any of their horses with them, but had four other horses provided for them from another source. As soon as the man of the Lord had enlisted these three, whom he had chosen as the most loyal, four of the best chargers were brought up, and were kept outside the door of the house, as if they belonged to visitors, until the appropriate time. Even the time and hour of the blessed man's flight seemed to be aided by divine support. For such a torrent of rain fell for the whole night that no one thought of opening the door of their house. Indeed such intense darkness prevailed from both the density of cloud and rain and the natural darkness of night, that nothing in the open could be seen. And since they expected that all the gates of the town would be diligently watched, they tried to find out through which of the gates the man of God might be able to pass most easily and safely. It was found that guards had not yet been posted on the northern gate. So, with everyone assuming that the archbishop was still in the place which they thought had been prepared for him in the church, he and his three companions mounted their horses and directed their course through the middle of the town to the northern gate. They had, with God's co-operation, the darkness of the night as a veil, and the violence of the downpour muffled the clattering of the horses' hooves. And thus with no one at all knowing, they went out through the northern gate.

All that night they hastened their flight, and eventually with day approaching they reached Lincoln. The archbishop had endured so much that night from the pouring rain that, unable to bear the weight of the water, twice before daybreak he cut off part of his cloak for the sake of comfort. When he came to Lincoln he lodged with a certain townsman called James, who was well acquainted with one of the brothers who had accompanied him.

But the next morning the bishop of Winchester, not knowing what had happened, came to speak to the archbishop. Osbern, the blessed man's chamberlain, who that night had guarded his bed in the church, met him, and when he was asked what the archbishop had done he said, 'He did well, for he has already taken his leave of us, and we do not know where he has gone'. When the bishop heard this, he drew a deep breath, burst into tears and said, 'With God's blessing!' But the king, when he learned that the archbishop had left, realising he had been outwitted, and stung by inner anxiety, was dumbstruck in indignation and fury. But recovering himself after a little, he said, 'We have not finished with this fellow yet'. Then quickly sending word, he ordered all the shores of the sea everywhere to be watched.

25. Reflections on the flight

The justifications of Thomas's flight are based ultimately on a letter of Augustine which features in canon law discussions of the subject.[3] The vision of the hedgehog echoes similar allegorical stories which punctuate Eadmer's account of Anselm's decision to go into exile.[4] The Icelandic Saga provides an elaborate gloss: the hedgehog represents Thomas, the stiffness of his hair his defence against assailants, and its roughness his harsh manner of life; the Acts of the Apostles on his back represents Thomas's adherence to their footsteps; the blind are those who hate godly light and walk in the darkness of worldly indulgence; the one-eyed are those with wisdom to see what they ought to do but who are blinded by evil desire; the lame also know what they ought to do but trip their foot against evil habits and limp away from God's path; those with mutilated lips refrain from rightfully admonishing and chastening wrongdoers; those of mutilated nose have no conception of whether their deeds are foul or fragrant; the darkness covering the face of the earth represents sin filling an earthly conscience; the shower of blood reflects the bloody counsel given against the archbishop; the king's white robe represents temporal power and its winding folds the shadowy evil counsellors; the garland of foxes' tails symbolises the wily deceits that turned Henry against Thomas.[5] Clearly the image of blood filling the king's mouth is also a comment on his rash words which led to Thomas's murder.

William of Canterbury, *MTB* 1. 40–2.

So, in the dead of night he left the town, not finding any town guard. At the appropriate time he escaped the premeditated crime and the exertions of evil counsels, deciding to cross to a safer place, just as the Lord promised and did, Who chose to flee so that authority for flight, when reason demands it, be given. Our patriarch Jacob fled from the presence of his brother Esau, and this on his mother's advice, so that

3 *Epistles* 228.
4 *Vita Anselmi* ii, 18.
5 *Saga* I. 233–9.

later by God's arrangement he would return home with blessed and excellent fruit. Paul fled so that he would be preserved for other things for which he was necessary. The most brave David fled the perils of battle lest the light of Israel be extinguished, but he acquiesced in the request of his people, he did not propose it himself. Thomas fled to protect the Church's liberty from danger. He fled so that he could die more proven and perfect. He fled, not as a mercenary, who sees the wolf coming and leaves the sheep and flees,[6] since those who could supply ecclesiastical ministry were not lacking, but in order to tend from afar the sheep whom he was unable to tend under the jaws of the wolf. He fled from the battle but did not flee the battle. He fled the renewed machination of the evil and the clamouring disorder of the defeated. Peter, because he would not flee, denied; John, so as not to deny, fled.

This is the vision of the fugitive hedgehog, which a certain deacon saw. The king of England was hunting in Wabridge forest with all his archbishops, bishops, barons, nobles, priors and abbots, when a hedgehog jumped out in front of them, roused by the clamour of the hunters. When they saw it they all began to chase it, harrying it with shouts and mockery. But the hedgehog outran the throng and hastened to the sea, not in a straight line but through a more winding path, carrying on his back the book entitled *The Acts of the Apostles*. None of those who followed was without a bodily flaw, but seemed either blind, one-eyed or lame, or to have mutilated lips or nose. And when eventually the hedgehog came to the sea, it plunged in and did not emerge again. Seeing this, those who had been in pursuit turned back. And behold a thick dark cloud arose and covered the face of the earth, and a shower of blood fell. The king then turned aside to the royal hall set up in that place, and he sat in it, after he had put on a long white robe of linen, and placed around his head wolves' tails as a garland. But the blood did not cease from spilling down upon him, because the house, being in a deserted place, did not have a water-proof roof, and through the wolves' tails hanging down it flowed into his garment. And when it had filled his garment and its winding folds, it began to flow out, and as it overflowed it filled even his mouth.

6 See John 10.12.

26. Thomas's itinerary (October–November 1164)

Herbert of Bosham, *MTB* 3. 322–35.

So, the next morning,[7] with the flight now known, the bishops and
nobles gathered together, and the king in his confusion asked what
was to be done. Their common advice was that the senior bishops by
birth, especially those who, as we have mentioned, had bound themselves to the king, should go to the pope and accuse the archbishop of
perjury, and of disturbing the peace of the realm and the priesthood.
Meanwhile all of his possessions should remain in place until they
reported the pope's judgement. So it was immediately announced to
the people by royal proclamation that no one was to molest the
archbishop's men or possessions, or to take anything away from him,
but everything of his was to remain untouched. And these wise men
gave this counsel to do evil, so that in this way they might more
easily justify their cause and denigrate the archbishop's: that although
he had rashly and disgracefully exasperated the king, recklessly
disturbed the peace of the crown and the priesthood, and foolishly and
indiscriminately abandoned the Church by fleeing in the night, still
after all this, out of royal clemency he undeservedly enjoyed the
benefit of royal peace. In this way the bishops along with the nobles
secretly laid a trap for the one who fled, and so straightaway Archbishop Roger of York, Bishops Gilbert of London, Roger of Worcester,
Hilary of Chichester and Bartholomew of Exeter set out. Besides these
a number of clerks of the court and certain other great and distinguished men from the king's party were sent with them as witnesses.
Through them the king wrote to Louis of blessed memory, then king
of France, and Philip, noble count of Flanders, bitterly intimating that
Thomas, formerly archbishop of Canterbury (for that was how the
letter began), had fled the realm as a traitor, and that they ought not
receive him in their lands.[8] So these men set out, but first let us relate
the itinerary of the fleeing Thomas as an example of humility.

As we have said, fleeing secretly by night [from Northampton], with

---

7 14 October, the morning after Thomas's flight.

8 'Know that Thomas, formerly archbishop of Canterbury, has been publicly judged
in my court by the full council of my barons to be a hostile and perjured traitor to
me, and under the plain appearance of a traitor has departed wickedly, as my
envoys will tell you more fully. For this reason I urgently pray that you do not
allow a man guilty of such great crimes and treasons, or his men, in your kingdom'
(*MTB* no. 71, 5. 134).

one brother of the order of Sempringham[9] with him to lead the way, he directed his path to the north to that noble city of Lincoln, being watchful and careful, travelling off the track, so that in this way, if men were sent after him, he would more easily escape his pursuers and evade ambush. And that night he came to the district of Grantham, about twenty-five miles from Northampton. He allowed himself a little sleep there, and the next day he hit the road and came to Lincoln, a journey of around twenty-five miles, where he lodged in the house of a certain fuller. Then he sailed down the river which flows through the city[10] for about forty miles until he came to a deserted place set in the middle of the water, which is called The Hermitage and belongs to that holy and devout community of Sempringham.[11] There he hid for three days quite untroubled, on account of the solitude of the place and the difficulty of access, being surrounded by water, and recovered his energy for the journey that remained. But on one of these days when the brother who ministered to him saw him sitting alone at table to eat a dish of pottage, profoundly affected, he was unable to contain his tears. And he withdrew immediately lest his flood of tears disturb the man of God at the holy banquet.

From the Hermitage he travelled ten miles to Boston, and thence by water he came to Haverholme, which belonged to the same holy community. But from then on he travelled only by night for fear of detection. And now turning east he headed for Kent, where he was better known by sight to the people. So he proceeded for eight nights, travelling by night and hiding by day, until he came to the district of Eastry on the Kent coast, where he arranged to cross the sea. He stayed there securely because of his caution, that village being part of the estate of the community of his metropolitan see, only eight miles from Canterbury. The future light of the world hid in this place for eight days until the feast of All Souls. But on All Souls – which was a Tuesday,[12] a fortnight from that Tuesday, that day of battle, when he fought the beasts at Northampton – a little before daybreak he set out to sea in a skiff without any baggage. Around vespers he landed on the seashore commonly called Oye in Boulogne, one league from the port of Gravelines. The man of God proceeded on foot as far as he could, but little could he do so, because, sailing in a small craft, a skiff

9 The Gilbertine order, founded by Gilbert of Sempringham (d. 1189).

10 The Witham.

11 Probably Catley.

12 All Souls, 2 November 1164, actually fell on a Monday.

as we have said, he was tossed by the ups and downs of the sea, and arrived quite exhausted. So after a little he lay down on the grass unable to proceed, and said to the brothers who were with him, 'I cannot leave here unless you carry me or you seek transport for me'. And they found him a packhorse for a shilling, which did not even have a harness around its neck but only a halter, and they put their clothes on its back and made him sit on top.

What a sight to see Thomas, once on chariots and horses, now astride a packhorse, with only a halter around its neck for a bridle and the rags of the poor brothers and lay brothers on its back for a saddle! What a change of circumstances, Thomas! Where are all those horses and knights you used to have, all those rich and ostentatious trappings? Look at all these now reduced to one packhorse and one halter, and not even your packhorse or halter but another's. As you change, the things belonging to you also change, as your old things pass away and all become new.[13] Truly God is marvellous in his saints,[14] Who leads them down a wonderful road, from tribulation gladdening, from pressure expanding, from temptation proving, by destroying building, by persecuting healing, by killing giving life. This is plain to see in, among others, Thomas. And so he came to the port of Gravelines, sitting like that on a packhorse. In this way he landed across the sea on the feast of All Souls, on a Tuesday, which is commonly called the day of Mars, a fortnight, as we have said, from the day he fought in Northampton as described above. I do not know by what foreshadowing of events – if nevertheless the foreshadowing more than the fulfilment – he began his flight on a Tuesday, set out across the sea on a Tuesday, departed from the sea on a Tuesday, again on his return from England landed on a Tuesday, and finally fell to the sword on a Tuesday, precisely a month from the day of his return landing. In this way, what was the day of Mars would also become the day of the martyr,[15] the day on which, as a portent of the future, he was frequently prepared thus for martyrdom. On a Tuesday, then, the feast of All Souls, he landed across the sea, and at vespers came to Gravelines.

When at a late hour he sat down with three brothers, companions of his journey, he was recognised by his host as he was breaking bread. This despite the fact that no more deference was paid to him at table

13 See 2 Corinthians 5.17.

14 Psalm 67.36.

15 *quae fuit dies Martis, fieret et martyris.* Mars was identified as the God of war, as well as being associated with Tuesday.

than others, rather less, as one would expect of someone who had not first place at table but last. Indeed throughout this journey he had changed his name along with his dress, and was called Father Christian by his brothers, the companions of the way, the name Christian chosen specially, all so as not to be recognised. However, this observant innkeeper noticed that among those dining he stood out by his manner of eating and his fondness for giving. For from the little amount that was set before him, he distributed among the children and the others in the house.

To gain more certain proof of the identification he had already conceived, he inspected the build and posture of the whole man: the great height, the large brow and serious expression, the long and handsome face, the long hands, and their elegant and quite exquisite fingers. Seeing then that this man was quite different from the others in his way of eating and in the nature and posture of his body, he quickly judged that he had taken in some great man, and for a certainty suspected that this was the archbishop of Canterbury. For already the rumour had widely spread in the land around how the archbishop of Canterbury had secretly left Northampton, and had either already landed in these parts or was soon about to land. Therefore the innkeeper immediately took his serving-girl aside and privately informed her that it was the archbishop of Canterbury to whom he had given lodging. But hardly had he said the words than she, in her impatience, rushed to the table, and after a little observation she soon returned and said with a smile, 'Certainly, sir, it is he'. Consequently the serving-girl began to run more busily this way and that, hastening to put now nuts, now fruit, now cheese before Father Christian. But Father Christian, now suspecting that he had been found out on account of some disclosure or other, preferred to abstain from these things which the serving-girl had affectionately placed before him, and kept up his pretence.

When the meal was finished, the innkeeper approached with a newly cheerful face. When Father Christian wished to place him on a seat beside him the innkeeper insistently refused and sat on the ground beside his feet. And after a little he said, 'Lord, I thank God that I was considered worthy for you to enter into my home'. Straight away Brother Christian answered, 'And who am I then? Am I not just a poor brother called Christian?' The innkeeper said, 'For sure, whatever you say, I know you to be a great man, the archbishop of Canterbury'. So, since no covering of words could free Father Christian from his innkeeper, and he found himself with the choice of either admitting the truth about himself with constancy or falsely denying it, he admitted and did not deny that it was he. And so as not to betray himself, stroking him with flattery, he led the innkeeper with him the next day. How far-reaching was the danger to the man of God, who even now in port was imperilled![16]

The king spread abroad by letter and word to the noble count of Flanders, his brother, and his friendly nobles of the land that Thomas, 'formerly archbishop of Canterbury' (for such was the opening of the letter), had fled from his realm like a traitor. When royal power is extensive, so the danger to the one who flees the royal power is far-reaching, and therefore everywhere there is suspicion, and no security. The reason he feared to be revealed in these parts was that by the arrangement of the lord king of England, Matthew, the brother of Philip count of Flanders, then count of Boulogne, had contracted a profane marriage detestable to all future generations, to a certain abbess, daughter of Stephen, formerly king of England.[17] The archbishop, then royal chancellor, had objected to the shameful deed, and protested as much as he could, and so the count of Boulogne had hated him intensely from then on. So it was that he was afraid and, not without reason, did not wish to make himself known in those parts. Therefore, because of the length of the following day's journey and the difficulty of the road, and the traps which he feared, he set out the next day at the break of dawn. The man of God travelled on foot from Gravelines all that day, along a very muddy and slippery road in very wintry weather, and at night he came to the monastery of the holy order of Cistercians known in the land as Clairmarais, a journey of twelve leagues by local calculations. This monastery is situated near that noble fort which we have mentioned before, St-Omer.[18]

The disciple who wrote these things had preceded him by around four or five days, as mentioned was enjoined on him,[19] and was now awaiting the arrival of his lord in the noble, distinguished and all-holy

16 Other writers relate how Thomas was almost discovered by his conspicuous interest in a falcon which he saw on a young knight's wrist: see *MTB* 2. 335, 4. 56–7.

17 Mary of Blois, abbess of Romsey.

18 While Thomas was at Clairmarais he is reported to have had an interview with the justiciar, Richard de Lucy, who urged him to return to England, When he saw that his efforts were in vain, the justiciar told the archbishop that from now on he would be his enemy. 'The holy man said to him, "You are my man, and you ought not say such things to me". "I hand back my vassalage to you", he replied. "You did not borrow it from me", answered the archbishop' (*MTB* 4. 57).

19 Herbert had been sent to Canterbury to take some of the church's revenues for Thomas's expenses. All he managed to lay his hands on was a hundred marks and some precious vessels.

abbey of St Bertin's.[20] An envoy came to announce the arrival of the archbishop and the same night he came. I was delighted to see my lord, but nevertheless felt sorry for him when I heard, in his own words, the difficulties and dangers of his journey ...[21]

But the same night that the archbishop embarked, the aforementioned envoys of the king set sail with great provision. Suddenly a storm arose and in difficulty and danger they were hardly able to land, whereas the sea was very peaceful for the archbishop and his men in the skiff.[22] So testified the brothers who were with the archbishop in the skiff, and others from the other party who crossed in ships. Truly this is the work of Him Whom the wind and sea obey, Whom when He wishes disturbs the sea, and when He wishes stills the roaring of the waves.[23] It also closely resembles the seventh in the catalogue of plagues of Egypt, in which Moses stretched forth his rod towards heaven, and the Lord sent thunder and forked lightning upon the earth, raining hailstones upon the land, and a mixture of hail and fire was brought forth. Only in the land of Goshen, where the sons of Israel were, did hail not fall.[24] Similarly also, in the ninth plague a thick darkness fell over the whole land of Egypt, but wherever the sons of Israel lived there was light.[25] Indeed the most powerful God of Israel, the same then and now, distinguishes both in reward and in the lash the righteous from the impious and the fearful from the scornful.

Therefore the said envoys of the king set sail on the same night as the archbishop, and also on the same day as the archbishop they came to the fort of St-Omer. It was widely known in the land that the archbishop of Canterbury had intended to come to that monastery of Clairmarais, to which he now came. So, that same night, after he had sung the night office, he entered the large and spacious pool in which the monastery is situated, and came in a skiff to a certain hidden place surrounded by water called Oldminster by the inhabitants, formerly the hermitage of the blessed and glorious confessor Bertin. For he

20 Thomas's predecessors Anselm and Theobald had both stayed in this monastery when they were in dispute with their kings.
21 Herbert recaps, and mentions his limited success in retrieving revenues from Canterbury.
22 This seems to contradict Herbert's earlier statement that Thomas suffered from a difficult journey, above, pp. 121–2.
23 See Psalms 65.7 and 89.9.
24 See Exodus 9.22–6.
25 See Exodus 10.21–3.

feared that if he tarried until the next day in that monastery he would be revealed by signs of some kind to the locals, and in particular to the king's envoys, who would perhaps turn aside to see him. To see him there would cause scorn to the rich and disdain to the proud,[26] and they would freely jeer that he had fallen from such former fortune to such present poverty. So the same night he departed, and hid in the said hermitage for three days. And on the fourth he came to the abbey of St Bertin at the request of the then abbot Godescal and the community of the place. And like days of cloud and fog a little brightened, a ray of true light now tentatively emerged and showed itself to the world.

But leaving the archbishop for the moment in the monastery of St Bertin's at St-Omer, let us first follow the journey and activity of the envoys. The day after their arrival they left St-Omer and travelled for three or four days until they found Louis of pious memory, then king of France, at the royal castle of Compiègne. They greeted the king and offered him letters in the name of the king of England. Their form was similar to those which as we have said above had been sent to the count of Flanders, namely that Thomas, 'formerly archbishop of Canterbury', had fled from the realm as a traitor, and he begged him as his lord not to receive him in his land. But when he heard the opening of the letter, 'Thomas formerly archbishop', zeal immediately seized the king, as a most devoted son of the Church, and he was greatly angered at the expression. The insolent phrase caused offence, and as is the saying of the wise man, 'He who restrains his speech is clever and prudent'.[27] And the king straight away enquired again and again who had deposed him, and added, 'Certainly, like the king of England, I am also a king. Nonetheless I do not have the power to depose the lowliest clerk in my kingdom'. So those who had been sent could not give a prudent answer to the king's question, nor did they take home the answer they desired to their petition.

But the disciple who wrote these things, and another circumspect and learned man from the archbishop's fellowship, on the advice and command of the archbishop, followed every day in the envoys' footsteps without their knowledge, so that they were always a day ahead of us. And indeed this was done deliberately and diligently, so that thus we might more carefully and certainly ascertain their words and labours against us. But as soon as we gained access to that Christian king of

26 See Psalm 122.4.
27 Proverbs 17.27.

the French, from whom the envoys had departed the previous day, we greeted him faithfully and humbly in the name of the archbishop. The king had admired and favoured him since the time he was chancellor on account of his greatness, honesty and industry, and since we had previously been unknown to him he repeatedly asked us, in his way, if we were from the archbishop's house and retinue. When he learned that we were, he immediately welcomed us with a kiss and graciously listened to us. When, according to the archbishop's mandate, we recounted our tearful story, our troubles and dangers, royal clemency was touched to the core, and he deigned to tell us how and in what terms the king had written to him against the archbishop, and how he had responded. And he added, 'The lord king of England, if it pleases him, before he dealt so harshly and so fearfully with such a great friend of his, an archbishop and such a great person, ought to have remembered the reading, "Be angry and sin not".[28] And my companion on the way and fellow-envoy quickly answered in jest, 'Lord, perhaps he would have remembered this verse if he had heard it as often as we have in the canonical hours', and the king smiled. But the next day, before we left, the king took counsel with his men who were there with him, and according to the archbishop's petition delivered through us, he granted peace and security to the archbishop in his realm. And indeed he added that it was an ancient privilege of the French king that exiles, and especially ecclesiastics, should enjoy the peace and security of kings and of the realm, and be protected from the injuries of their persecutors …[29]

Therefore, enjoying the benefit and security of royal peace, in exultation and joy the French king dismissed us in peace. But we did not return immediately to the archbishop, nor did we report anything about this, because we hoped we would quickly return to him, but as he had instructed us, we hastened to the lord pope, and came to Sens, where the envoys who preceded us had arrived the day before. That evening we were admitted to the lord pope, whom we greeted in the name of the archbishop, as father and lord, with appropriate devotion and humility. We said that we were just two who had escaped from the house of Rechab, and had come to the feet of his holiness to announce that his son Joseph was still alive, but was not ruling in the land of Israel,[30] rather, oppressed by the Egyptians he had almost been

28 Ephesians 4.26.
29 Herbert praises God for inspiring Louis to turn to the archbishop's cause.
30 See Genesis 45.26.

destroyed. As he listened with fatherly compassion we freely related
the pressures on his son the archbishop, the hardships and sorrows,
the dangers in that fight with the beasts at Northampton, danger with
false brethren, dangers in flight, dangers on the way, dangers in the
sea and even in port, trouble, want and difficulty, and how he changed
his dress and name to escape ambush.[31] And hearing this the father of
all fathers was moved to the depths of fatherly piety towards his son,
and unable to hide his paternal affection he wept, and stung in this
way he turned his speech to us who had spoken and said, 'The lord
lives yet in the flesh, as you say, and indeed while still alive he lays
claim to the dignity of martyrdom'. And as it was now very late and
we were tired from our journey, he gave us blessing and apostolic consolation and sent us quickly to our lodgings to return the next day.

27. Discussions with the pope at Sens (November 1164)

Both sides had an audience with the pope, a few days apart, at his residence
in exile at Sens.

Alan of Tewkesbury, *MTB* 2. 336–45.

Meanwhile a wild confusion disturbed the state of affairs, everyone
conferring with each other, and according to the wish of the king
seeking an opportunity to destroy the Lord's anointed. Therefore the
archbishop of York and the bishops of London, Chichester, Exeter,
Worcester and Lisieux were sent by the king to the pope, and with
them a large number of earls and barons, in great splendour, with
presents and gifts with which for the sake of men they might pervert
justice and blind the eyes of the wise. For, as certain bishops advised
against the archbishop of Canterbury, they believed that in this way
they could turn the Roman curia to their will in this regard whenever
it was wavering. Indeed, on their arrival, very many of the cardinals
were caused to falter, on the one hand because of the fear of public
disturbance that the king's anger could bring about, and on the other
because of the hope of gain, and a dispute arose among them. Some
said that he was a defender of the church of Canterbury, and for that
reason was advancing a just cause, and others that he was a disturber
of peace and unity, and therefore the force of his presumption ought
to be restrained rather than supported. As it happened, the prompting
of the enemies prevailed to such an extent that the envoys of the lord

31 See 2 Corinthians 11.26–7.

of Canterbury, men of great virtue and zeal, gained no favour from the cardinals, nor were they received with a kiss. And these were distressed to see the looming danger to their lord's cause.

The next day,[32] nevertheless, the envoys from Canterbury attended a papal assembly in the presence of the cardinals in the hope of seeing a result. On the other side the king's envoys rose, and their leader and standard-bearer the bishop of London began. 'Father', he said, 'to you the care and attention of the Catholic Church looks, so that through your prudence the wise may be encouraged to good behaviour, and the foolish may be rebuked and corrected by apostolic authority and thereby learn wisdom. But your wisdom would not consider wise the man who, relying on his own wisdom, seeks to disturb the concord of brothers, the peace of the Church and the devotion of the king. For recently, for a trivial and unimportant reason, a conflict has arisen in England between the crown and the priesthood which could have been avoided had a restrained approach been taken. But the lord of Canterbury, following his own individual counsel in this business, and not ours, took too vigorous a stand, not considering the evil of the time, or the danger that could result from such an impulse, and laid traps for himself and his brethren. And had we given our assent to his proposal, matters would have turned out even worse. But because, rightly, he could not have our connivance in his plans, he attempted to turn the blame for his own recklessness around on the lord king and us, and indeed the whole realm. For which reason, in order to discredit our mutual brotherhood, with no one using force or even making threats he took to flight, as is written, "The wicked man flees when no one is pursuing"'.[33] To this the lord pope said, 'Have mercy, brother', and the bishop of London replied, 'My lord, I will have mercy on him'. But the pope replied, 'I am not telling you, brother, to have mercy on him, but on yourself'. In this way the Lord so struck and confused the bishop of London through this apostolic voice and trumpet that he could not mutter another word.[34]

Then the fluent Hilary, bishop of Chichester, took up the argument, trusting more in his own eloquence than in justice and truth, as later became apparent. 'Father and lord', he said, 'It concerns your blessedness that what has been wrongly done to the harm of all, be returned quickly to its proper state of peace and concord, lest the immoderate

32 26 November 1164.
33 Proverbs 28.1.
34 See above, pp. 111 n. 126.

obstinacy of one man be allowed to wreak havoc on many, and bring schism in the Catholic Church. The lord of Canterbury paid little attention to this, when he abandoned more mature counsel and consulted himself alone, thereby bringing grave hardship and trouble to himself and his men, to the king and the realm, and to the clergy and people. And certainly it was not becoming for a man of such authority, nor was it proper, nor was it right'. (In this way Hilary of Chichester made a grammatical mistake saying *oportuebat*.)[35] 'Besides, it would not have been proper for his people, if they were wise, to have given assent to him in such things.' When they heard then this fluent man of grammar leaping from port to port, all were dissolved in laughter, and one of them quipped, 'Painfully you have reached port at last'. With which words the Lord so confused this bishop, that from then on he became mute and speechless.

But the archbishop of York, observing the ruin of those who had gone before, took care to temper the passion of his feeling. 'Father', he said, 'the character and inclination of the archbishop of Canterbury are known to nobody more than me. I have known the way of his mind from the beginning, that once he seizes upon an opinion, he cannot easily be turned away from it. And therefore it should be recognised that this obstinacy resulted from his usual unreliability. And the only way I see of correcting him is for your discretion to apply the heavy hand. I think I have said enough to an intelligent man.'

The bishop of Exeter[36] was next. 'Father', he said, 'we should not linger much upon this. This case cannot be brought to issue in the absence of the archbishop of Canterbury. Therefore we ask for envoys to hear the case between king and archbishop, and then decide upon it.' And he was silent. Nor did any of the bishops add anything after him.

Seeing this, the earl of Arundel,[37] who was standing in his company with a number of knights, asked for an audience. Silence fell, and he said, 'Lord, we unlettered[38] men are entirely ignorant of what the bishops have said. Therefore we ought to explain, as much as we can, why we were sent. We have certainly not come to argue, or throw insults at anyone, in the sight of such a great man, to whose will and authority the whole world rightfully bends. Rather we have come for

---

35 Confusing the imperfect tense, *oportebat*, with the perfect, *oportuit*.
36 Bartholomew, one of the bishops more sympathetic to Thomas.
37 William d'Aubigny.
38 I.e. without Latin.

this purpose, that we represent in your presence and that of the whole Roman Church, the devotion and love of our lord king, which he has been accustomed to show towards you, and continues to show. Who, then, represents the king in this way but the greatest and noblest subjects in all his lands, archbishops, bishops, earls and barons? Higher than these are not found in his dominions, and if he could find higher, he would have sent them specially in deference to your reverence and that of the Roman Church. May we add that your fatherhood was made sufficiently aware at the beginning of your pontificate of the fidelity and devotion of our lord king, when he placed himself, his men and all he owns entirely at your will.[39] And certainly we believe that there is no one within the unity of the Catholic faith, which you hold in Christ to rule over, more faithful, or more devoted to God, or more suited to the conservation of that peace to which he had been enlisted. Nevertheless the lord of Canterbury is equally capable in his rank and order, prudent and discreet in the things which concern him, although, as it seems to some, a little too sharp. And were it not for this present dispute between the lord king and lord archbishop, the crown and the priesthood would rejoice together in mutual peace and concord under a good ruler and an excellent pastor. This then is our prayer, that your grace look out more attentively for the removal of this dissension, and the restoration of peace and love'. This the earl elegantly said, but in his own tongue,[40] so that his modest discretion was commended by all.

Paying careful attention to these words, the pope answered, 'We know, Earl, my son, and well recall with how much devotion the king of England conferred many rich benefits upon us. And we, given the opportunity, heartily wish to repay them as deserved, as much as in God we are able. But since you ask for envoys, you will have envoys.' They kissed the lord pope's foot and withdrew, believing they had succeeded in their cause because the cardinals had given them hope that they could be corrupted. Therefore after consultation the bishop of London returned, asking from the lord pope with what powers the cardinals would come. 'With what is right', said the pope. 'Rather', said the bishop, 'we ask that they be allowed to decide the case free from appeal.' 'That', said the lord pope, 'is my glory, and I will give it to no other.[41] And certainly, when a judgement is to be made it will be

39 A reference to Henry's support for Alexander in the papal schism.

40 French, presumably.

41 See Isaiah 42.8.

made by us, because no reason allows that we return the archbishop
to England to be judged by his adversaries and among his enemies.'
Their hope frustrated at hearing this, the hostile party withdrew in
indignation to inform the king of the answer they had received.

When these things had happened at Sens, for that is where the pope
was, and these men returned, the lord of Canterbury came to [the
papal] court with his men.[42] There he was received coldly by the
cardinals, whose nostrils had been poisoned by the odour of lucre in
the pursuit of profit. Nevertheless, he was brought into the lord's
presence, and while this and that was being discussed there, he was
eventually instructed to set out the cause of his exile before the
brethren the next morning. So the next day it was demanded that he
present himself in person before the lord pope, and when the exiles
discussed in conclave which of them would put forward their case,
each excused himself, and the burden of speaking fell on the archbishop. Sitting next to the lord pope, he wished to rise on account of
reverence, but was ordered to sit down again to discuss the case in
detail, and, not prepared by himself but instructed by God, he began:
'Although we are not so wise, nor are we so foolish that we have left
behind the king of England, his men and possessions, for no reason.
For if we had wished to please his desire in all things, there would
have been no one in his dominions or in his kingdom, who would not
have obeyed us with pleasure. And since we served him on these terms,
what was it that did not meet our wish? But from this we entered
upon another path and were made mindful of the profession and
obedience which we had undertaken on God's behalf, and the previous
fondness which he had towards us undoubtedly cooled. But still, if we
had wished to shrink from this objective to regain his favour, we
would have acted without anyone's intervention. But since the church
of Canterbury is accustomed to be the sun of the west, and in our time
its lustre has been obscured, we would more willingly have taken on
in the Lord any torment, or even a thousand kinds of death, should
they have occurred, than bear in silence the evil which it suffers these
days. Moreover, lest I seem to have begun upon this in a meddlesome
or vainglorious way, let us establish it with keensighted faith.' And
producing the charter in which those contentious customs had been
written, with tears he said, 'See what the king of England has set up

42 A few days later. As the king's envoys passed the River Seine on their way north
   they saw 'more than 300 horsemen of the archbishop's retinue' on the other side
   (*MTB* 3. 74).

against the liberty of the Catholic Church. You will see if you may dissimulate about these things without loss to the soul.'

When it was read through all were moved to tears. Nor could those who first acted in opposition on men's behalf contain themselves, but with common voice they praised God that he preserved if only one for them who in that tempest dared to go up against adversity on God's behalf.[43] And they who earlier seemed to disagree about this case were now united in one opinion, that they ought to come to the aid of the universal Church in the person of the archbishop of Canterbury.

The next day the lord of Canterbury attended a meeting in a private chamber with the lord pope and the cardinals, where he made this speech: 'My father and lords, no one ought to lie anywhere, least of all before God and in your presence. Therefore willingly, but also with sighs, I confess that my wretched fault brought these troubles upon the English Church. I ascended to the sheepfold of Christ not through Him who is the door,[44] as one called by canonical election, but as one intruded by pressure of public power. And although I took on this burden unwillingly, nevertheless human and not divine will induced me. What wonder then, if it turned out badly for me? But if at the king's threat, as our brothers insistently urged, I had renounced the privilege of episcopal authority granted to me, it would have left a pernicious example to the hopes of princes and the wishes of the Catholic Church. Therefore I waited until I met you. But now, recognising my appointment to be uncanonical, and fearing lest the outcome turn out even worse for me, indeed seeing my powers unequal to the burden and afraid lest I lead to ruin the flock to whom I have been given in whatever way as pastor, I resign into your hands, father, the archiepiscopate of Canterbury.' And he cried, sobbing, but also brought the pope and all present to tears.

And who hearing this could contain themselves from tears? The archbishop sat apart with his men, who had been thrown into confusion by these words and were now certainly beginning to despair. Meanwhile the lord pope began to confer with the cardinals about what had been said, and received various and diverse opinions. It seemed to some that this afforded an easy opportunity to allay the anger of the king, since he could be given another position in the church of Canterbury, and another more competent person could be provided as archbishop.

43 See Ezekiel 13.5.
44 See John 10.1–2.

This view came from Pharisees.[45] But to those who had their eyes open it seemed on the contrary, that if he who risked not only riches and glory, dignity and authority, but also his life to protect the Church's liberty in the greatest danger and crisis, should be deprived of his right so as to please the king, it would be an example to others trying to resist kings in similar cases and preserve their righteousness intact. So if he fell all bishops would fall, so that never in future would anyone dare to stand up to the will of a ruler, and so the prestige of the Catholic Church would totter and the pope's authority would perish. 'It is better then', they said, 'that he be reinstated even if unwilling, and that assistance be given to him in every way, he who fights for all'. This opinion pleased everyone, except the Pharisees.

The archbishop was called in along with his men, and the lord pope said this in judgement: 'Now finally, brother, it is clear to us, what zeal you have had and still have for the house of the Lord, with what a sincere conscience you have stood as a wall against adversity, how pure a confession you have made since your entrance. The resignation you have made can and ought to wipe away blame of wrong. Now you can securely receive the care of episcopal office anew from our hand while we arrange for its full restoration to you. And deservedly, as we know you to be a man proven by many kinds of temptations, prudent and discreet, dear to God and men, faithful in everything to us and the Holy Roman Church. And just as you have been made an indivisible partner and consort in our persecution, so, with God's help, we will be unable to fail in any way in our duty to you, as long as a breath of life remains in this body. But you who have up to now delighted in riches ought to learn to be the comforter of the poor, and this you cannot be taught except by poverty, the mother of religion. We have decided therefore to commend you to be trained by the poor of Christ, that is the abbot of Pontigny' – who was present by prior arrangement – 'and his men. Not, I say, to be trained in splendour but in simplicity, as befits an exile and an athlete of Christ. You will live among them for a time with just a few companions and those necessary, the others dispersed among friends, until the day of consolation approaches, and a time of peace descends from above. But meanwhile be strong of heart, and manfully resist those who disturb the peace'.

---

45 The prominent religious sect among the Jews at the time of Jesus, usually characterised as hypocrites: see Matthew 23.1–36.

28. Henry's measures against Thomas (Christmas 1164)

William Fitzstephen himself escaped such measures, making his peace with
the king by presenting him with a royal prayer to God (*MTB* 3. 59, 78–81).
William Fitzstephen, *MTB* 3. 75–6.

At Marlborough on Christmas Eve the king of England received his
envoys and a personal legate of the lord pope. Unsuccessful in his
plan, on the first day of Christmas he ordered the archbishop to be
immediately deprived of all his possessions, and the church of Canterbury, with all its lands and appurtenances, and all the churches and
revenues of all his clerks to be taken into royal hands. And all the
archbishop's relations, and the clerks and laymen of his household
were to be proscribed and banished from his kingdom. On the second
day of Christmas the king's servants and officials came to London.
Among them was Ranulf de Broc, 'more monstrous in crime than all
others',[46] the cruellest of laymen and most hostile to the archbishop,
to whom the king committed that holy church of Canterbury, the
primary see of England, to keep, or rather destroy. He with certain
others was the executor of the king's mandate. 'They do what they are
ordered, and worse than they are ordered.'[47] Outside the city, in
Lambeth, in the archbishop's own house, these knights ordered into
exile all his relatives found in the city of London. They were to leave
from the seaport, and from their native soil, at the first suitable wind,
and go directly to the archbishop. In other words, his flesh would be
ground down with his own flesh and sorrows be added to his sorrows.
And for every one of his people expelled for his sake who appeared
before him, a sword pierced his heart. It was not a happy group of
good people, rather a distressing exodus. Relatives of his of both sexes
emigrated, and infants, some in cradles, others clinging to the breast.
Indeed all his clerks and servants who were found were expelled, but
also anyone who had taken him in for even one night as he wandered
through England as a fugitive from the king. But to what end? This
noble France welcomed all in pity: the king of France himself took in
some, archbishops, bishops, abbots, priors, counts, barons, governors,
castellans, and individuals others. Nuns took in women and children.
Noble men divided among themselves the poor of Jesus Christ, the

---

46 Virgil, *Aeneid* i, 347. Ranulf, doorkeeper of the king's chamber and royal brothel-
keeper, was to play a central role in the events of December 1170. See Barlow, p.
301 n. 55.

47 Probably a quotation, unidentified.

good archbishop's tattered procession, his desolate household, nor did any of them go in want among those noble French. This bounty and generosity has not been forgotten. Such are the sacrifices which God approves.[48]

29. Thomas's learning at Pontigny (1164–66)

Pontigny, founded in 1114, was the second daughter house of Cîteaux, and was to be, in the following century, a place of refuge for Thomas's successors Stephen Langton and Edmund Rich. There Thomas engaged in a programme of spiritual study under Herbert's guidance, and was also trained in law by Peter Lombard, who was later to become bishop of Benevento. In January 1165, at the beginning of Thomas's sojourn there, John of Salisbury wrote him a famous letter in which he stressed the benefits of spiritual studies: 'Who ever rises contrite from the study of civil or even canon law? And further: scholarship sometimes swells learning into a tumour, but never or scarcely ever inflames devotion. I would rather have you ponder on the Psalms and turn over the moral writings of St Gregory than philosophise scholastically'.[49]

Herbert of Bosham, *MTB* 3. 357–8, 379.

When we had spent about three weeks in court, with apostolic blessing and licence we came to Pontigny, where we were received by the whole community with as much joy as if the heavenly host had been sent. Showing great consideration to us, with a ready and willing spirit they allowed us to eat meat, and certain other indulgences contrary to the rule of the order. Indeed the generosity and kindness of the order was apparent around us more than there is time to say. But on the third or fourth day of our arrival, the archbishop entered the chapter house and committed the cause of the Church which he bore to the Lord and their prayers. Our packs were set in order, and we received neighbouring but separate dwellings within the precincts of the monastery, and immediately we began to direct ourselves zealously, whatever the time, to reading holy writings.

The archbishop certainly, after all the troubles we have described, as if after a time of dense cloud, soon began to turn himself with all his mind to the serenity and tranquillity of divine light, giving himself entirely to reading, prayer and meditation. For this was the time which,

48 See Hebrews 13.16.

49 *LJS* no. 144, pp. 32–5. 'The moral writings are St Gregory' are, presumably, his *Moralia in Job*, a fitting text for Thomas at this point.

as I heard from himself, he had always longed for, from the beginning of his promotion as archbishop, even during his time among the vanities of the world as chancellor. Knowing that, as the wise man said, 'Wisdom depends on leisure',[50] he was taught and he learned. That monastery was to us like a training-school for combat, in which we were exercised together, a school of virtue in which we were educated together, so that every day we would say to the Lord, 'It is good for us that we are afflicted, that we may learn thy statutes'[51]

[…][52]

As we have begun to say, our banished and proscribed by God's grace were comforted in this way at Pontigny. In solitude among the stones and the monks we solitary men now hid ourselves away remote from the world, more free because more peaceful, more fruitful because more private, and turned with all the mind to spiritual things. But the archbishop above all was stirred with an ardour wonderful to speak of. As if to illuminate what was great in the firmament of the heavens he perpetually clung to holy scripture, to apostolic ordinances, but devoting the greatest effort to theology. For this was the time which, as we have said above, he had always longed for, when now at last he might make up for the loss of squandered days, so that he who had been chosen to rule over souls should at some time, even if late, learn how to rule them. He was such a lover of scriptures that every day after the regular hours the sacred books would hardly leave his hands for the whole day, especially those two holy books the Psalms and the Epistles, like two spiritual eyes, mystic and moral.[53] As he said himself, he learned ethics fully from one of these, and contemplation in particular from the other. Indeed from this love of scriptures and from hard work he progressed so far in a short time, that in his wisdom he gained an even greater grasp of the rocky and knotty meanings of scriptures than our teachers.

50 See Ecclesiasticus 38.25.
51 See Psalm 119.71.
52 Herbert discusses Thomas's physical exertions (see Grim's version below [30]), before returning to his scholarship.
53 It was during this time that Herbert began, at Thomas's request, his revision of Peter Lombard's *Great Gloss* on the Psalms and Epistles.

30. Thomas's asceticism at Pontigny (1164–66)

Edward Grim, *MTB* 2. 412–13.

The lord pope had commended Thomas to Pontigny, and during his sojourn there he revealed many grave and deliberate sufferings to God alone. Mindful of the holy command, 'Let not your left hand know what your right hand is doing',[54] whatever he saw in himself of holy religion or devotion, as much as was in himself, he concealed with his conscience as witness. Therefore from this time content with eating vegetables and coarser feasts and removing lighter things, he furtively withdrew certain delicacies from himself, without the knowledge of his fellow diners, and used them to minister to the infirm poor. He would also lower himself into the stream which ran between the workshops of the monastery where he would remain for longer than human fragility can take. The extent of bodily torment inflicted by the extreme cold, in his efforts to purge himself of the stings of desire that still seemed to dwell in him, was revealed by his consequent illness. For shortly after, he developed an abcess which festered as far as the inside of his throat, and grew into an ulcer. He suffered for a long time in this agony, with much trouble and sorrow, until, after the extraction of two bones,[55] he eventually recovered.

But one night, exhausted by repeated prayer and genuflection, he fell asleep and saw in a dream that a serious conflict had arisen between him and the king, and that he stood alone before the lord pope and the cardinals to set out his case. But the cardinals who took the king's side, greatly angered because the archbishop had acted against the king with such constancy, attacked him and exerted themselves to gouge out and tear apart his eyes with their fingers. The pope cried out, but the clamour and tumult of the cardinals was greater, and served to smother the apostolic cries. Then when these had departed he saw others come in as if executioners destined for him, who was there alone. These men, terrible in appearance and full of fury, approached the archbishop, drew their swords and sliced off the top of his head, as much as the width of the crown, so that the part sliced off fell down on to his brow. Disturbed by the strangeness of this horrendous vision, and on the deep consideration of his heart judging that it would not have been shown to him without reason, the man of God privately delivered more and more prayers to God, and steeled himself to suffer all injuries.

54 Matthew 6.3.
55 From his jaw.

31. Thomas decides on vigorous action (spring 1166)

At Pontigny Thomas was effectively prevented from taking any serious action until April 1166. His attempts to win influential mediators, including Henry's mother Matilda, were unsuccessful, and in April 1165 Henry pulled out of a projected meeting with Thomas at Pontoise. Also in April 1165 Pope Alexander left Sens to return to Italy, and was accompanied by Thomas as far as Bourges. Meanwhile Henry had been flirting with Frederick Barbarossa's party. In spring 1165 he received an embassy from the emperor led by Archbishop Rainald of Cologne, and discussed a marriage alliance between Henry's daughter Matilda and Henry the Lion, duke of Saxony. Rainald returned to Germany with two of Henry's men, John of Oxford and Richard of Ilchester, and at the Diet of Würtzburg on 23 May 1165 they joined in an oath to renounce Pope Alexander and recognise the new anti-pope, Paschal. Henry's party quickly retreated from this position, and John of Oxford swore to Alexander that he had done nothing against his honour. Still, it was probably the threat that Henry might switch sides in the papal schism that prompted Alexander to write to Thomas from Clermont that summer urging moderation: 'Since the days are evil,[56] and many things must be tolerated because of the times, we request your discretion. We advise, counsel and urge you, that in everything you do regarding your own affairs and those of the Church, you show yourself cautious, prudent and circumspect, and do nothing hastily or precipitately, but act seasonably and responsibly, and strive in every way possible to recover the favour and goodwill of the illustrious king of England, as much as can be done saving the liberty of the Church and the honour of your office. And until next Easter you should forbear with the king, so that you take care not to act against him or his lands until the prescribed time. For then the Lord will grant us better days, and both you and we will be able to proceed in this business with greater security' (*CTB* no. 54, pp. 224–5; *MTB* no. 95, 5. 179–80). The following spring, new opportunities opened up for Thomas when on Easter Sunday, 24 April 1166, Alexander granted him a papal legation within the province of Canterbury. The following month Thomas sent Henry three letters 'of mounting severity',[57] the first two delivered by Urban, abbot of Cercamp, the third by Gerard, a 'squalid barefoot monk'. Many of the arguments in favour of resisting secular authority found in those letters, which were drafted by Thomas's clerks, including Herbert, may be found in this extract.

Herbert of Bosham, *MTB* 3. 380–4.

In the second year of our pilgrimage,[58] the archbishop came to realise how hardened were the hearts of our enemies, for they had not shown any sign of penitence for their sins against us, but on the contrary

---

56 Ephesians 5.16.

57 *CTB* nos 68, 74, 82, pp. 266–71, 292–9, 329–43; *MTB* nos 112–14, 5. 266–94. The first is certainly the mildest, but there is disagreement as to which of the others came first.

58 *Peregrinatio.* The exile is frequently described as such.

continued to sin. Now, since we were living far away and in solitude
they could not persecute us in deed, they hurt us with detracting
tongues. Perceiving this, as I say, the archbishop began to reflect
within himself and meditate in his heart, and in this meditation a fire
began to kindle, a fire not of malice but of love. For he saw his own
sons, even if they had now turned into enemies, every day rushing
headlong into destruction and ruin. And as the father of fathers, he
could dissimulate no longer. Because even if they had withdrawn filial
feeling, it was by no means right for a good archbishop to withdraw
his paternal affection. So his heart grew warm for his lost sons, and a
fire kindled, not driven by vindictiveness but by justice and fatherly
compassion. He wished to show them also how a father shows compassion to his sons, by punishing their iniquities with the rod and
their sins with lashes.[59] Therefore he realised that on the one hand
ardent zeal on account of insults to justice was especially fitting for a
priest, but on the other hand that intense compassion for erring sons
was especially appropriate for a father. And so he who up to now had
been silent, who had patiently borne all, now seeing his patience
trampled underfoot in pride and abuse, was now no longer patient,
now no longer slept, but rising and shaking himself out, as a true son
of the shaken out,[60] immediately began to confer with his men about
what to do, as if he had suddenly been roused by the Lord's prophetic
command to the prophet, 'And you, son of man, I placed as a watch-
man over the house of Israel. If you do not speak to keep the wicked
from their evil ways, and the same wicked remain in their iniquity, I
will require his blood from your hand'.[61] Therefore he first addressed
a speech in deliberation to us, his comrades in battle: 'Men and
brothers', he said, 'my cohorts in the cause of Christ's church, you
know and understand much better than I do that there is a time for all
things,[62] a time of suffering and a time of rebelling, a time of mercy
and a time of justice. "When I receive the time", he said, "I will judge
justice".[63] And the Master said to the disciples, "You are serving time".
But we up to now have served time, up to now have sustained, up to
now have borne the sinners building above the door of the Church,[64]
patient to all. At the same time they prolong their iniquities, day after

59 See Psalm 89.32.
60 See Psalm 127.5, above, p. 98 n. 85.
61 Ezekiel 3.17.
62 See Ecclesiastes 3.1.
63 Psalm 74.3.
64 See Psalm 128.3.

day abuse goodness and patience, and pile sins upon sins, laying up only anger for themselves, not mercy. The Lord through the prophet said of someone who is hardened and does not come to his senses, adding sin to sin, "Do you not in three or four impieties go against him?"[65] Therefore, brothers, form a plan, see what we ought to do now. Up to now we have been silent, but does that mean that we will always be silent? "Woe is me", said the prophet, "for I was silent".[66] Surely, frightened by the prophet's example we will not be silent in the same way? And we, who up to now have slept in solitude between these monks and these stones, do we not also awake? Yes, it is good and pleasant for us to sleep here in this way and enjoy in leisure the sweet embraces of the beloved Rachel.[67] But still, while not wishing to prejudice sounder advice, it certainly seems to me that from now on the business of the bride[68] draws us and the duty of our office, the pastoral care which we have undertaken, urges us to the performance of necessary things. Look how the foxes demolish the vines[69] and the wolves continue to prowl openly in the sheepfold. And above all, none among the prevaricators turn to their hearts, but perhaps they would do so if they were struck. Any pastor who does not ward off the wolves carries the staff without cause, and a judge who does not reprimand transgressors carries the sword without cause. And now I say this especially to you brothers, because the brutality of what has been done against us, in our expulsion and proscription, makes justice against our adversaries all the more urgent ...[70]

Let us do, therefore, what the Lord of the garden enjoined on certain of His gardeners, to whom He committed its care: "Behold", He said, "I have constituted you today above the peoples and kingdoms to root out and destroy and scatter and dissipate and build and plant".[71] But you, brothers, as experienced men in scripture, and learned in the

65 Amos 1.3.

66 Isaiah 6.5.

67 Patristic writers interpreted the two wives of Jacob, Rachel and Leah, as representing contemplation and action respectively. Contemplation was regarded as the 'more preferable' way of life, but action on behalf of one's neighbour was often 'more necessary'. In the twelfth century writers such as Bernard of Clairvaux praised the benefits of the contemplative life, but also pointed to a pastor's duty to revive to action. See C. Butler, *Western Mysticism* (London, 1926), pp. 227–87.

68 I.e. the Church.

69 See Song of Songs, 2.15.

70 Herbert expands upon the image of the wolves destroying the vines in the Lord's garden.

71 Jeremiah 1.10.

examples of many Fathers, know what to do in such circumstances
better than I do. Still, with my conscience dictating this to me, I tell
you what I feel. And to add to what I have said, it seems to me also
that among other things, if we wish to be his imitators and we are his
disciples, following the Samaritan of the gospel,[72] a true guardian and
carer, to cure sins we should first pour on oil, and later, if it is necessary, wine.[73] First then, because it is more appropriate to heal the
wounds of the powerful, let the smoothest oil of leniency be poured
on. First let our lord king be met in all leniency and humility. Perhaps
with anger and indignation satiated by our misfortunes, royal
clemency might have regard for us in our humility'.

32. Thomas's clerks meet the king (1 May 1166)

In late spring 1166 King Louis and others secured an audience with the king
for three of Thomas's clerks. The reception of Thomas's most important
advisors, John of Salisbury and Herbert of Bosham, is related here. The third
clerk, Philip of Calne fared better, the king allowing him peace and
restoration of his goods without asking for an oath.

William Fitzstephen, *MTB* 3. 98–101.

At one point the king, counts and magnates of France approached the
king of England on behalf of the archbishop's principal clerks, who
had remained with him, asking him to restore their revenues to them
in entirety: 'If because of their office they served the archbishop, this
is no wonder. The king's cause and that of the archbishop did not concern them. For what follies these two did between them, these clerks
were unworthily punished.'[74] So the king granted these clerks peace in
coming, tarrying and returning.

They came to Angers on the first Sunday of Easter week, where the
king had celebrated the Easter feast, and one day he sat among his
men to hear these clerks. The first called in was John of Salisbury.
When he had been greeted by the king, he first asked for peace, and
the restitution of his ecclesiastical benefices, since he had not know-
ingly earned the disapproval of the king, and as his follower and
subject he would be prepared to obey the king as his worldly lord,

---

72 See Luke 10.

73 See Gregory the Great, *Moralia in Job* xx. 5; Gratian, *Decretum* 45, c. 9.

74 See Horace, *Epistles* 1, ii., 14. An interesting view, considering that Fitzstephen
    served as a clerk to both Thomas and Henry.

saving his order. He was reminded on the king's behalf that he had
been born and raised in the king's land, that his relatives had
possessions there, and that he had derived great fruits of benefits and
riches from the advantages of the king's land, and as a native of the
king's realm he ought to be faithful to the king before the archbishop
and all men. And a form of oath was put before him to swear that he
would be faithful to the king in life and limb, and preserve his worldly
honour before all men, and specifically that he would duly observe his
written customs and royal privileges, whatever the pope or any
archbishop or bishop might do. He agreed to all this but hesitated on
the customs, saying that he had been nourished from youth by the
benefits of the church of Canterbury, and that he had sworn obedience
to the pope and his archbishop. He could not abandon the church of
Canterbury or his lord the archbishop, nor could he adopt the observation of any customs contrary to the lord pope and the church of
Canterbury. But, he said that with the lord pope and the archbishop
he was prepared to accept what they accepted and reject what they
rejected. The king was not satisfied and on his order John left.

Master Herbert of Bosham was called in. As he entered the king said to
his men, 'See, here comes a proud one'. Of noble stature and handsome
appearance, he was very splendidly dressed, wearing a tunic and cloak
of green cloth of Auxerre, hanging from his shoulders in the German
style and falling to his ankles, with suitable adornments. The king
greeted him and he sat down. He was interviewed in a similar way to
John and began to answer in the same way, but hesitated when he came
to the matter of the archbishop and fidelity, and these written customs.
He warmly praised the rectitude of the archbishop's life and his faith
to the king, saying that he alone is faithful to the king who does not
allow the king to err, when he can be restrained, for he who tries to
please the king when he speaks to him and glosses over his sin, if that
is what it is, and supports it with silence, is not faithful to the king but
rather neglects faith and goes back on his oath. Therefore, he said, he
could not swear this true faith to the king unless he were to adhere to
the king as an inseparable follower and correct him when he justly
ought be corrected, but he knew the king to be of such habit of
mind that he would not need him or tolerate him. Regarding the
customs, he spoke as John had, and added that it seemed amazing to
him that the king had put them in writing. 'For there are also in other
realms other evil customs inimical to God's Church', he said, 'but they
are not written down. And because they are not written down, there
is a better chance that by God's grace they will be annulled by kings'.

Trying to catch him out, the king said, 'So what evil customs are there in the realm of our lord the king of France?' 'Customs of toll and passage', answered Herbert, 'which are even exacted from clerks and pilgrims. And, when a bishop dies, the goods from his house, his money and all his moveables, even windows and doors, are taken away and become the king's. Also, as it happens, similar and additional evil customs apply in the realm of the king of Germany, but they are not written down.' 'Why', said the king, 'do you detract from his dignity by calling him that, rather than calling him the emperor of Germany?' 'Because he is the king of Germany', said Herbert, 'but when he *writes*, he styles himself "Emperor of the Romans, ever Augustus"'. 'For shame!', said the king, 'Why should my kingdom be disturbed and my peace unsettled by the son of a priest!' 'Far be it from me', said Herbert. 'But nor am I the son of a priest, since I was not born to a priest, although later my father became a priest. Just as someone is not a king's son, if he was not born to a king.'[75] Then one of the barons sitting nearly, Jordan Taison, interjected 'Well whoever's son he is, I would give half my land for him to be mine!' The king took this bitterly and was silent. After a little he ordered Herbert to leave, and he did.

33. Excommunications at Vézelay (12 June 1166)

In late May Thomas went on a pilgrimage to Soissons, where he spent three nights in vigil before the altars of the Virgin Mary and St Gregory, the founder of the English Church, and the tomb of the former bishop of that place St Drausius, the patron saint of those about to face combat. He then proceeded to Vézelay where Bernard of Clairvaux had preached the second crusade in 1146. He condemned the Constitutions, excommunicated John of Oxford for his communication with the German schismatics and his uncanonical intrusion into the deanery of Salisbury, and suspended his bishop Jocelin for allowing that appointment. He also excommunicated Richard of Ilchester for schismatic communications, Richard de Lucy and Jocelin de Balliol for their treatment of the English Church, and Ranulf de Broc, Hugh de St Clair and Thomas FitzBernard for usurping Canterbury possessions. John of Salisbury reports that Thomas intended to excommunicate the king, but had mercy on him when he heard that he was seriously ill (*LJS* no. 168, pp. 112–15). The biographers are quite reticent about this episode.

Herbert of Bosham, *MTB* 3. 391–2.

---

75 Henry's father was, of course, Geoffrey, count of Anjou.

As both our cause and the wrongdoing of the opposite side were very well known to the whole Christian world, [Thomas] determined to act, not under a shelter, not secretly, but publicly and solemnly, so he came to a busy place at a festive time. That is, he came to Vézelay, as the principal festival of that church was approaching, the feast day of the blessed Mary Magdalene,[76] in whose honour that church had been founded, and where her body gloriously lies, and where also for the day of the feast many nations from diverse kingdoms gathered. So, at such a busy festive time we came to the celebrated place, a day's journey from our residence at Pontigny. We travelled there and arrived shortly before the feast day, we who followed not knowing the reason for his visit – because as explained above he did not wish to inform us[77] – and believing that he had come solely on account of the feast day. But the next day, the feast day, at the request of the abbot and chapter he celebrated a public Mass. When the gospel had been read, he ascended the pulpit, and delivered an elegant and profitable sermon to the people. Then in the hearing of all he set out the cause of the conflict between him and the king, how harshly and dreadfully he and his people had been treated, and how the king had been approached so many times but had still not been moved to pity, but become even more inflexible, and he commended the cause of the Church and himself and his people to their prayers. Then suddenly, to the astonishment of all, he was inflamed in a remarkable way, and in a tearful voice and with earnest compassionate zeal for his King Henry of England, by name he announced the threatening proclamation. And when we, the allies of his struggle, unexpectedly heard this, we were immediately astonished that he had acted in this way without consulting us. He, as he disclosed to us shortly after, wisely and prudently had concealed this from us, excusing himself for the aforementioned reason from doing it with our consultation. But what had been done was soon spread throughout the lands by the many and various nations which had come together for the day of the feast and heard it with their own ears, and it certainly reached the ears of the king. And the king, not without reason, was angered and disturbed more than there is now time to say or write, as were all who were with him.

---

76 In fact, this occurred on Whit Sunday, 12 June 1166, rather than this date, 22 July.

77 So as to spare them from incurring the king's hatred (*MTB* 3. 387).

34. The bishops appeal against the censures (June 1166)

Immediately upon hearing of the news from Vézelay, Henry summoned the archbishop of Rouen and the bishops of Normandy to an assembly at Chinon where it was decided that the English bishops must appeal to the pope against the archbishop's censures. Thomas had written to those censured, and also to all the bishops of his province ordering their implementation, but in anticipation the king had ordered the ports to be watched and so the letters were delayed in reaching England. A monk delivered the sentences to Salisbury, and, as a deliberate insult, a stranger served the letters on the bishop of London at St Paul's on 30 July, St Paul's day. With the pope now back in Italy, receipt of his confirmation of the sentences was further delayed until the autumn of 1166.

William of Canterbury, *MTB* 1. 56–8.

After a little, when many of the bishops and abbots of the realm had gathered together in the city of London at the king's command, they were ordered to appeal against the archbishop.[78] For it was feared that he would extend the hand of correction towards crimes which were being performed throughout the kingdom. Therefore the bishops of London and Salisbury, the tinders of provocation and prevarication, appealed.

The bishop of Exeter could not be forced to appeal. And when he was pressed very insistently to do so, he answered, 'You press me to appeal against the sentence of my metropolitan that you fear. But you know that I neither acknowledge nor associate with either the brothers or the bishops on whose behalf you appeal, when he against whom you appeal sets them apart as excommunicates. Nevertheless, so as not to be viewed with mistrust by the lord king, as if I were plotting something ominous against him or his realm, I appeal, but saving honour to God and the lord king, saving obedience due to the Roman Church, and saving reverence for the archbishop of Canterbury'. Those who were in charge of the administration of justice took this ill, and laboured to bend him back to the others' form of appeal, but he could not be constrained to a different appeal. The monks of Canterbury also, along with their sub-prior, had been ordered to take part in the meeting. When they had met to make the appeal, they asked for a postponement before they agreed to the wish of the king, who, before he crossed the sea, laid down that they ought not be disturbed by any business. The bishop of Rochester excused his absence on the grounds of illness, feigned, so it is said. The bishop of Winchester too excused

78 Around 24 June.

his absence, saying in a letter, 'Summoned by the highest pontiff, I do not appeal, nor do I wish to appeal'. And it was thought by the ambiguity of the title that he had been called to an audience of the highest pontiff, that is the lord pope. But he himself understood it to mean the highest Pontiff, the highest Judge, to whose tribunal now at last he was being summoned for examination, he who had passed through many days and was approaching the end of his life.[79]

Still, the archbishop often admonished the king with paternal charity, through letters, or through men who deserved to be heard on account of their esteem, to desist from the oppression of ecclesiastical liberty. Again and again the pope worked on him with much prayer through the archbishop of Rouen, through the former empress of the Romans, the king's mother,[80] and through the bishops of Hereford and London. But although each approached their commission diligently, the bishops of Hereford and London following the king as he led an army up to the Welsh frontier,[81] they gained nothing, except that the archbishop could return home on his own initiative, as he had left on his own initiative. It is believed, however, that the bishop of London did not carry out the mandate faithfully, because when he wrote back to the lord pope regarding its execution and the response received from the king, he was not ashamed to advise against the punishment of ecclesiastical severity directed against the prevaricators, preferring that the church of Canterbury should lament the exile of its pastor for ever and the English Church its shipwreck.

35. Thomas is removed from Pontigny (autumn 1166)

The summer and autumn of 1166 were marked by an exchange of polemical writing. Gilbert Foliot first appealed to the pope in the guise of the clergy of the province of Canterbury (*MTB* no. 204, 5. 403–8), and then to Thomas in the guise of the clergy of England (*CTB* no. 93, pp. 372–83; *MTB* no. 205, 5. 408–13: see below, no. **59**). John of Salisbury denounced the latter as the work of Doeg and Achitophel, the evil counsellors from the Old Testament (*LJS* no. 175, pp. 152–65, *CTB* no. 100, pp. 456–69; *MTB* no. 231, 6. 13–21; see 2 Kings 15–17, 1 Kings 22), and Thomas's clerks wrote three lengthy letters

79 Henry of Winchester died in 1171.

80 Matilda, daughter of Henry I, was married to Emperor Henry V of Germany from 1114 to 1125 before marrying Geoffrey, count of Anjou in 1128.

81 Henry seems to have been in Feckenham, Worcestershire in early March 1166, but left for Normandy shortly after: see R. W. Eyton, *Court, Household and Itinerary of Henry II* (London, 1878), pp. 91–2.

in his name in response to the clergy (*CTB* no. 95, pp. 388–425; *MTB* nos 221–3, 5. 459–512). Thomas then wrote directly to Gilbert (*CTB* no. 96, pp. 426–41; *MTB* no. 224, 5. 512–20), and this prompted the bishop of London's masterly response, *Multiplicem nobis* (*LCGF* no. 170, pp. 229–43; *CTB* no. 109, pp. 498–537; *MTB* no. 225, 5. 521–44). See the discussions below, p. 223.

Edward Grim, *MTB* 2. 413–15.

When [Henry] recognised that the archbishop lacked no human requirement while he was established safely in Pontigny, nor could he or any of his men be caused any trouble as long as he remained there, he laboured to remove him from that place. But as he could not accomplish it through the king of France, a lover of goodness who always revered the archbishop with the greatest fondness and supported him with devoted assistance, he turned to other schemes. He wrote to the abbot of Cîteaux, whom by rule of subjection Pontigny and the other houses obeyed as the head of its order, that his order had sheltered his public enemy and the public enemy of his whole kingdom. And he assured the abbot that if the archbishop remained there or was allowed refuge elsewhere in the order, he would expel without argument every Cistercian monk he found in his realm.[82] But when the holy archbishop heard this from the abbot of Cîteaux, he answered calmly and generously, 'Far be it from me to allow by my own cause so many virtuous men, so many innocent souls, to fall into desolation, so many places, so many monasteries, which had been acquired with such exertion, to be reduced to eternal solitude. For He will ease my want Who raises the destitute from the land, and lifts the poor man up from the dirt, and may our Father repay the debt of mercy to you, and recompense the act of charity which you showed me'.

Likewise he informed the king of France by what artifice the king of England had removed him from Pontigny, and said that he was ready to take up the offer that had long ago been made to him. For when he first came to King Louis as a fugitive from England, the king offered him, and begged him with great entreaty to stay with him in whatever way or wherever he chose.[83] But at that time he declined the offer in case it allowed anyone to accuse him of injuring his lord the king of England by obliging himself to the king of France as one more powerful. On the pope's advice he chose Pontigny where he would enjoy a more frugal and sober existence. Now the king hastened to

82 This was reported to the general council of the Cistercian Order which met on 14 September 1166.

83 Louis had offered his support to Thomas at Soissons in November 1164.

Pontigny to put the archbishop's wish into practice with all devotion, and there he gave thanks to the abbot and brethren who had given honour to France by taking in such a guest. 'And now', he said, 'lest he suffer the offence and hatred of the king because of helpful favours bestowed by you, let him come with me'. Moved to tears the monks lamented the departure of their father and comfort, and calling to mind how he had lived among them with so much gentleness and humility as if he were one of them, and his presence that they had cherished, they sent him on his way with mourning and sighs. He set out with his men after two years in that place, and made his way further into France, to St Columba's, a great monastery near the town of Sens. He was welcomed most attentively by the king's officials who had been sent in advance, and spent four years there, maintained by royal provision. He could easily have spent this time with bishops or abbots, and he received many offers. But eager to keep more safely warm in silence the fire of heavenly love, which the Saviour had instilled in his bones and with which he now burned fully, the holy man avoided the public, and far away from crowds and commotion, he occupied his time, especially at night, with holy meditation, prayers and tears, with which he overflowed abundantly. He did not cease from this pursuit except when forced by the care of household business, or matters which he could not avoid.

IV: DIPLOMACY AND DISCORD (1167–70)

36. Conference between Gisors and Trie (18 November 1167)

Before the end of 1166 both sides had sent low-key missions to the pope. John of Oxford's efforts on the king's behalf brought the pope to relax some of the archbishop's censures on 1 December 1166, and to suspend him from further sentences. He also promised to send legates to settle the dispute. In spring 1167 Alexander despatched a mission of Cardinals William of Pavia and Otto, and they arrived in northern France in the autumn of 1167.

Meanwhile Emperor Frederick had entered Italy and advanced on Rome, where he had himself crowned by his anti-pope Paschal on 1 August 1167, and forced Alexander to flee to Benevento, where he remained until February 1170. Although plague caused the German army to retreat ignominiously, this, along with mounting tension between the kings of England and France, made for an unstable situation.

Herbert of Bosham, *MTB* 3. 408–15.

We had not spent long at Sens when our pilgrims to Rome returned and reported that the lord pope was about to send cardinals as his representatives, who would address the peace between the king and archbishop and restore it if they could. Meanwhile, everything was to remain in a state of suspension, and no ecclesiastical discipline was to be exercised. So the pope in his sealed letters instructed and advised the archbishop through our envoys. Therefore we remained inactive for many days awaiting the arrival of the cardinals. They eventually came to Sens, coming first to us rather than to the king because we were on their way. These envoys, very upright and eloquent men, came as restorers of appropriate peace, of whom one was called William of Pavia, the other Otto, both cardinal-priests.[1] So these, coming to us first, explained the reason for their coming. And it pleased us greatly, that they would make a settlement between us and the lord king to the honour of God and without harm to the liberty of the Church. They then set out for Normandy to see the lord king – for the king was then outside his kingdom – and stayed with him for quite a while, not returning to us or reporting anything. The king wanted one thing, as was said, and as later the outcome of the matter proved, namely, to drag things out, not being willing to restore our peace, although he

---

1 William was cardinal-priest of St Peter *ad vincula*, Otto cardinal-deacon of St Nicholas in Carcere Tulliano.

pretended to be. Nevertheless the cardinals, lest they should seem to have come in vain, again and again approached the king for a reconciliation, diligently and attentively pursuing and searching out peace, but unable to find its path. But so as not to appear to have come in vain and to have done nothing, they eventually called us to a conference. So a conference was held between us on the frontier of France and Normandy, between those two castles, Trie and Gisors.

But the night before, the archbishop had a vision in a dream, as he told us the next morning on the way to the conference, that he was given poison to drink in a golden cup. And so it happened. For one of the cardinals, William of Pavia, a man of elegant fluency and persuasive words, offered us smooth and charming speeches, which nevertheless, if one looked more closely, detracted greatly from the peace and liberty of the Church. As we heard his words we thought of the nocturnal vision earlier related to us, and soon arrived at a conclusion. From which point we viewed with mistrust everything that the cardinals proposed to us, and were careful not to be taken in by speeches which were mollifying and honeyed, but dangerous. To summarise here what was said at length there, the central advice of the cardinals, which they urged in every way, was this: that if no express mention were made between the archbishop and the king regarding the customs – which as we have said had been reduced to writing, and our objection to which prompted our exile – the archbishop would return to his church, if this could be obtained from the king. They said that expression would only cause damage and would act as a stumbling-block to the progress of peace. For, as they added, it would be disgraceful and unfitting for the king to renounce these customs plainly and explicitly, which had been recognised by the senior and great men of the realm, by the bishops, and indeed by us, to belong to royal privilege and have a bearing on the crown. 'But if the king grants you peace', they said, 'though no reference will have been made either to the retention or the abolition of the customs, you can take it that they have been abolished. This is particularly the case since these customs were the root and the entire substance of this bitter dispute between you and the king. Therefore if the king grants you peace, even if you neither concede these things nor bind yourself to their observation, in this way they will be understood as expunged, and you will have succeeded in your cause. For the king, even if not explicitly, nevertheless implicitly may be understood to have conceded their abolition.' And they drew parallels, saying for example that if someone were raised by a bishop to holy orders, he would have tacitly agreed to celibacy, even if it were not expressed. And being practised in divine and human law, they brought forward many other examples to prove it: examples in which either kind of law speaks sometimes of express consent, and sometimes of tacit, unexpressed consent.

But we on the other hand sought the explicit abolition of the customs, and that the charter in which the Constitutions were spelled out be annulled. Neither our peace nor that of the Church, we argued, would be secure unless the basis and the entire cause of the dispute and dissension, the root of all evil, be dug up, especially when, as we have shown above, the archbishop had been cheated and seduced to give his assent to them. So, if he made a settlement with the king without any mention of the customs, either specific or general, it would seem to bestow validity on his earlier assent, and to confirm what had been wrongly done, according to the rule of civil law, 'Ratification is retrospective and confirms things that were done' ...[2]

Besides, we very urgently sought the restitution of goods, both moveables and fixtures, taken away from us – or rather, from the Church – and we repeated again and again that rule of divine law, that a sin is not to be remitted unless the loss has been made good. We certainly asked for much, and the things which we most certainly knew could not be fulfilled through the king's men, because we had been warned, and discovered through certain courtiers, friends of ours but lying low, that they would not even obtain from the king what they had offered us. For the king had now made clear, indeed had publicly sworn, that while he reigned, the archbishop would not return to his church. But the cardinals, one of whom was partial to the king,[3] had set out some form of peace, so that in this way they might excuse the king, as though it were not his fault that peace was not achieved, and, as we have said, so that they did not appear to have come in vain and to have achieved nothing. And so, with peace corrupted, and with all hope of achieving peace through them lost, we departed from them, and they immediately returned to the king.

But in the city of Le Mans many clergymen of the realm gathered. And seeing that peace by no means could come about through the cardinals, before the cardinals they renewed their appeals to the apostolic see, on behalf of the king, the realm, their own persons and their churches.[4]

2 Herbert expands upon this point.

3 William of Pavia.

4 In fact this appeal on 29 November seems to have been made at Argentan.

But after a little the cardinals returned to the Roman Church, greatly honoured by the king and weighed down with ostentatious gifts, with our peace and that of the Church poisoned ...[5] But we decided not to heed this appeal from a lower judge, quite manifestly made to cheat justice and suppress the suppressors. Nevertheless many of us begged, warned and counselled our lord archbishop to leave the person of the king alone unharmed.

Therefore the archbishop readied himself, knowing from the prophet that cursed is he who keeps back his sword from bloodshed and he who does the work of the Lord with slackness.[6] And first he very sternly summoned some clerks of the court, who by reason of order or ecclesiastical benefice were obliged to him and bound to show obedience, to come to him without postponement or delay. But though he commanded them on their obedience in peril of their order and benefice, they did not come or show him obedience. Accordingly the archbishop, not heeding the appeal, struck them with the sword of God's word and bound them with the chain of anathema, and, as the canons teach, sending his letters as was right, as much as the evil of the time allowed he denounced the anathemised.[7] So he censured some clerks of the court, and lay courtiers, for various reasons: some as usurpers of property, others for violently and wrongfully detaining the things of the Church, others because they received estates of the church of Canterbury at the time of his pilgrimage[8] not from him but from the king. In short, he struck with anathema all who on the authority of the king took into custody the estates and possessions of the archiepiscopacy of Canterbury, or of those who went on pilgrimage with the archbishop. And he not only censured these, but also some bishops, on account of evident disobedience, and especially because they stood out as inciters of the whole dispute between the king and himself, which they did not cease from fomenting every day. Among those anathemised in this way was Gilbert Foliot, bishop of London. And among those anathemised were some of the courtiers most familiar and closest in counsel to the king. And hence now almost everyone in the court was either excommunicated by name, or at least cut off from

---

5 Herbert describes how they deliberated upon the appeal.

6 See Jeremiah 48.10.

7 Herbert's chronology seems confused here. It does not appear that Thomas issued censures immediately after Gisors and Trie, and Gilbert Foliot's excommunication, mentioned here, did not occur until 13 April 1169.

8 I.e. exile.

involvement with those named as excommunicate, whom they were
not allowed to avoid, so much that there was hardly anyone in the
king's chapel to offer that sacramental kiss of peace in the Mass to the
king unless excommunicated personally or through participation.
Therefore these were excommunicated, and those were excommunicated. For the archbishop was unable and unwilling to bear any more,
so he did not cease, he did not spare these or those. He did not forbear,
I say, he did not spare, even though the pope, by his own authority,
which is before all, had absolved some already of those he had bound:
namely, the bishop of Salisbury and that clerk of the court who, as
mentioned above had unlawfully conducted business with the schismatics of Germany against the peace of the church and against the
pope.[9]

But on hearing this the king was angered and troubled, and all the
other side, that the archbishop had neither deferred to the courtiers
for the king's sake, nor to the appeal for the pope's sake, and they sent
to the pope with all haste and sent again. Envoys, more envoys and
more again rushed, hurried and made speed to report these things to
the pope. We also sent envoys. But because we did not have gold and
silver, we sent only bare words, as before, unattractively written in
black ink, whereas they, being rich, sent words written in gold and
silver, and many more than before.

37. Conference at Montmirail (6 January 1169)

After the failure of the cardinals' mission, both sides sent further embassies to
the pope. In May 1168 the pope limited the suspension of Thomas's legation
until 5 March 1169, as a spur to a speedy settlement. The next papal mission
was led by three distinguished monks, Simon prior of Mont-Dieu, Bernard de
la Coudre prior of Grandmont, and Englebert prior of Val-St-Pierre. They
succeeded in arranging the first meeting between Henry and Thomas since
October 1164. Although most of our knowledge about the meeting at Montmirail concerns the Church, this formed only part of wider discussions
concerning Henry's dominions and his relations with the king of France.
Herbert of Bosham, *MTB* 3. 418–28.

It happened that the Poitevins and Bretons began to quarrel with the
king of England, and took up arms against him. In order to strengthen
their rebellion, they had entered into an alliance with the illustrious

9 John of Oxford.

king of France, whose relations with the king of England were at that time equally unfriendly. But after a conference of many days, peace was restored between all, and eventually attention turned to us, who were also present at the conference seeking peace. Many ecclesiastics and other great men came to mediate between the king and the archbishop, and the king spoke privately to those who were considered most favourable to the archbishop and on most friendly terms. To these he told of his intention to take the cross and set off to Jerusalem, as long as peace had first been made between him and the archbishop according to his honour, and he added that in this conference all he sought was honour before the king of France and others, if only verbally. After all the mediators had discussed the peace at length together apart from the king, those most familiar to the archbishop, to whom the king had spoken about taking the cross and about our peace, drew the archbishop aside. In private they informed him what the king had said privately to them, not reporting it in the king's name, but most faithfully maintaining that they had heard it from the king. Their basic advice, which they particularly urged, was that the archbishop, regarding the whole cause and what had been taken away from him and his people, should submit himself in every way to the compassion and will of the king. That is, that he place himself at the king's mercy concerning the whole dispute which had gone on between them, and unreservedly so, without qualification. Indeed the archbishop, at the insistence and advice of the mediators had already agreed before them all that he would do this, but added 'saving God's honour'. But those mediators who were more intimate with the archbishop, faithful men and experienced in counsels, whom the archbishop trusted as himself, attempted to remove that qualification, because, as they said, the king would be outraged at the phrase. And they also advised him with the utmost effort and application that he unreservedly submit himself to the wish and judgement of the king regarding the whole dispute. In this way, by giving honour and glory to the king before all, he would satisfy the king, and the king in turn would restore his peace and favour to him. In fact this expression was similar to that which had been added when we were still in England regarding observation of the royal customs. For, as we related above, the archbishop had said that he would observe the royal customs 'saving our order', whereas here he said 'saving God's honour'.[10] And with the same inducements and arguments which the mediators of peace had

10 At the Council of Westminster, October 1163: see above, p. 82.

used then in England regarding the phrase 'saving our order', here they attempted to remove the similar addition 'saving God's honour'. Indeed the archbishop would have used the first phrase again here, except that, as we have described, the king had then been offended by it, and now he was just as offended by this 'saving God's honour', as will soon be described.

What next? He was eventually urged, drawn, pushed and pulled so much that he seemed persuaded. And when he finally spoke apart with his learned companions for a brief time, as much as was allowed, and reported what the most friendly of the mediators had told him, all their wisdom was devoured.[11] For on the one hand they saw the good of peace and the much-desired royal favour. But on the other it could be seen as disgraceful, irreligious and ignominious to the Church if the archbishop were to submit himself in this way regarding the Church's cause to the will and judgement of a layman without any declaration concerning the Church's liberty or God's honour, especially since mention had been made of God's honour and the question had already been raised. Nevertheless the mediators, especially those faithful and religious men among them who were expert in counsel and most intimate with the archbishop, urgently advised and sought with every pressure what they most certainly hoped and asserted should be followed for our good and the good of the Church. Therefore every one of our learned companions hesitated and was afraid to give counsel, afraid that through them peace might be obstructed, or alternatively that through them the cause of the Church which they supported might be endangered. So in this situation every one of them was silent, and all counsel perished from our learned companions, just as no wisdom was found in Teman.[12] Wisdom and counsel, I say, perished from our learned companions, except for some who murmured softly that it would not be safe in such a situation to suppress or leave unspoken God's honour or ecclesiastical liberty for the sake of acquiring worldly favour. That would be no different, they said, from putting a light under a bushel,[13] as happened when, as shown above, that similar addition, 'saving our order', was similarly omitted in England for the sake of peace. So in these straits our wisdom and counsel perished. Therefore we did the only thing that seemed to remain to us: we

11 See Psalm 106.27.

12 See Jeremiah 49.7. A district in Edom, known for the wisdom of its people, but here criticised for encroachment of the land of Judah.

13 See Matthew 5.15; Mark 4.21.

called out to the Lord, praying that he furnish us with the spirit of counsel and knowledge.

And what happened? While we were suspending counsel and hesitating over what to do, the archbishop was swayed, pushed and pulled to such an extent by the mediators that they thought he had been persuaded. Surrounded then by the mediators and others he was led to the kings, for the two kings were still together awaiting the outcome of our peace. When, I say, he was being led like this, the disciple who wrote these things pushed himself forward, though with difficulty among so many and so great, and briefly and quickly (for he could not do otherwise), he whispered in his ear. 'Lord', he said, 'see that you tread carefully. In England you removed that phrase "saving your order" when you were pressed to observe the royal customs. I say to you most certainly, speaking from my conscience, that if in making an agreement with the king you omit this addition, "saving God's honour", certainly when there is now such pressure to suppress it to gain the king's favour, just as then, so now, your sorrow will be renewed, because you were mute and silent from speaking good. So also you will tearfully remember the reading from the psalm, "I was silent and was humiliated, and was silent from good, and my sorrow was renewed".[14] And your sorrow will be renewed more fully, because once punished for a similar silence you have not yet learned your lesson'.

Hardly had this been said, than the archbishop was led before the kings, with him looking at me alone and unable to answer, so great was the crowd surrounding him and trying to speak to him. Aware that humility, of all virtues, tends to soften the hardened heart, and is especially attractive to the proud and lofty – so much so that through it pride itself might allow itself to be overcome – knowing this, I say, the archbishop immediately in the first place prostrated himself at the king's feet. And according to his honour he had with him William, now archbishop of Sens, son of the great and distinguished count Theobald of blessed memory, who had succeeded on the death of Hugh of blessed memory who had been archbishop when we first arrived in Sens.[15] But as soon as he had prostrated himself at his feet the king immediately took hold of him and raised him up.

14 Psalm 38.3.

15 William of the White Hands was one of Thomas's most distinguished supporters. He was the son of Theobald IV, count of Blois, brother of Theobald V of Blois and Henry, count of Champagne, nephew of Henry, bishop of Winchester and King Stephen of England. He replaced Hugh de Toucy as archbishop of Sens, later transferred to Rheims and ended his career as cardinal-priest of St Sabina.

Standing before the king then, the archbishop began humbly and
zealously to solicit royal mercy towards the Church committed to him,
though, as he said, an unworthy sinner. As is the custom of the just, in
the beginning of his speech he found fault with himself and attributed
the Church's great disturbance and harsh affliction solely to his own
failings. And in the conclusion of his speech he added, 'Therefore, my
lord, regarding the entire cause between you and me, I now submit
myself to your mercy and judgement in the presence of our lord king
of France, and the bishops and nobles and others present here'. But, to
the surprise of the king, the mediators, and even his own men, he
added, '– saving God's honour'. As we have said, the mediators had
urged him, and had thought that they had persuaded him, not to add
such a phrase which might cause scandal to the king and an obstacle
to peace. And so it certainly happened. As soon as he heard this addition the king took strong offence and burned with anger towards the
archbishop, throwing many insults at him, condemning him a great
deal, reproaching him more, inveighing against him, accusing him of
being proud and haughty, forgetful of and ungrateful for the royal
bounty lavished on him. And because, as we have said towards the
beginning of this history, the archbishop's character was from the
earliest age so honourable, and even liars and detractors feared to tell
falsehoods about him on account of the integrity of his reputation, the
king explicitly cited this one charge against him: that when he had
still been chancellor, he had taken oaths of homage and fealty from
the king's men, both major and minor on both sides of the sea, as if, he
said, to disinherit his lord and king, who had conferred so much upon
him, and make himself lord of all. That is why, he added reproach-
fully, he had lived in such magnificence and acted with such munifi-
cence in his time as chancellor.

But the archbishop heard all this patiently, and seeming in no way
disturbed or confused, immediately answered his reproaches. Indeed
he responded with a calm speech of great humility and moderation,
tempering it so that he appear neither inflexible nor slack. He first
said a few things briefly in answer before turning to the king's accusation regarding his chancellorship. 'My lord', he said, ' in your anger
you now make this accusation about my time as chancellor, in this
angry state seeking a reason to blame me for something which ought
to have earned me your eternal thanks. It would not be right or
proper to recall now to my merit the things I did in your service, and
the fidelity then rendered to you. For our lord the king of France, who
is here, knows, all others present also know, the whole world knows

and works testify, how, when I was still in the court I carried out my duties to your benefit and honour. It would be shameful and indecent to bring up the benefits of past service as a reproach, the cost of which the world saw and knows.' The king would not put up with any more and interrupted his words, turning to the lord king of France and saying, 'My lord, take note, if you will, how foolishly, how proudly, this man abandoned his church. Neither I nor anyone else expelled him from my realm, but he himself took to flight secretly by night with no one forcing him to do so. And now he seeks to persuade you that he is advancing the cause of the Church, and is suffering for justice, and in this way he has deceived many men. Indeed I have always wished and allowed, and still wish and allow, that he hold and rule the church over which he presides in the full liberty in which any of his saintly predecessors ruled it more fully and freely.' And the king of France, seeming to have turned somewhat against the archbishop and to favour the king on account of what he had said about the saintly predecessors, laconically said to the archbishop, 'Lord archbishop, do you wish to be more than a saint?' These words, said as if in insult to the archbishop, pleased the king and his party no little. For their aim and effort had always been to justify their cause and denigrate ours before everyone, and especially before the king of France, and in this way alienate the king's heart from us, which by God's favour had been an unimpaired and secure refuge for us in our troubles.

Although the kings now seemed to be hostile to him, trying to catch him out in whatever way they could, the archbishop was not disturbed or shaken but with a composed and balanced spirit as before he immediately answered the king. Certainly, he said, he wished willingly and eagerly to receive the church committed to him with those liberties with which his holy predecessors ruled it, but he refused to accept other new customs, introduced to the detriment of ecclesiastical liberty. Rather, he would vanquish and condemn them as contrary to the precepts of the saintly fathers. But when the archbishop began to justify his flight, which the king had accused him of effecting secretly by night without good cause, and sought to argue that its cause was just, the mediators present, many great men, drew the archbishop aside out of the hearing of the kings. For they cautiously observed that such exchanges between the king and archbishop would provoke great dissension rather than peace. And so drawing him aside they urged him, cried out again and again, pushed and pulled him, so many calling out together, 'Give glory to the king and suppress the phrase which offends him, be silent, and subject yourself absolutely to the will and judgement of the king, especially when we have such an opportunity for peace, with the lord king and the nobles of France present, and everyone agreed to peace except you and your men'. The many and the great urged this on the archbishop, both secular and ecclesiastical potentates, French, English, Norman, Breton and Poitevin, and some from the religious orders who had come to the conference specially on our behalf and on the mandate of the pope as mediators in the hope of restoring our peace. This alone everyone proposed, advised and urged, that as a compromise he remove and be silent about that little phrase, 'saving God's honour', and in this way he and his men would soon achieve honourable and glorious peace in the sight of kings and nobles. You would have seen then the archbishop standing as a sacrificial victim, the others as executioners, armed not with steel but with words, standing around and seeking to extinguish God's honour, thinking at the same time that they were serving God. But shortly after, many blamed themselves for being clearly and undoubtedly tricked and deceived, as the following will show. But now let us proceed with what we have begun.

With the archbishop standing like that, truly standing as a bold tower directly situated facing Damascus,[16] he was pressed by the many and the great, but was not turned, declaring again and again to this one and that one that he would do as they urged, 'saving God's honour'. For he said that it was not fitting for a priest and archbishop to submit himself in any other way to the judgement of a worldly man, especially regarding the cause of ecclesiastical liberty, and certainly when the question of this phrase had already been raised; and it would be honourable and ought to suffice if it should be thus, if the cause of ecclesiastical peace did not urge fuller submission. Truly as the psalmist says, 'the righteous man bathes his hands in the blood of the wicked'.[17] And as the saying of the wise man attests, 'Strike a scoffer and the wise man becomes wiser',[18] just as it is commonly said that something about to be boiled fears the water. As we have described earlier, in England the king was offended by the similar phrase, 'saving our order', and hoping that the king's favour would be restored to him, the archbishop followed the advice of certain people and was silent. But the king's favour did not result, and instead by being silent from speaking good the archbishop's sorrow was increased and renewed

16 See Song of Songs 7.4.
17 See Psalm 58.10.
18 See Proverbs 19.25: 'Strike a scoffer and the *fool* becomes wiser.'

much more than before. And now he feared it would happen again. So he stood among the many and the great pushing and pulling, immovable like a house built upon a firm rock, like a city placed on a mountain, like an iron pillar, and like a bronze wall against the land, kings, princes and priests,[19] in heart, voice and deed, as if in the middle of a battlefield, singing, as it seemed, 'The God who guided me with strength for war, so that my arms can bend a bow of bronze'.[20] And not unmindful of that legislator, he said, 'You shall not follow a multitude to do evil; nor shall you bear witness in a suit, turning aside after a multitude, so as to pervert justice'.[21] Also as the philosopher said, 'And that of the few is more to be chosen'.[22]

Therefore all the mediators, seeing him immovable and inflexible in this way, soon departed from him, and he remained alone. Alone, I say, who bore the pressure of the wine-press alone;[23] he bore it bravely and trod it triumphantly. So the mediators departed from him and the athlete of the Almighty remained alone in the battlefield, alone in the hall of the wrestling-school (the conference was in fact held on the plain of a battlefield). They soon reported the obstinacy of the man to the kings, interpreting his great constancy as such. And the kings left on their horses with great haste – for night had cut the conference short – without bidding farewell to the archbishop or receiving it from him. In fact, as he was leaving the king did not cease from abusing the archbishop, though not to his face, saying among other things that that day he had now taken revenge on his traitor. Equally the courtiers and mediators who had been there made numerous accusations on their return even to the archbishop's face, that he had always been proud, haughty, wise in his own eyes, ever following his own wish and judgement. And they added that it was a great evil, and enormously damning and dangerous to the Church that he had ever been made a ruler of the Church, and that through him it had already been almost destroyed, and would soon be destroyed completely. But the archbishop held his tongue when sinners stood against him in this way, seeming to meditate on that psalmist and to say to the Lord, 'You are my refuge and my fortress, for you delivered me from the

19 See Jeremiah 1.18.
20 See Psalm 18.40, 34.
21 Exodus 23.2.
22 Unidentified.
23 See Isaiah 63.3.

fowler's snare and the hostile word',[24] and, 'Deliver me, O Lord, from
lying lips, from a deceitful tongue'.[25] Therefore to the reproaches and
insults he was like someone who did not hear and in whose mouth
were no rebukes.[26] Except to one of bishops – John the bishop of
Poitiers, an Englishman and very familiar, dear and acceptable to him
from everyday conversation and society – who reproached him about
the destruction of the Church, he responded humbly and gently,
'Brother, watch out that the Church of God is not destroyed through
you. With God's grace it will not be destroyed through me'.

38. The exiles are abandoned by their supporters (January 1169)

The falling-out and reconciliation with King Louis may have had less to do
with the French king's view of Thomas and his cause than with his fluctua-
ting relations with Henry. At Montmirail Thomas had proved an irritant to
the new peace between the kings, but when the peace quickly began to falter,
Louis again saw the value of Henry's rebellious archbishop.

Alan of Tewkesbury, *MTB* 2. 349–51.

When the conference broke up, not without the murmur of many, the
archbishop returned home, with his fellow exiles of Canterbury in a
state of deep desperation. For it was the French king's custom to go
down to the archbishop's lodgings after these conferences under the
pretext of consolation and reverence, but this time he showed no
regard for him either in person or through his men. He travelled for
three days in the company of the king of France and the king came
neither to him nor to his party. And whereas in such situations the
archbishop of Canterbury was used to being looked after by royal
generosity, after this conference and during this interval we have
spoken of he received nothing at all from that source. On his journey
he was supported as a beggar once by the bishop of Sens, another time
by the bishop of Poitiers, or someone else upset at his pitiful condition,
which terrified many of his men, believing they were now destitute of
all human aid.

But on the third day, their journey completed, they were sitting in their
lodgings discussing these things among each other, and asking each
other where they could turn. Whereupon the lord of Canterbury, with

24 See Psalm 91.2–3.
25 Psalm 120.2.
26 Psalm 38.15.

a little laugh, as if he were suffering no adversity, and invincible to all blows of fortune, joked with these men in their agony. 'I alone', he said, 'am under attack, and when I am gone there will be nobody to persecute you more fiercely, or abandon you more desolately to the kindness of friends. So take comfort, and be not afraid.' 'It is for you', they said, 'that we feel more pity, because we do not know where you can turn, a man of such authority abandoned by friends, high and low.' 'I commit my care to the Lord', said the archbishop. 'Entry to either kingdom is closed to us, nor does any hope of consolation advise us to hurry back to the Roman mercenaries, who steal the spoils of the poor without discrimination. But there is another way for us to proceed, for I have heard that men are more generous around Burgundy's River Saône up to Provence. I and one other will go to these by foot, and when they see our distress perhaps they will take pity on us, supplying us with bodily sustenance for the time being, until God visits us. God can support his people even in the worst crisis, and he is worse than an unbeliever who despairs of God's mercy.' And immediately God's compassion appeared before the door. For a certain servant of the king of France rushed up and said, 'the lord king summons you to court'. '– To expel us from the realm', said one of the household. 'You are not a prophet, nor the son of a prophet', said the archbishop, 'do not start prophesying doom'.

So they came to the lord king and found him sitting with a sorrowful expression, nor did he rise for the archbishop according to his habit, and in the beginning this seemed to them a grim portent. After this cool invitation they sat down, and there was a long silence while the king bowed his head as if he were sorrowfully and unwillingly considering expelling them from the kingdom as they feared. Whereupon, to the astonishment of those present, exploding into tears and bursting forth with sobs, he flung himself down at the archbishop's feet. The archbishop bent down to lift up the king, and hardly had he recovered himself from his distress than the king said, 'Truly, my lord of Canterbury, you alone could see. We were all blind, we who against God advised you in your cause, or rather God's, to yield God's honour at the command of a man. I repent, father, gravely I repent. Forgive and absolve me, I pray, from this blame. And I lay myself and my kingdom open to God and to you, and from this hour I promise that I will not fail you or your people, as long as with God's favour I live'. When the king had been absolved and given blessing, the lord of Canterbury and his men returned in joy to Sens, where the king of France splendidly provided for him until he returned to England.

39. New excommunications (April–May 1169)

On 7 February 1169 a fruitless meeting was held at St Léger-en-Yvelines
with Thomas, the two kings, the papal mediators and many intermediaries.
On 28 February the pope announced a new mission in the form of Gratian, a
papal notary, and Vivian, archdeacon of Orvieto and an advocate in the papal
court. On 5 March the term of suspension imposed on Thomas in May 1168
(see above, p. 154) lapsed, allowing Thomas to announce fresh censures. The
bishops of London and Salisbury, expecting excommunication, sent an appeal
in advance to the pope. On 13 April these two, along with Ranulf and Robert
de Broc and various invaders of archiepiscopal property were excommunicated. Further offenders were excommunicated on Ascension Day, 29 April.
It was on the same day that Thomas's letter excommunicating Gilbert Foliot
was announced in St Paul's cathedral by a young man called Berengar, who
had made it past the royal observers at the ports.

William Fitzstephen, *MTB* 3. 87–90.

On Palm Sunday,[27] after the procession and sermon, in the presence of
the religious and faithful at Clairvaux, the archbishop excommunicated
the bishop of London who had been corrected for threefold disobedience, but proved incorrigible. He also excommunicated certain others
living in England or within the king's court for reasons which he made
clear in his letters. For the archbishop sent out letters to everyone he
excommunicated in which he outlined their crimes and added the
grounds for excommunication according to the laws and decrees, so
that it would be clear that it was not heat of anger or enmity that drove
him to severity, but was rather a response to their outrages prompted
by a pious feeling of fatherhood. The report immediately spread to
England: 'Rumour thrives by mobility. Speed lends her strength, and
she wins vigour as she goes'.[28]

As soon as the bishop of London heard this he immediately entered the
city and came to the cathedral church. He called together the canons
and clergy of the city of London, the abbots and priors also, and the
beneficed clergy of neighbouring churches. He announced the report
about himself, and made known that he had been excommunicated,
but to the astonishment of wise men, he did not accept his excommunication. Not much later he summoned a general synod, and again
made this announcement, but with no one from the opposing side
responding, as none had been summoned. But it was not easy to find
someone to carry over the letters of threefold citation or others of

27 13 April 1169.
28 See Virgil, *Aeneid* iv. 175.

summons, for a great chasm, not only of sea and lands, but of the king's anger and threats, had opened between them. The solemnity of the citations could not be performed through an envoy, when an envoy did not dare to declare his name or that of the archbishop. Besides, the bishop of London claimed that he was not obliged or subject to the archbishop or church of Canterbury. He said that he had formerly been bishop of Hereford, and had given profession to the archbishop of Canterbury, but was now free of that obedience, since he had been translated to the church of London, and the bishop of London made no profession to the church of Canterbury. And he claimed on the testimony of chronicles that he ought to be archbishop, since in the time of the Britons, before the island had been subdued by the Angles, London was the metropolitan see.[29] So he declaimed, but no opposing case was made. When he had been heard he was left to himself and everyone returned home ...[30]

The archbishop found one young man, who carried these letters into England, exposing himself to great danger, but not afraid to die for God. On the feast of the Lord's Ascension, a certain vicar called Vitalis, a God-fearing and honourable priest, was celebrating at the high altar of the episcopal church of St Paul in London. When the offering was being sung, and the priest had offered the bread and wine and arranged the cup, Berengar appeared, bent the knee, and offered the letters to the priest as if they were his offering. The priest, astonished, held out his hand and took the offering. Berengar said, 'The bishop of this see is not here, nor the dean. I see that you are the minister of Christ here. On behalf of God and the lord pope I hereby give you the letter of excommunication passed by the archbishop of Canterbury on the bishop of this church, and also the letter to the dean, so that he and the clergy of this church observe this sentence. And I instruct you by the authority of God not to celebrate any other Mass after this one, until you show the bishop and dean their letters'. This he said, and left amidst the dense throng of people returning home as is customary on a feast day. The next day he heard Mass in the parish churches. Those who had drawn close to the altar began to murmur, asking the priest if the divine celebration had been put under

29 The claim that London was the metropolitan see since the time of the Britons has no basis in fact, though it is true that in 596 Gregory the Great had instructed the founders of the English Church to site metropolitan churches at London and York. The political situation of the time meant that Canterbury was a more suitable site for the southern metropolitan see. See *Gilbert Foliot*, pp. 151–62.

30 Fitzstephen describes how Gilbert awaited the letters of censure.

interdict in the city. But when he said no, the people were silent and did not pursue Berengar, and the priest continued with the celebration. Meanwhile certain officials of the king secretly and diligently sought the messenger in the city and outside and at crossroads, but did not find him. He later came to York with letters of the pope containing bitter words, but nevertheless escaped unharmed.

40. The mission of Gratian and Vivian, and the Council of Montmartre (autumn 1169)

In June 1169 the pope wrote to Thomas asking him to suspend the recent sentences until the outcome of negotiations became known. Meanwhile Gilbert Foliot had appealed to Rome against the sentences. In July the papal envoys, Gratian and Vivian, came to Vézelay and had an interview with John of Salisbury. Shortly after, they informed Thomas that he would be free to renew his sentences if peace were not made by Michaelmas, 29 September 1169. Meetings with Henry at Domfront and at Bur and subsequent negotiations in the summer and early autumn came to nothing. Though the diplomatic intensity suggests that all sides were serious about a settlement, as the deadline loomed, a despondent Gratian returned to Italy, and Henry strengthened his blockade. As soon as he was able, Thomas renewed the sentences of April and May and added some more. On 18 November the king and archbishop came to Montmartre to make another attempt at a settlement.

Herbert of Bosham, *MTB* 3. 440–2, 444–51.

The king of France and others wrote to the pope, so affectionately, so pungently, so insistently knocking at the door of papal piety and justice and rousing the heart of papal compassion. When the pope had received all these prayers and commissions he found himself in a more difficult position than before. On the one hand he realised that peace could not make progress through the mediators.[31] But on the other hand he understood that, as we have already sufficiently shown, in such a difficult time, a time of schism, it would be dangerous to extend the severity of ecclesiastical discipline to someone who had so many allies,[32] even though such serious and outrageous offence to us, and the cause of justice which we were advancing, demanded such discipline. The pope, when he heard what had happened in the aforementioned conference with the kings,[33] supported our cause much more. In

31 Cardinals William of Pavia and Otto.

32 Henry was Alexander's most powerful supporter in the papal schism.

33 Montmirail.

particular the pressure of so many and such great people pleading on our behalf had distressed him, knowing that great scandal would result not only to them but to all the Church if peace were not rendered to the archbishop, his men and his church either through justice or amicable agreement.

The pope, in such straits and seeing these things, decided to appeal to the king according to the canons, to advise, exhort and order that he desist from vexing and disturbing the Church, and that he restore peace to the archbishop and his men. So he sent as his representatives not cardinals, which as we have shown above he had previously done, but other very erudite and industrious men, to carry out the papal commission. One of them was called Gratian, the nephew of the former pope of happy memory Eugenius, the other Vivian, one of the advocates from his court. These came quickly and readily – not having as much baggage with them as the cardinals did, not so many ornamented trappings, not so many burdensome packs – and straight away, before they saw us, went to the king. And according to the pope's mandate they confronted him again and again regarding our peace and that of the Church, sometimes advising and encouraging in all leniency, at other times arguing and harshly threatening. One of the legates in particular did not flatter, did not defer or spare, but on the authority of a papal legation rebuked and threatened the king with all authority,[34] and stood up him. This was Gratian, more vivacious than his companion Vivian, sharper and more insistent, truly Gratian, gracious in name and character ...[35]

When they had already approached the king again and again regarding peace, he and his companion eventually came to us. They reported that in the whole core issue which they had come to investigate they had found the king evasive, shifty and crooked, hiding what he was doing and always seeking through whatever evasions, dissembling, and meticulous and ingenious tricks to stall the business of peace for which they had come, and with the utmost effort labouring to justify his side and denigrate ours. Gratian in particular did not hide, was not silent and did not conceal this from us. Perceiving quite clearly that neither through them nor through other mediators could peace be achieved saving the honour of God and the Church, without delay he speedily returned to the pope and the Roman Church, not detained by

34 Titus 2.15.

35 Herbert reflects at length on Gratian's refusal to accept gifts and how such a stance was appropriate to a papal representative.

quibbling over words, nor seduced by promises, nor stuffed with gold and silver. He returned as a faithful legate, and reported fully and completely to the pope what he had seen and heard. But though he quickly returned, the other, his companion in his journey and embassy, remained with us over here. For he was so infected with the poison of our western isle, and so stuffed full of our silver, that he was unable to return as quickly and promptly.

When the king saw that Gratian had returned in this way as a faithful legate, not seeking the things of his own and in the business for which he had come appraising offence and favour in a balanced way, he began to deliberate on what to do. For he thought, not without reason, that returning in this manner to the lord pope he would disparage his cause and justify ours. Indeed he worried that the king of France, angered by the violated peace of his nobles, would influence the pope to be more inclined against him and in our favour. And so he tried to figure out what stratagem would pacify the upset king and either remove entirely or suspend the ecclesiastical censure which he now feared. With this in mind he decided to placate the king through some appearance of humility, knowing that a gentle and mild man is easily won over by humility, which indeed is most pleasing even to the proud. Therefore he said that he would make a pilgrimage to the glorious martyr Denis, apostle of the French, and in this way he would see his new lord the son of the king, who was then a boy and he had not yet seen. That is that beloved boy Philip, beyond all hope given by God to the king, or rather to the whole people, after many years of his reign, the only son of his father, who later succeeded to his father's kingdom and still reigns.[36] And may he reign happily and powerfully for many years. Therefore after a few days the king unexpectedly and without warning entered France. He did not seek any conference between himself and King Louis, for he knew that the upset king would avoid this, but on the pretext of pilgrimage he came to the glorious martyr Denis, apostle of the French. He certainly hoped that when the king heard of his arrival in the land he would come to him, and that the archbishop would equally rush to him, and as had happened before, sue for peace. For now, as we reliably heard, he regretted that in the previous peace conference described above he had not agreed to peace, even in the form including the phrase 'saving our order'.

And of course it turned out as the king had planned it. The lord king of France went to meet him, as did we, turning aside to that place

36 Philip II Augustus, born 1165, king 1180–1223. Louis VIII became king in 1137.

between Paris and St Denis commonly called the Holy Martyrdom, that is, the chapel at the foot of the hill of Montmartre. This chapel was called that because, as they say, the glorious martyr Denis was beheaded there. So we came to this chapel, the place of the holy martyr. The kings had already come together and the beloved boy whom we have mentioned had been brought outside Paris to meet them. They had preceded us to Montmartre and were now waiting for us on a level plain outside the chapel. And when one of us pressed the archbishop to make haste, saying that the kings were now waiting just for him, he answered that a priest ought only to walk with dignity. We took our place in the chapel, the kings outside. The other legate of the holy see who had remained behind when Gratian had returned, now seeing an opportunity, began through the king of France, through other men and through his own agency to encourage the king of England with great urgency towards our peace. And he did so with greater application because with his one fellow mediator now returned, he alone remained, and he hoped, if the Lord would grant it, that peace would be made through him alone to his great glory. In human things glory is greater because more singular if in great and energetic acts it has neither equal nor accomplice. The gentle king of France, and the nobles and bishops present, intervened painstakingly and attentively, pursuing peace with great diligence. And so as restless mediators they came and went, going back and forwards again and again between king and archbishop. To what end? After many objections from this side and that, after many suggestions, now in private, now in public, with the day nearly at an end everything was smoothed out and the path laid for the tranquillity of peace. All the evil customs which might enslave the Church were abandoned by the king, in essence if not explicitly, and with good will, as it seemed, he embraced the liberties of the Church to its honour and the glory of the clergy. Still, nothing concerning this or that was given expression by either side. For, as everyone agreed, to give these terms expression here would only do harm and would disturb the tranquillity of the peace now set in shape. Nor was there any recollection or mention of that added phrase 'saving God's honour', which had been the bone of contention in the last conference, that great wrestling-match. Nor was it necessary, because now the archbishop was not being asked to submit himself regarding the Church's cause in any way to the king's wish and judgement. This alone the king said, that the archbishop should return to his kingdom – from which, nevertheless, he claimed he had not expelled him – and there carry

out the duties of an archbishop, and in customs and other things defer
to the king as his king, and not usurp what did not belong to the
Church but the king under ecclesiastical pretext. And he, he said, would
not usurp anything that did not belong to the king but the Church.

But the archbishop spoke with great urgency to the king of France
and the other mediators among other things about his dispossession
and that of his men, reminding the lettered and lay in common
language[37] again and again of that rule of divine law, that a sin must not
be remitted until the loss has been made good. And he added that it
was in no way fitting to royal magnificence to turn the things of
paupers or the confiscated goods of the Church to his own use, or to
make grants of the possessions of another, which would be like strip-
ping one altar to clothe another, or crucifying Paul to save Peter. He
reckoned the sum of money taken away from him and his men at
30,000 marks. But the king of France and others replied to this that it
would be dishonourable and unfitting to obstruct the peace which was
so necessary and desirable to the realm and the Church for the sake of
money, especially a peace between so great a king and so great an archbishop. And in persuasion they reminded him of the old friendship
between them, and the benefits and services conferred by each side on
the other. And they added that with everything smoothed out, and the
Church's liberty restored, a just and pious pastor would not spurn his
Church, his bride now offered to him, and stay in exile because of a
money matter. Rather, rejoicing he ought to take his bride in his two
loving arms, even if she is naked, even if torn to pieces and broken,
and as the spiritual groom render what the spiritual bride demands.
Even so, the mediators said that they would petition the king frankly
and assiduously regarding his demands. The king answered their
petition by saying that he was prepared by the counsel of wise and
religious men to restore what was owed as soon as his financial agents
had assessed the sum. And since the archbishop had raised the issue of
fixtures as well as moveables, the king added that he would also speak
about those in good time.

And after so many various storms it seemed and was hoped by all that
we were about to enter port, when the archbishop through his mediators demanded a guarantee of peace. He explained that while he
suspected nothing sinister of the king, he was wary of the king's men,
not without reason after such prolonged animosity, especially if no
outward symbol of guarantee was given which would act as a clear

37 I.e. French.

sign that peace had been re-established and favour restored. Being a prudent man, he had consulted the pope some days before as to what he should do, what guarantee of peace he should demand, if it should happen that after so much enmity he be reconciled to the king and allowed to return to his land and his church. The pope answered that in such a case it would not be fitting to demand as surety a pledge or an oath from the king as a guarantee. He added that since the cause that he was advancing was the cause of justice, the cause of the Church, the peace if it should result, should also be the peace of the Church and the peace of justice, for which, whether peace were made or undone, it was precious and good to die, and the more precious because more secure. Therefore the pope answered that no formal guarantee should be demanded in this situation for such a cause. It is worldly and secular people alone who may ask for such guarantees, rather than ecclesiastics, priests and bishops, for whom, if they advance the cause of justice, life is loss and death is gain. So, as he wrote, if by God's will peace were granted between him and the king, the archbishop should demand no other secular guarantee, but be content with a kiss of peace alone.[38] This alone ought to suffice for a priest who was advancing the cause of justice, and none other should be demanded, unless spontaneously offered.

Finally now, when peace terms had been drawn up after much difficulty and effort, the archbishop turned in the last resort to the pope's counsel, and demanded as a sole guarantee from the king a sign of concord and favour between them, that is, the kiss of peace, saying that after such great and prolonged hostility he would be content with that alone. When the king of France and the mediators informed King Henry of this, he answered that he would freely do so, had he not at an earlier point publicly sworn in anger that he would never allow the archbishop a kiss of peace, even if it happened that in the fullness of time he should restore his peace and favour to him. For no other reason than this oath would he now deny him the kiss, certainly not because he harboured any anger or resentment in his heart. But when the king of France and many of the mediators heard this, they were immediately suspicious that under the honeyed speeches which had gone before, there lay poison. They returned straight away to the archbishop, who was waiting in the Chapel of the Martyrdom to hear

38 It was not unusual for an agreement to be sealed with a kiss of peace. The biographers claim that Thomas wanted it as a signal to Henry's men that the peace between them was real, but he must have known that Henry had sworn never to admit Thomas to such a kiss.

the king's response. As timid men, who now saw everything as
suspect, they neither persuaded nor dissuaded him either way, but just
reported the king's answer without embellishment.

But as soon as he heard it, the archbishop, being the wariest of the
wary and very experienced, like the others became suspicious, and
some of the remarks which he had circumspectly and privately made
earlier now appeared prophetic. He did not pause to take counsel, but
soon answered simply and categorically that he would not for the
present make peace with the king unless it were accompanied by the
kiss of peace, according to the pope's counsel. And with this unambi-
guous answer the conference broke up. Night was approaching, and
the kings still had to make a long journey to their lodgings in Mantes,
twelve leagues from Paris. As he left, the king of England, exhausted
by the whole day, and with the night journey still ahead of him,
cursed the archbishop again and again, repeatedly recalling the
trouble, vexation and nuisance he had caused him. When the kings
departed, we immediately retired to our lodgings at a Templar house
called the Temple just outside Paris. And as we left the Chapel of the
Martyrdom where we had conducted our negotiations for peace, one
of the company went up the archbishop and said, 'Today the peace of
our Church was discussed in the Chapel of the Martyrdom, and I
believe it is only through your martyrdom that the Church will gain
peace'. The archbishop, turning around to face him, said in a few
words, 'How I wish that it were liberated, even with my blood!'

41. The coronation of the young king (June 1170)

Thomas responded to the failure of the conference at Montmartre in familiar
fashion, reimposing the sentences of the previous year and threatening further
measures. In January 1170 the pope launched yet another mission under
Bishop Rotrou of Rouen, Bishop Bernard of Nevers, and Cardinal William of
Pavia, who were commissioned to threaten interdict if the king failed to agree
to peace.

On 3 March Henry landed in England, after four years in his continental
territories, with the intention of having his fifteen-year old son crowned. The
coronation of a designated heir during the king's lifetime had precedents in
France and Germany. It was designed to avoid the succession disputes which
had occurred on the death of each Anglo-Norman king, and to form the basis
of a division of his dominions between his sons. On hearing of Henry's plan, the
pope forbade it, but it seems that his letter was not delivered. Thomas issued a
prohibition against the English clergy's involvement in such a coronation,

and appealed to the pope. The coronation was celebrated on 14 June at Westminster in the presence of almost all the English bishops.

'Roger of Pontigny', *MTB* 4. 65–7.

The king of England called together a council of bishops and magnates at Clarendon, and demanded that they swear an oath that they would not provide any comfort to the archbishop or direct a commission to him, and especially that they would not receive letters from him. He added to the oath that they were to accept no letters or envoys of the lord pope, or appeal to him in any business, except with his permission. Also he decreed that no one was to cross the sea without his licence and letters. And he put guards on the ports to prevent anyone from crossing the sea, and to examine carefully anyone coming from overseas to make sure that no one brought letters from the pope or the archbishop into his realm. Besides, he ordered that if anyone was caught with letters they would be put in a battered old boat and led out to the high seas, to be left alone without an oar to the mercy of the waves. The bishops, however, shrank from the oath of guarantee in what ways they could, and after much persuasion the king finally conceded that they need only promise verbally. The laity then swore. The king was employing such cunning because he had heard that the lord pope had arranged to summon all the bishops of the realm to him.

With the kingdom then closed, the king again ordered them all to present themselves at London, and when they had gathered there the king began to discuss the coronation of his son. The bishops murmured and spoke with each other, saying that such a coronation would be illegal in the archbishop's absence, when no one doubted that it was his privilege alone to anoint kings. Nevertheless, three bishops were found, Roger of York, Gilbert of London and Jocelin of Salisbury, who said that it ought not be delayed on account of his absence, and that they were prepared to carry out the king's wish in this regard. So the king did not delay but had his son crowned with these three bishops performing the celebration and the others not able to escape, but unwilling to apply their hands.

Therefore in different ways the cause of the church of Canterbury was stirred up, but still peace could not be achieved, although King Louis of France, in the many conferences which he had during this time with the king of England, urgently promoted the restoration of peace and concord. The lord pope also sent many of his envoys, inciting the king towards the peace of the Church of God with fatherly affection in letters and words, but to no avail. Understanding that it could only be achieved through force, he eventually wrote to the king, commanding and exhorting, requesting and advising him to restore peace to the church of Canterbury which had suffered for a long time now without a pastor, and that he re-establish harmony with the archbishop. Indeed he secretly sent other letters, and put them in the hands of a certain French bishop, in which was contained explicit sentence of interdict on the realm of England. That is, so that if the king defied papal admonition his realm would immediately be placed under interdict, which the pope did not hide from the king. So the kings arranged a date for a conference between them to settle the peace of the Church.

42. The settlement at Fréteval and its aftermath (July–November 1170)

The coronation of the young Henry outraged the pope, his envoys and others, including King Louis, whose daughter Margaret, the young king's wife, had not been present. In late June Henry crossed the sea. The papal envoys Rotrou of Rouen and Bernard of Nevers served an ultimatum on him, and Henry agreed to their terms for reconciliation, apart from the proposed kiss of peace. A meeting between Henry and Louis was arranged for 21 July between La Ferté and Fréteval, and the next day Henry and Thomas met a little further south between Fréteval and Viévy-le-Rayé.

William Fitzstephen, *MTB* 3. 107–17.

The king agreed to a meeting that summer. So, before the end of Archbishop Thomas's sixth year in exile, the day before the feast of the blessed Mary Magdalene, there gathered at Fréteval the archbishops of Rheims, Sens, Rouen, and Tyre, and the lord king of France, and the bishop of Nevers, and the abbot of Grandmont, on behalf of the lord pope, and the bishop of Poitiers, and almost all the bishops of Normandy, almost all the counts and magnates of France, to restore the peace between the king of England and the archbishop of Canterbury. No bishop of England was there except Roger of Worcester. That day the king of England came to the French king's lodgings, and when they had spoken together privately, after a little the king of England said to him in jest, 'And tomorrow your thief will have his peace, and will have it good'. 'By the saints of France', said the king of France, 'what thief?' 'That archbishop of Canterbury of yours', said Henry. 'Would that he was ours as he is yours', said Louis. 'You will have honour before God and men if you grant him a good peace, and we will be grateful to you.' These things were said publicly; in private they spoke their minds. The next day all went out to the conference ...[39]

Various people said many things from this side and that in support of the good of peace and the restoration of their favour. The king agreed to every detail of the Church's peace and liberty, to render esteem and restitution to the church of Canterbury and the person of the archbishop, to restore lands and churches taken from the archbishop's clerks and supporters, and to leave the presentation of vacant churches belonging to the archiepiscopal see – which the king had given to his clerks – to the archbishop. Then the good archbishop, unwilling to hide from the king anything that might later occasion an obstacle or stumbling-block between them – for the wise man wishes neither to deceive nor be deceived – made a speech like this: 'My lord king, I often call to mind the many benefits from my first and second promotions, and the great reverence, which you have bestowed upon me. I hold them dear and consider them pleasing, and I thank you in every way. I am indebted and accountable to you as my king and worldly lord, saving honour to God and Holy Church, especially now when you have just recalled and admitted me to your peace and favour. But among all the individual evils which in your anger and resentment I have endured – proscription, plunder, my banishment and that of my people, and whatever oppressions of the church of Canterbury – there is one that disturbs me most, and which I neither can nor ought to leave untouched or uncorrected: that you had your son crowned by the archbishop of York in the province of Canterbury. You despoiled the church of Canterbury, the church which anointed you as king with the unction of God's mercy, of its privilege of consecrating kings. This among all its privileges it has considered particular, its own and special, for a long time past, since first the blessed Augustine established the metropolitan see of Canterbury.' To this the king replied, 'I have heard and been informed that one of the royal privileges of my realm is that if a king of England while still living wishes to appoint his son king, he is allowed to do so wherever and through whatever archbishop or bishop he pleases. My great-grandfather William, the conqueror of England, was consecrated and crowned at London by the archbishop of York, and my grandfather King Henry by the bishop of Hereford.'

'Yes it is true', replied the archbishop, 'that they crowned those kings,

---

39 Fitzstephen explains that Louis decided not to attend the conference, so as to avoid the suspicion that he had put pressure on Henry to make peace.

but in their coronation the dignity of the church of Canterbury was not encroached upon. When William of York anointed the king, the see of Canterbury was effectively vacant, for Stigand who then appeared to be ruling the church of Canterbury, was not archbishop – he had never received the pallium from the Holy Roman Church. And with the church of Canterbury vacant, in the English clergy the archbishop of York was pre-eminent, and the suitable person.'[40] When King Henry was meant to be crowned, St Anselm was archbishop, but he was far away, an exile in Cluny. And since the delay of his recall could have been very dangerous to the kingdom, to guard against the outbreak of war in the land, one of his suffragans, the bishop of Hereford, took the place and office of the absent archbishop.'[41] The king replied, 'That could well be true. What I said on the matter I did not say against the church of Canterbury. It anointed me and I wish its dignity to be safe in all circumstances. If I offended it in any way, I am prepared for my sake to make correction according to the judgement of the lord pope and the Roman Church. And you may make complaint about the injuries inflicted by the archbishop of York and the bishops of England on the church of Canterbury and on you'.

The archbishop was satisfied, and in view of this answer and concession he got off his horse intending to give thanks to the king by falling down at the king's feet. Realising this the king more promptly jumped down from his horse, embraced the archbishop and raised him up, showing him approval with a cheerful expression, a happy countenance, and pledging peace and returning favour to him. And showing deference to the archbishop, he held his stirrup for him as he inserted his right foot. All men of good will present burst out into pious tears.

40 Stigand had received the pallium from the schismatic Pope Benedict X (1058–59), and since his appointment to Canterbury was widely regarded as invalid, neither Harold nor William sought his participation in their coronation. According to Eadmer, a champion of Canterbury rights, 'although the king himself and everyone else knew well enough that such consecration ought to be performed by the archbishop of Canterbury as being his special and peculiar privilege, yet seeing that many wicked and horrible crimes were ascribed to Stigand, who was at that time archbishop of Canterbury, William was unwilling to receive consecration at his hands, lest he should seem to be taking on himself a curse rather than a blessing' (*Historia Novorum*, ed. M. Rule, London, 1884, p. 9).

41 Henry I's particularly swift coronation on 5 August 1000, three days after the death of his brother, William II, was justified by Hugh the Chanter on the grounds that otherwise 'the kingdom might have been disturbed' (Hugh the Chanter, *The History of the Church of York, 1066–1127*, ed. C. Johnson, rev. edn, Oxford, 1990, p. 18), though Henry's aim was clearly to gain the advantage over his brother Robert, a rival claimant. Anselm had been in exile since 1097, and did not return until September 1000.

Then the king was asked to give him the kiss of peace.[42] Long before, when peace was being negotiated between them, and the king had granted return and restitution and all other clauses of this kind, only the kiss was denied, and peace came to a standstill for a long time.[43] For the king said that he had once sworn in anger that he would never kiss him. The lord pope was consulted on this matter and he absolved the king of his oath, if he had made it, and enjoined on him on the security of his soul to give the kiss to the archbishop in sound peace. The king said, 'In my land I will kiss his mouth, his hands and his feet a hundred times, a hundred times will I hear his Mass, but let us put it off for now. I do not speak deceptively. It is part of my honour, that in this thing he appear to defer to me, and in my land the granting of a kiss will seem to spring from grace and benevolence, while here it would seem to be prompted by necessity'. With the assent of all the archbishop agreed. Everyone who saw and heard these things was happy, clergy, knights and people of every age and rank. Later the lord king and archbishop alone engaged in secret counsel apart for a long time. The meeting broke up.

It was agreed between king and archbishop that the archbishop would return to France[44] to give thanks to his benefactors, and to the lord pope, his envoy and staff. And with licence, when he had made arrangements for his return home, he would come back to the king, who would lead him back to England in his own person if possible, or else send the archbishop of Rouen, so that he would be met with reverence as he resumed his former position. Meanwhile the king gave instructions that all the possessions taken away from him and the others were to be restored ...[45]

The restitution to the archbishop's clerks was observed, though not fully enough, but not to the archbishop himself. The king, as was said above, had granted away certain vacant churches of the archbishop during the dispute, and according to the terms of the peace he revoked

---

42 Herbert of Bosham, also an eyewitness, insists that the kiss was neither sought nor granted: 'There peace was made between us, but the kiss, which as we have said had been sought but denied at [Montmartre], was now neither demanded by the archbishop nor offered or refused by the king. Indeed no mention was made of it there, but the king granted us peace and security publicly in the presence of the prelates and lay magnates assembled' (*MTB* 3. 466).

43 See above, pp. 170–2.

44 I.e. across the frontier between Normandy and the French king's domain.

45 Here Fitzstephen inserts letters from Henry announcing the reconciliation and restoring the archbishop's property.

these grants, and relinquished them to the archbishop. The officials of the clerks to whom the archbishop had granted them returned, but not much later these were expelled by the king's officials, and those to whom the king had earlier granted them returned. Besides, the king's officials, rather than the archbishop's, received the revenues and pensions of the archiepiscopal manors for the next Michaelmas term. Many wise men silently considered these things, and took note.

The archbishop immediately sent his envoy to give thanks for peace to the lord pope and the Holy Roman Church, and he sent with him the terms of the peace, and the king's concession regarding the vengeful injury of the coronation, and he awaited his return. Meanwhile he visited his religious and helpful friends throughout France and gave thanks to each individually and from them he received licence to leave. These French nobles fully equipped him and his men with horses, clothes and all necessities, so as to send back to their homeland with great honour the exiles whom they had supported. He sweetly and affectionately received licence from the king of France, with every expression of thanks, and said among other things, 'We are going into England to play for heads'. 'So it seems to me', agreed the king of France. 'In truth, lord archbishop, without the kiss of peace if you trust me, you should not trust your king. Why don't you stay here? While King Louis is alive, you will not lack wine, food and all the riches of France.' The archbishop replied, 'May God's will be done'. With tears they bade each other goodbye for the last time. In the same way he warmly kissed the bishop of Paris and said among other things, 'I go into England to die'.

In England a certain man who served in the king's court confessed his sins to Richard de Haliwell, a religious and honest priest, and said among other things that with his own hands he had sealed letters sent into England, ordering the archbishop to be killed. And Nigel de Sackvill,[46] he said, had written them in tears. And he added that he had made confession to a certain bishop of England, and had asked for penance to be imposed on him. But that bishop said to him, 'What for? Do as your lord commands', and imposed no penance, as if he had committed no sin. One day Reginald of Warenne[47] entered the chapter of the canons of Southwark, to whom he was bound by intimate love, community with their brotherhood, and generous payment of benefices.

---

46 Keeper of the seal, whom Thomas had excommunicated in 1169.

47 A royal justiciar, and one of those who challenged Thomas upon his return to England: see below, p. 183.

Among other things he spoke to them about this unclean world, about the evils of wicked men, about vices, which, falling away from the nobility of our fathers, challenges and stands in comparison to the present corrupt age, and he said to them, 'I beg you, pray to God for me more urgently. I need it. Soon you may hear of things done in England that have not been done or heard of ever. As far as I am concerned, they are against me and my wish, but I am not my own master'. The canons who heard this recoiled, not knowing what he was speaking about, until, though this Reginald was innocent of the killing of the righteous man, eventually the deed was carried out through others.

Meanwhile the king of England wrote a letter of recall to the archbishop through Hugh the clerk, saying that he found this delay of his in France suspicious, and urging him to return quickly to England. When everything had been prepared the archbishop returned to the king, as agreed. First he visited him at Tours, where the king was not asked for and did not offer a kiss. The archbishop did not ask in case he should appear too hasty and precipitate. Again he visited his court at Amboise. That day the king was yet to hear Mass. Nigel de Sackvill, the king's clerk and seal-bearer, to whom the king had given one of the good churches of the archbishop, and which he was now afraid he would have to give up, announced to the king that the archbishop was in the chapel. Perhaps, he said, the archbishop was being opportune in arriving before Mass so that during it he would receive the kiss of peace. But, if the king wished, he could cheat the archbishop of the kiss. 'How?', asked the king. 'Let the priest say Mass for the faithful departed',[48] he replied. The king agreed and it was done. After the Mass, as is customary in veneration of Our Lady the ever Virgin Mary, 'Hail, holy mother' was said, and then the priest kissed the text of the Gospel. Then he handed it over to the archbishop to kiss, which he did and handed it over in turn to the king. When the king had kissed it, the archbishop said to the king, 'Lord, just now I have come into your land to see you. Give me, as is fitting for the time, the place, and the promise, the kiss of peace'. The king said, 'You will have enough another time', a rebuff which the archbishop and all present silently noted. That day the king and archbishop spoke alone together for a long time. As a final stipulation of the peace it had been agreed that the king would come to Rouen to meet him, and free him from all debts to creditors, and make amends for the other money of the

48 From which the kiss of peace is omitted.

archbishop which he had received. There he was also to admit him to
the kiss of peace, and to accompany him into England or send the archbishop of Rouen with him to his son the king, to make good anything
that might be lacking to the full restoration of the archbishop or his
men. Then he sought licence and took his leave of the king of
England for the last time.[49] The king said to him, 'Go in peace. I will
follow you and will see you in Rouen or in England as quickly as I
can'. The archbishop said, 'Lord, my heart tells me that in taking my
leave of you now, I will not see you again in this life'. 'Do you think
I don't keep my word?', demanded the king. 'Far be it from you, lord',
replied the archbishop.

The archbishop left the court and following the wish of the king came
to Rouen. But there he received only an envoy of the king, the dean of
Salisbury[50] to guide his journey. The king's excuse for not coming
with him was that the king of France was preparing to attack his men
in the Auvergne.[51] When the dean of Salisbury told him why he had
come, the archbishop said to him, 'How things change! Once it would
have been up to the archbishop of Canterbury to provide a safe conduct to England for you, and one a little safer than that which you can
provide him'. And he asked the archbishop of Rouen, through whom
the settlement had been agreed, 'What has happened to the agreement
between me and the king? Why is the king not here in person? Where
is our kiss of peace? What is happening about money? I have brought
forward my creditors. The king does not honour his word'. Next he
asked him if he had received an order from the king to accompany him
to England, and the archbishop of Rouen replied, 'Not at all'. He
would have escorted him nevertheless out of love, if the archbishop
had wished, but he had not been put under an obligation. He said that
all things were assured, his peace and security had been established
and confirmed by such great authority and in presence of such great
men. Then the archbishop of Rouen gave him £300 as a gift from his
own money.

As the archbishop made his way to the sea at Flanders, accompanied
only by John dean of Salisbury as an escort, he went over these things

---

49 At Chaumont-sur-Loire, probably in late September.

50 John of Oxford, whom Thomas had excommunicated in 1166, and whom Thomas
still considered excommunicate.

51 So Henry claimed in a letter to Thomas (*CTB* no. 322, pp. 1338–9; *MTB* no. 722, 7.
400). There does not seem to be any other evidence of such preparations, though
the Auvergne had been an area of dispute between the two kings.

in his heart, especially the absence of the kiss of peace which had been agreed in the settlement. Nevertheless he set out on his journey secure in the Holy Spirit, not afraid to die for God and the cause of the Church. For now he had received an envoy and a letter of encouragement from the lord pope, telling him to return fearlessly to his church and resume his ministry. He also received a letter of most uncompromising justice regarding the presumptuous coronation of the new king, suspending the archbishop of York and all the bishops who took part in the coronation, apart from Bartholomew of Exeter alone, and letters renewing the earlier excommunication of the bishops of London and Salisbury.[52] His envoy was sent ahead with these letters of justice, and he found the archbishop of York and the bishop of London at Canterbury waiting for the right time to cross the sea. The pope's letters of thundering judgement, which included the phrase, 'Let us fill their faces with shame',[53] were read, and their faces were pushed to the ground.

---

52 These had been issued by the pope on 16 September.
53 See Psalm 83.16.

V: MARTYRDOM (1170–74)

43. Thomas is warned as he embarks (?30 November 1170)

William of Canterbury, *MTB* 1. 86–7.

On the 1170th year from the Incarnation of the Lord, with the most serene Pope Alexander presiding over the Roman Church, the schismatic Frederick ruling in Germany, the glorious Louis beloved of God king of France, Thomas archbishop of Canterbury of venerable memory on his return from exile, now in the seventh year of his deportation, came to the sea which flows between Dover and Wissant. As he was walking on the seashore, assessing the state of the weather, as those who cross the sea do, he saw a certain Milo, dean of Boulogne approaching. Thinking that he was coming to exact a fare, the archbishop engaged him with a smile. However, as he approached he said, 'I am have not come to exact a fare but to deliver a message. For my lord the count of Boulogne[1] says this: "Watch out for yourself. There are those lying in wait who seek your life, blockading the sea ports, so that as you leave the ship they might seize you and butcher you or put you in chains".' He replied, 'Believe me, brother, not if I were to be torn limb from limb would I leave off from the path I have begun. Neither danger, nor force, nor torture will recall me now. It is enough that the Lord's flock has lamented the absence of its pastor for seven years. I implore with all my heart as a last request from my men – and there is nothing more bindingly owed to a man than that his last wish, when he can do nothing more, be fulfilled – that they do not disdain to carry me even dead to the church from which I have been kept away during my life, if the Lord has decided that this is the time to lead his servant from the body to his death.'

44. The archbishop's return (*c.* 1–3 December 1170)

Shortly before he crossed to England, Thomas had sent his servant Osbern to England with the papal letters of censure. He served them in person on York, London and Salisbury in Dover, where they were waiting to cross the sea.

Herbert of Bosham, *MTB* 3. 476–80.

---

1 Matthew, whom Thomas had feared on his arrival, see above, p. 124.

On the second or third day after the feast of St Andrew the apostle,[2] in the season of the Lord's Advent, we set sail by night as desired with a favourable wind. Suspecting ambushes, which, as we heard, were now set for us, we landed safely, not at Dover as expected, but at Sandwich. For that harbour was more secure because the men living there held their lands from the lord archbishop, as a fief of the church of Canterbury. As he reached the shore, the archbishop's boat could be distinguished from the others by the cross, which as primate of all England the archbishop of Canterbury is accustomed to carry before him, towering erect. Soon a crowd of poor people gathered to meet him, some striving to be first to receive blessing from their father as he landed, others humbly prostrating themselves on the ground, some wailing, some weeping, for joy, and all crying out together, 'Blessed is he who comes in the name of the Lord,[3] father of orphans and judge of widows!' So much for the poor.

But the knights[4] who, as we have said above, had expected us to land in a different port, hurried to us with great speed. Hardly had they greeted the archbishop than they began boldly to ask him why, at the outset of his return which was meant to be tranquil and peaceful, even before he had embarked, he had suspended and excommunicated the king's bishops. And they threatened that soon, when the great disturbance in store for the king became known, not only the crown but the priesthood would be disturbed. But the archbishop gently answered that the king would not be offended on this account, nor had he by his actions done anything against the king or the realm. In fact, he said, it had been done without injury to the king or the realm on the permission of the king himself, so that in this way the injury which the bishops had inflicted on himself and his church in the coronation of the king's son, would not remain uncorrected, lest such a great usurpation henceforth become a pattern. When they heard the king cited as the source of these actions, they spoke with greater restraint, nevertheless insistently demanding that he absolve the excommunicated and suspended bishops. The archbishop, wishing to take counsel, postponed further discussion until he came to Canterbury the next day, so the knights withdrew.

But the next day the archbishop set out for Canterbury from that port, a distance of about six miles, and was welcomed with as much

2 St Andrew's Day is 30 November. There is some confusion among the biographers over the date of Thomas's landing, but 1 December seems the most likely.

3 Psalm 117.26; Matthew 21.9, etc.

4 Gervase of Cornhill, sheriff of Kent, Ranulf de Broc, and Reginald of Warenne.

thanks and celebration as a heavenly host, as an angel of God. But why do I say with celebration? Rather – if it is fitting to say so of the poor – the poor of Christ met Christ's triumphant anointed with a victory procession rather than a celebration. For wherever the archbishop passed, a throng of paupers, the small and the large, the old with the young, ran up to him in a group, some prostrating themselves on the road, others tearing off their garments and spreading them on the road, crying out again and again, 'Blessed is he who comes in the name of the Lord'. Indeed the parish priests who had, along with their parishioners, arranged a procession with their crosses, went out to meet him as he passed, and greeted their father and asked his blessing, again and again crying out, 'Blessed is he who comes in the name of the Lord'. What can I say? If you had seen it, he with his passion[5] now imminent, among the boys and the infants and the poor, following the path prepared by the Lord, you would have said without question that the Lord was for the second time approaching his passion, and that He who once died at Jerusalem to save the whole world had come again to die at Canterbury for the English Church. With such a closely-packed throng coming to meet him, even though the road was short, he was hardly able to reach Canterbury that day, but eventually to the sound of bells and organs, hymns and spiritual songs, he was received by Christ's poor, his sons, namely his holy community of monks, with the devotion and reverence due to a father. What a face of the man you would have seen as he first entered the church! As some noticed and marvelled, it seemed as though with his heart aflame, his face was also on fire …[6]

But the next day the said knights returned seeking an answer to the previous day's petition. Clerks of the three bishops mentioned above, who were still waiting in harbour, also came in the bishops' name, and demanded absolution for their lords. But the archbishop answered that these three and the other bishops, some of whom had been excommunicated, others suspended, by the authority of the lord pope not himself, being bound by such a great judge, could only be released through him. But when the clerks pressed on most insistently in their purpose, the archbishop eventually answered that, trusting in the clemency of the lord pope, he would in this regard for the good of peace usurp what belonged to the pope and submit the cases of the

5 A term used of the suffering and death of Christ: see Acts 1.3.

6 Herbert expands upon this description of Thomas's countenance, drawing scriptural parallels.

excommunicated or suspended to the judgement of the Church, as long as they took an oath of guarantee.[7] In no other way, he categorically insisted, would it be done. At this these men left in indigation, making many arrogant and abusive comments as they left, and Ranulf de Broc went especially far. But among them the archbishop, a very patient man, was like someone who does not hear and in whose mouth are no rebukes.[8] But the bishops' clerks returned to their lords and reported the archbishop's response to their petition. And as was said, two of the excommunicated bishops, London and Salisbury, would have perfomed the oath demanded by the archbishop, had the third, York, not objected. Truly is it written, 'The third voice disturbs many'.[9]

45. Thomas is prevented from visiting the young king (c. 8–13 December 1170)

William Fitzstephen, *MTB* 3. 121–4, 126–7.

After a delay of eight days in his see, the good Archbishop Thomas sent an envoy to the young king, indicating that he was coming to see him as his king and lord. And he brought with him three valuable destriers, of remarkable speed, elegant stature and beautiful appearance, which walked tall, lifting supple legs, flickering their ears and quivering their limbs, standing restlessly, clothed in flowered and parti-coloured blankets, which he had arranged to give as a new gift to his new lord.[10] For he loved him very much as his lord king, whom as a boy he had reared in his house and court when he was chancellor to his father the king.

On the first day the bishop and the church of Rochester came out to meet him with due veneration. At London he had a third procession, to the church of the canon regulars of the Blessed Mary in Southwark.[11] And there an infinite multitude of clergy, men and women went out from the city to meet him returning from exile, praising and commending God for his long desired homecoming. Around three thousand poor scholars and clerks of the churches of London had gathered to meet him on their own initiative outside the city, and

7 That they would stand by the pope's judgement.

8 See Psalm 38.14.

9 Unidentified.

10 As king, the young Henry was now Thomas's lord.

11 Priory of St Mary Overy.

when they saw him approaching they began to sing most loftily and serenely, 'God, we praise you', and almost all those who heard this too, weeping for joy were provoked to tears of pity. He shared in their devotion and exultation in the Lord, giving thanks, and reaching into his pocket where he kept his alms, distributed money to them with great compassion. When he eventually came to the canonical church of Southwark, where the bishop of Winchester was to give him lodgings, and went in, the religious canons who had made a procession to the door met him with great joy, and bursting out with many pious tears they began to sing the response, 'Blessed Lord God of Israel'. There the infinite multitude of clergy and people of every age and every order with great rejoicing and loud voice honoured him with a hymn of thanks and common joy. Among them, a certain foolish, shameless and prattling woman called Matilda, who tended to force herself on public courts and gatherings, cried out and repeated a number of times, 'Archbishop, watch out for the knife', so that everyone wondered what portents or treachery she had heard of, which she had signified to him with these words.

There in the bishop of Winchester's lodgings, after a delay of one day, he received the envoy of the young King Henry. Jocelin of Arundel, brother of the queen,[12] told him that the king did not wish him to visit, nor for him to travel through the cities and towns of the realm, but rather that he return to Canterbury, and remain in his see, and not leave it. The archbishop was surprised, judging that such a statement was not in the young king's nature, and he asked Jocelin if the king was saying that he was expelled from the communion and security of his peace. 'His orders are just as I have said', he replied. And leaving with a scowl on his face he saw in his path a certain citizen of London, a rich man known to him, and he said to him, 'Have you come to see the king's enemy? Return quickly, I advise you.' The man replied, 'If you consider him an enemy of the king, I know nothing about it. I heard and saw the letter from the king across the sea confirming his peace and restoration. If something else has escaped my notice it is unknown to me.' So, even before the event there were signs heralding evil.

The next day he returned to Canterbury when he was told that Ranulf de Broc had seized a transport ship of his carrying his wine, cut the rigging and weighed anchor, killed some of his sailors and imprisoned others at Pevensey Castle. There and then he sent the

12 Queen Adela, wife of Henry I.

abbot of St Albans and the prior of Dover to the young king, who
reported what had been done to him, and at the king's command the
ship was restored to him. Returning to Canterbury, Archbishop
Thomas was accompanied by some knights, as a precaution against
the possibility, at a time of so many recurring signs of evil, that some
ruffians lying in wait by the side of the road might attack him. In his
company he had five knights in all with shields, destriers and lances.
Immediately it was announced to the king across the sea that he was
roaming about the kingdom preparing to attack cities and drive the
king's son from the realm ...[13]

The good Thomas came to Canterbury, these five knights returned
home, and he remained there with only priests, clerks and his domestic
household. That infamous family de Broc, his neighbours at Saltwood
Castle, laid nocturnal ambushes for him at the exit of the roads everywhere around Canterbury, and so as to exasperate him and provoke
his men to violence, they hunted without licence in his drive, and
caught a stag, and captured and kept the archbishop's own dogs, which
he employed in his woods. Further, one day before Christmas, a certain
Robert de Broc, who had once been a clerk, and then a Cistercian
monk, but later an apostate who defected to the world, happened to
come across a pack-horse of the archbishop's heading from one of the
estates of the church with his supplies. And he had his grandson John
de Broc cut off the whole of the horse's tail, as an insult to the archbishop. But Thomas the lover of God, chariot and charioteer[14] of the
English Church, equally enduring in prosperity and adversity, a
dwelling-place of outstanding virtue, thought over all these indications
of his imminent martyrdom, and steadied his soul for his exit from
Egypt.[15] So from day to day he prepared himself, more prodigal in
alms-giving, more devoted in prayer, more anxious in the care of his
soul. Indeed several times in speaking with his clerks, he said that this
affair could not be brought to completion without bloodshed, and that
he would stand by the Church's cause up to death. At the time, his
men did not understand what he was saying, but later those who saw
what happened recalled these words. And the archbishop wrote to the
lord pope that nothing was in store for him except death and the
sword, and begged him to pray to God more attentively on his behalf.

13 Here Fitzstephen relates how Thomas encountered a poor priest who had received
   a vision concerning the archbishop, and how royal officials enquired as to who had
   welcomed the archbishop on his return to Canterbury.
14 See 2 Kings 2.12; 13.14.
15 A reference to the deliverence of the Israelites from the Pharoah in Exodus.

46. The bishops complain to the king (*c.* 23–24 December 1170)

The bishops set off shortly after their clerks' negotiations with Thomas. They arrived in Bur-le-Roi a few days before Christmas, by which time the king had already been informed of the recent sentences imposed upon them by Thomas.

Garnier, 4971–5010. Language: Old French. Translation by Janet Shirley.

When Roger of Pont-l'Evêque learned that he had been excommunicated and set apart, he would not make amends or ask for forgiveness, for his heart was evil, full of arrogance and presumptuous pride; the devil had enthroned himself within him. The other prelates, however, his two companions, Gilbert Foliot and Jocelin, did wish to make atonement and to make to their archbishop those reparations which were justly due; they acknowledged between themselves how wrong they had been. But this man Roger of Pont-l'Evêque made them go astray, made them persist in acting against God and against reason; he wanted helpers for his evil plans.

'Don't', he said, 'don't, I beg you, adopt that course, lest your religion should change you; he could so easily turn you about and cheat you. But I have got £10,000 in my treasury; I will spend every one of them, I promise you, to bring Thomas's pride to a fall. He won't be able to do much against me. Now, we will cross the sea and go to the king on the other side; he has supported us so far and will go on supporting us and our cause against that man. As long as you don't weaken, he will finish him off. Do you know what he will do if you desert him? If you change now and go over to his enemy, you will never enjoy his affection again, however long you live, you will never recover his good will. And he will say that you are running away from right reason. If he does justice upon you, you will lose everything you possess. Then what will you be able to do? Where will you go and beg? And if you stand fast by the king, what else is there that Thomas can do to you? He has passed a sentence on you which cannot be binding because it is not based upon the truth.'

And so he cajoled and persuaded them, and they agreed to go with him. They reached the boat, and put to sea. Roger of Pont-l'Evêque could not hide his feelings; he exclaimed, 'Thomas, Thomas, how you will regret making me cross the sea! I am going to get an uncomfortable pillow for your head.' As soon as they had landed, they sent the king the letter from the pope by which they had lost the exercise of their profession. When the king saw it he was very angry; he struck his hands together and exclaimed against it vehemently. He went away into his room, white with fury, and said that he had brought up evil men and cared for them, he had given his bread uselessly to an evil people, not one of those nearest him took any share in his griefs. All this terrified his people. 'Why', they said, 'does the king distress himself so dreadfully? If he were to see his sons or his wife being buried, and all his lands in flames, burning, he ought not to grieve like this. If he has heard anything he ought to have said what it was. Besides, one ought not believe everything one hears. We are ready to carry out his orders, to assault and batter down cities and castles, to risk our bodies and our souls as well. He is wrong to complain to us, when he will not say what it is'.

'A man', the king said to them, 'who has eaten my bread, who came to my court poor, and I have raised him high – now he draws up his heel to kick me in the teeth! He has shamed my kin, shamed my realm; the grief goes to my heart, and no one has avenged me!' Then the whole court stirred and murmured; they began to blame themselves severely and to utter fierce threats against the holy archbishop. Several men started to bind themselves together by oath to take swift vengeance of the king's shame.

When they had crossed the sea, the three companions made straight for Bur. They found the king there and fell at his feet and begged his forgiveness, lamenting and grieving before him, groaning and weeping in sorrow and affliction. Then King Henry's manner quite changed: he told the bishops to get up on to their feet and asked them why they were so unhappy. Archbishop Roger spoke first – he knew all about scheming and wickedness! 'My lord king', he said to him. 'We ought indeed to grieve; and I am able to talk about it and explain it, but no one may speak to these two others, or he too will lie under the same sentence that Thomas laid on them after he crossed the sea. Thomas has excommunicated everyone who was with your son at the consecration, and all those also who approved of it.'

'Then by the eyes God sees with', exclaimed the king, 'I am not exempted, for it has my approval.'

'If, my lord', said the archbishop, 'you have to share our sufferings, it will be the easier for us to bear it. He is forcing your free men to leave Holy Church and your bishops to lie under excommunication. And he does not mean to stop at that – since he returned to the country he has gone about your land strongly reinforced with men, he has knights and soldiers with him, all armed and ready, in the fear that he may be exiled again; he is seeking assistance everywhere, to make himself stronger. We do not mind, we do not complain, that our loyalty in your service has led to our expending so much of our own resources and to our weariness and suffering, as long as we are not cut off from your love – but we do complain at his doing us this injustice, disgracing and dishonouring us as if we were evil-doers. You would certainly not be blamed if you were to follow a different policy. But wait until he feels secure; then you will be able to take your revenge without any disturbance'.

The letter from the pope cutting off these three prelates from their calling was brought forward and was read out in audience and listened to by everyone. Then indeed ill will blazed out everywhere, with insults and threats against St Thomas. Christmas Day this year was on a Friday; it was on the eve, Thursday, that this council and God's enemies met together and swore the death of God's friend. They thought they could bring him down, but it was they who reaped the disgrace. They swore now on holy relics and pledged each other that wherever in the world they might find him, they would pull his tongue down past his chin and dig both his eyes out of his head; neither church nor altar nor season should protect him.

47. The conspirators

The conspirators were important barons. Reginald FitzUrse was a descendent of Henry I. Hugh de Morville held large estates in the north of England, including Knaresborough Castle where they sheltered after the murder. William de Tracy was descended from the sister of King Edward the Confessor, and held lands in Gloucestershire, Somerset and Devon. Richard le Bret held lands in Somerset, but seems to have been lowlier and younger than the others. The leader of the conspirators was really Ranulf de Broc, but he did not take part in the murder itself.
William of Canterbury, *MTB* 1. 128.

The first is Reginald, afraid of no crime, as they say, and from his father Urse[16] deriving the savagery of a beast.

Hugh de Morville – a vill of death or the dead: whatever way it is said it translates as a village of death. It is told that his mother was passionately in love with a young man called Litulf, but he would not consent to debauchery. So with perfect womanly trickery she suggested

16 Meaning 'bear'.

a game, in which he would enter the castle on his horse with his sword drawn before him. But as soon as he did this she exclaimed in her native tongue to the aformentioned man, '*Huge de Morevile, ware, ware, ware, Lithulf heth his sword adrage*', which translates as 'Hugh de Moreville, look out, look out, look out, Litulf has his sword drawn'. For which reason the blameless youth, accused of stretching out his hand to shed the blood of his lord, was condemned to death and stewed in boiling water, thereby attaining martyrdom. What can we expect from the brood of vipers?[17] Are grapes gathered from thorns, or figs from thistles?[18] If a bad tree cannot bear good fruit,[19] as God declares, it follows that a harmless seed cannot grow from a poisonous root.

The third is called William de Tracy, who however bravely he often acted in military contest, nevertheless because of his sinful way of life, deserved to fall headlong into parricide or another disgraceful act.

The fourth is Richard le Bret, who on account of the depravity of his life turned from Bret to brute. And though fighting under the name of a tyro, he incurred the infamy of Thraso.[20]

48. The king consults his barons (*c.* 24 December 1170)

Shortly after the four knights set out from Bur, Henry held a meeting with his barons in which he bitterly complained of the archbishop's actions.

William Fitzstephen, *MTB* 3. 128.

The next day after those who were to kill the archbishop left the king's court, the king addressed his barons in his chamber, and complained of the archbishop that he had entered his kingdom like a tyrant; that he had suspended the archbishop of York and all his bishops and excommunicated others for obedience to the king; that he had disturbed the whole realm; that he intended to deprive his son of his crown; that he had sought out a legation over his head; and that he had obtained a privilege for himself and the bishops from the lord pope by which they would have power over presentations to churches without any reference to the earls or barons, or even himself.

17 See Luke 3.7.
18 See Matthew 7.16.
19 See Matthew 7.18. This may also be a reference to Thomas's prognostic: see below, p. 227.
20 A braggart knight in Terence's *Eunuch*.

First the earl of Leicester answered, 'Certainly, lord, the archbishop and my father the earl were very friendly, but you can be sure that from the time he departed from your land and your goodwill, I have not been in touch with him, nor he with me'. Enjuger de Bohun, an inveterate of evil days and uncle of the bishop of Salisbury, who as an excommunicate had the mark of the beast on his forehead, said, 'The only way to deal with such a man is to hang him on a gibbet, twist stiff branches into a crown and crucify him'. William de Mandeville, the nephew of Eudo count of Boulogne, spoke third: 'Once', he said, 'as I was returning from Jerusalem I passed through Rome, and while I was there I asked my host about, among other things, the popes, and was told that a certain pope had been killed for his insolence and intolerable impudence.'[21] When these had finished the king immediately sent William de Mandeville, Saher de Quincy and Roger de Humet into England after these four knights, and it is said that they were ordered to capture the archbishop. Earls William and Saher got as far as the harbour but did not cross, but Richard crossed from another port. The young king was at Winchester, and Richard sent messengers to his guardians, Hugh de Gundeville and William Fitz-John, instructing them to go to Canterbury with knights from the king's household, without informing him. He would lie in wait around the coast, so that if the archbishop tried to flee to any port he would be caught. Earls William and Saher did likewise across the sea, so that if he happened to cross he would be caught there.

49. Thomas prepares for death (*c. 25–27* December 1170)

Herbert of Bosham, *MTB* 3. 484.

On Christmas Day, which, if I am not mistaken, was around the twenty-seventh from our arrival in England,[22] the archbishop ascended the pulpit and delivered a sermon to the people. At the end of the sermon he predicted that the time of his death was at hand, and that he would soon leave his people.[23] And when he made this prediction, tears more than words came forth, and the hearts of those listening

---

21 Possibly Lucius II, who was mortally wounded in 1145 after he led a campaign against his Roman enemies, but a number of other popes met a violent death.

22 This does not tally with Herbert's earlier statement, above, p. 183.

23 William Fitzstephen reports that at this point Thomas said that Canterbury already had one martyr, Elphege, and would soon have another (*MTB* 3. 130).

were also very disturbed and contrite. Throughout the whole church you would have seen and heard the tears and laments of the congregation, who murmured among themselves, 'Father, why do you desert us so soon, and to whom do you leave us the desolate?'[24] For these were not wolves but sheep, who knew the voice of their shepherd,[25] and felt compassion, hearing that their shepherd was soon to leave the world, but not knowing when or how it should happen. But eventually after he had preached at length to the people and predicted his end, no longer crying, no longer weeping, but after the tears, as could be seen and heard, so furious, ardent and bold, he inveighed against the arrogant and hateful men of the land explicitly and by name. Not now, as it seemed, peaceful towards those who hated peace, he did not sheathe the sword in the presence of his enemies, but wielded it boldly and confidently, and in a spirit of ardour struck with anathema many of the courtiers closest to the king, especially that provocative family we have mentioned.[26] And among others he inflicted perpetual anathema on Ranulf de Broc and Robert, who, as we have said above, had mutilated a packhorse in contempt of the archbishop.

Certainly if you had seen these things, you would have immediately said that you had seen and heard in the flesh the prophetic animal who had the face of a man and the face of a lion.[27] After he had done these things, for the rest of the day the archbishop showed himself devoted in the table of God and later at the secular table he displayed his usual good spirits, eating meat as on other days, even though it was a Friday and Christmas Day, pronouncing that on such a day it was more religious to feast than to fast.

But now certain courtiers and others, friends many in number but secretly hidden, intimated to him that his death had been discussed with studied sedition, and so suggested and advised that he should look after himself and forestall traps. The archbishop then with keen sighted faith clearly saw that the land had been stirred up against him, and on the information of the many secret friends, as we have said, believed that traps were now being laid for his death. Therefore the day after Christmas Day, that is the feast of the protomartyr Stephen, he secretly called the disciple who wrote these things to him and said, 'I have decided to send you to our lord king of France and to

24 Sulpicius Severus, *Ep. ad Bassulam, PL* 20. 182.
25 See John 1.14.
26 The de Brocs.
27 See Ezekiel 1.10.

our blessed brother the bishop of Sens, and to other princes of the land, and report to them what you hear and see of our peace: namely, what to us is truly peace, and what is not peace but discord'.

The disciple, unable to control his tears, immediately replied, 'Holy father, why have you decided this, why do you do this? For I know for certain that I will never again see you in the flesh. I offered to stand with you loyally, but as it seems to me, you wish to defraud me of the fruit of your consummation, I who have up to now been with you in your trials. Now I see that I who was a companion in your struggle will not be a companion in your glory'. The archbishop, now bursting into tears, said, 'Not so my son, not so. You who fulfil the instruction of the father and follow his advice will not be deprived of fruit. Still, what you say and lament is true: you will never see me again in the flesh. Even so, I wish you to leave, especially as the king sees you as more troublesome than others in the cause of the Church'.[28]

So, on the third day of Christmas, the feast of St John the Evangelist, in the dead of night on account of suspected traps on the way, in great sorrow, with tears pouring forth, having repeatedly received licence and fatherly blessing, I took my leave of my father, who, as he predicted, I never did nor ever will see again in the flesh. At the end of this history,[29] then, I pray with all my heart, with all my soul and with all my strength, that I be found worthy to see in heaven him who I will never see again in this world, and share in his crown, I who was a companion in the battle.

50. The conspirators gather a force (December 1170)

The knights arrived at Saltwood Castle on the evening of 28 December. The next day they set out for Canterbury where they stopped to dine at St Augustine's Abbey, the abbot of which place, Clarembald, was hostile to Thomas.
William Fitzstephen, *MTB* 3. 131–2.

Now then the knights called up soldiers to garrison the castles around Canterbury, Dover, Rochester, Saltwood and Bletchingley. This was so that, if the archbishop and his men decided to shut themselves up within the church of Canterbury, they could lay siege to them with whatever multitude of soldiers were placed in the vicinity. If the good archbishop

28 This was presumably the central reason for removing Herbert.
29 This is not in fact the end of Herbert's book.

wished to flee, whatever way he came, he would encounter the enemy. And if, by God's zeal, the citizens of Canterbury or the people of the neighbourhood were to rise up in vengeance for the murder against these vagabonds, these evil men could either take refuge in one of the castles, or seek support from these castles to fight in their defence.

So, on the fifth day of Christmas, these four barons of the king with all their men and the de Broc family left Saltwood Castle and came to Canterbury. They added many knights to their number, whom they had called out by edict from the castles and the neighbourhood of Canterbury, as if to the king's service. Of these about twelve went directly to the archbishop's court with the four knights. Meanwhile others made a proclamation throughout the city to the officials and major citizens and commanded on the king's behalf that all the citizens should come with them, armed in the king's service, to the archbishop's house. But when the people of the city, astonished at their madness, objected, they were immediately ordered to hold their peace, and do nothing, no matter what they saw or heard. Their intention was that the inhabitants of the city would help them in their crime, but if not, at least that they would not impede them, or fight for the archbishop.

51. The murder (29 December 1170)

There are five eyewitness accounts of the murder, by William Fitzstephen, John of Salisbury, Benedict of Peterborough, William of Canterbury and Edward Grim. Despite some discrepencies, there is broad agreement on detail, as one would expect of a very memorable event witnessed by many people. Edward Grim's has pride of place because of its influence on other writers, because of its combination of the narrative and the reflective, and not least because of Edward's own supporting role in the episode. For a collation and analysis of the different accounts, see E. Abbott, *St Thomas of Canterbury, his Death and Miracles* (1898), vol. I.

Edward Grim, *MTB* 2. 430-8.

So these men, not knights but miserable wretches, when they first landed, met up with the king's officials who had already been condemned by sentence of anathema. They assembled a force of knights and henchmen from the county, giving the false impression that they were acting on the king's order and in his name. The crime was easily recommended, by this claim that they had come to the business on the king's command. Now gathered together and ready for any impiety,

on the fifth day of Christmas, that is the day after the feast of the Holy
Innocents, they came together against the innocent. The hour of dinner
had finished[30] and the holy man and his servants had withdrawn to an
inner room to transact some business in private while a crowd waited
outside in the hall. At this point the four knights with one attendant
entered. They were met with honour, as servants of the king and well
known. They were invited to table, as those who had served the
archbishop were still dining, but they refused food, thirsting instead
for blood. Thereafter at their instruction it was announced to the archbishop that four men had come who wished to speak to him on behalf
of the king. This was granted and they were introduced, whereupon
they remained in silence for a long time, not greeting the holy archbishop or speaking to him. But nor did the man of great counsel greet
them immediately as they entered, so that, as it says in the scriptures,
'By your words you will be justified',[31] from their questioning he
might discover the inner desire of their hearts. But after an interval
he turned to them, and carefully examining the face of each, he greeted
them in peace. But the evil men, who had made a contract with death,
immediately responded to his greeting with curses, and sarcastically
prayed for God to help him. At these bitter and malicious words the
man of God flushed deeply, now fully aware the men had come with a
passion for doing harm.

Therefore he who seemed to be the leader and more ready to sin than
the others, FitzUrse, breathing fury burst out in these words: 'We
have something to say to you on the king's orders; if you wish us to
say it before all, speak'. But the archbishop knowing what they were
about to say, said, 'These things are not to be uttered in private nor in
the chamber, but in public'. But the wretches burned so much for the
murder of the archbishop, that if the doorkeeper had not called back
the clerks – for the archbishop had ordered them all to leave – they
would, as they later confessed, have impaled him on the staff of the
cross which stood nearby. When those who had withdrawn had returned, he who had earlier slandered the man of God now said, 'Peace
was made between you, the king sent you back free to your own see,
and all disputes were settled, as you requested. But you violated the
agreed peace and now perversely and arrogantly, adding insult to
injury, you occupy yourself in evil against your lord. For with stubborn pride you condemned with sentence of suspension those who

30 The knights arrived around 3 pm.
31 See Matthew 12.37.

assisted in crowning the king's son, and raised him to kingly honour, and you also tied with the chain of anathema the servants of the king by whose counsel and wisdom the business of the realm is conducted. From this it is clear that you would take the crown away from the king's son, if you had the means. But now everyone knows how you have laboured to bring to effect that which you have contrived against your lord. Therefore if you deign to respond to these charges in the presence of the king, say so. That is why we have been sent.'

The archbishop replied, 'It never was my wish, as God is my witness, to take the crown away from my lord the king's son, or to diminish his power. Rather I wish he had three crowns, and I would help him to conquer the greatest realms of the earth, according to reason and fairness. But it is unfair for the lord king to be angry with me, as you suggest, if my men accompany me through cities and towns, and if those who were because of my proscription denied the comfort of my presence for seven years now come out to meet me. And indeed now, where it pleases him, I am ready to make amends to my lord, if I offended in any way. But he has forbidden me with threats from entering his cities and towns and even villages. Besides, it was by no means by me, but by the lord pope, that the bishops were suspended from office'. 'They were suspended by you', said the furious men, 'now you must absolve them!' 'I do not deny', he said, 'that it was indeed done through me, but it is beyond me, and entirely incongruous with my rank, to absolve those whom the pope had bound. Let them go to him, to whom flows the contempt shown to me and their mother church of Christ, Canterbury.'

'Now then', said the executioners, 'this is the king's command, that you and all your men leave the kingdom and the lands over which he has dominion. For neither you nor any of your men will have peace from this day on, you who violated the peace'. To this he said, 'Cease your threats and quiet your brawling. I trust in the King of heaven Who suffered for His people on the cross. From this day forth no one will see the sea between me and my church. I did not come back to flee. He who seeks me will find me here. But the king ought not make such demands. I and my men have had enough insults thrown at us without further threats.' 'This your king ordered', they said, 'and this we will make good. For you who ought to have bowed to royal majesty, and deferred vengeance to his judgement, followed the decree of your furious passion, and disgracefully cast the ministers and servants out of the church.' To whom the athlete of Christ, standing up to his slanderers in fervour of spirit, said, 'I will not spare anyone, no matter who he is, who presumes to violate the traditions of the Holy Roman See or the laws of Christ's Church, and does not voluntarily make amends, nor will I hesitate to correct the offender with ecclesiastical censure'. Struck by these words the knights sprang to their feet, not bearing any further the constancy of his response. Coming near they said, 'We warn you that you have spoken in danger to your head'. 'Have you come to kill me then?', he said. 'I have committed my cause to the Judge of all, so I am not moved by threats, nor are your swords more ready to strike than my soul is ready for martyrdom. Look all you like for one who will run away; for you will find me foot to foot in the battle of the Lord.' Therefore as these left amid confusion and insults, he who was appropriately called 'The Bear',[32] savagely cried out, 'In the king's name we command you, clerks and monks, to seize and hold this man, so that he does not escape by flight before the king exacts full justice on his body'. As they left therefore with these words the man of God followed them to the door and called to them, 'Here, here you will find me', putting his hand on his neck, as if showing beforehand where they would strike.[33]

He returned then to the place where he had earlier been sitting, and consoled his men in the Lord, and told them not to fear. And as it seemed to us who were there, he settled down as undaunted, he who alone was being sought to be killed, as if they had come to invite him to a wedding. Soon after the butchers returned in hauberks with swords, axes and hatchets, and other weapons suitable for the crime which they had conceived in their minds to carry out. And when they found the doors had been barred and unopened when they knocked, they turned aside by a more private approach through an orchard to a wooden

32 FitzUrse.

33 Benedict of Peterborough reports that Thomas followed the departing knights to the door of the chamber, and called out to Hugh de Morville to return to speak to him. The knights continued on their way, and Thomas returned to his place, complaining of their words. 'One of his clerks, master John of Salisbury, an erudite man, of great eloquence and profound counsel, and what is more than these, grounded in fear and love of God, gave such a response to the complainer: "Lord", he said, "it is a matter of great wonder, that you accept no advice. And why did a man of such excellence find it necessary to rise to the exasperation of their malevolence and follow them to the door? Surely it would have been better to take counsel with these who are present and then to give a milder response to those who are aiming to carry out whatever evil they can against you, and catch you out by provoking you to anger." But the saint who yearned for the pain of death for the sake of justice and the liberty of the Church, as if for the pleasure of rest, said, "All your advice has now been received. I know well enough what I ought to do". And Master John replied, "Would that, by God's assent, it is good"' (*MTB* 2. 9).

partition, which they split open, cut down and demolished. Terrified by the fearful and uproarious din the servants and almost all the clerks were scattered this way and that, like sheep before wolves. Those who remained called out for him to flee into the church, but he, mindful of his former promise that he would not in fear of death run away from the killers of the flesh, refused flight. For in such a case one ought not flee from city to city,[34] but rather give an example to his people that everyone should prefer to succumb to the swords rather than see divine law scorned and the sacred canons subverted. But equally, he who had for a long time burned with love of martyrdom, having attained, as it seemed, an opportunity to fulfil it, feared lest it be deferred or even pass him by completely if he fled to the church. The monks persisted, saying that it was not right for him to be absent from vespers, which were just then being celebrated in the church. He remained immobile in the place of less reverence, determined to await the happy hour of his consummation which he had longed for with many sighs and sought with much devotion, lest, as has been said, the reverence of the sacred church prevent even the impious from their purpose and cheat the holy man of his heart's desire. For, sure that after martyrdom he would cross over from this misery, after he had returned from exile, he is reported to have said in the hearing of many, 'Here you have a martyr beloved of God and a true saint, Elphege. Divine compassion will provide you with another, and it will not be long'. What a sincere and untroubled conscience had the good shepherd, who in the cause and protection of his flock did not wish to postpone his own death, when he could have, nor evade the executioner, so that satiated with the blood of the shepherd, the fury of the wolves might keep away from the sheep. Then when neither by argument nor pleas could he be persuaded to take refuge in the church, the monks seized him unwilling and resisting, dragged, carried and pushed him, not heeding with how much protest he tried to get them to let him go, and guided him right up to the church. But the door, through which one entered the monks' cloister, had been carefully barred many days before, and now with the executioners pressing on their heels, all hope of escape seemed to be gone. Nevertheless one of them rushed up, took hold of the bolt, and to the great astonishment of all, he pulled it back with as much ease as if it were only stuck with glue.[35]

34 See Matthew 10.23.

35 In Benedict's version, two cellarers, Richard and William, heard the disturbance and rushed to the cloister, where they drew back the bolt from the other side (*MTB* 2. 11).

But as soon as the monks had withdrawn within the doors of the church, the four said knights followed on their heels with swift strides. Along with them was a certain subdeacon, armed with the same malice as the knights, called Mauclerk, fittingly on account of his worthlessness,[36] who showed no reverence to God or the saints, as what followed proved. When the holy archbishop entered the monastery, the monks broke off the vespers which they had begun to offer to God, and ran up to him glorifying God, now seeing their father, whom they had heard was dead, alive and unharmed.[37] And bolting the folding-door of the church they made haste to keep off the enemy from the killing of the shepherd. But the wonderful athlete turned to them and ordered them to open the doors of the church, saying, 'It is not right to turn the house of prayer, the church of Christ, into a fortress which, even if it is not closed is enough of a defence for its children. And we will triumph over the enemy not by fighting but by suffering, for we have come to suffer, not to resist'.[38] Without delay, the sacrilegious men came into the house of peace and reconciliation with swords drawn, instilling terror in the onlookers by the sight of them and the clatter of armour alone.[39] Those who were present were disturbed and shaken – for now those who had been singing vespers

36 Hugh of Horsea, called 'Mauclerk', i.e. 'evil clerk'.

37 William of Canterbury adds: 'As the monks were duly celebrating vespers, two boys ran up through the middle of them and announced, more by their fear than by what they said, the entrance of the enemy. Some of the brothers continued in their prayers, some tried to escape, and some tried to help. But one of the brothers went out and said, "Come in, father, come in. Stay with us, so that if it is necessary, we may suffer together and be glorified together. May we who were deprived by your absence be consoled by your presence"' (*MTB* 1. 131).

38 Benedict writes, 'But the holy father turned back and upbraided [the monks] straight away, saying, "Let my people enter". And he rushed up and opened the door, and thrusting aside the men who were standing by the folding-doors, with his most sacred hands he dragged his people, who had been abandoned to the jaws of the wolves outside, into the church, saying, "Come in, come in, quickly!"'.

39 William Fitzstephen describes how 'Reginald FitzUrse came in first wearing a hauberk, with his sword drawn, shouting, "This way, king's men!" Shortly after, his three companions joined him, likewise wearing hauberks, with their heads and bodies covered in armour, except for their eyes, and their swords drawn. Many others followed from among their followers and companions, armed but without hauberk, and some from the city of Canterbury, whom they had compelled to come with them'. He adds the reaction of the clerks: 'As [the archbishop] went down the steps to prevent the door from being closed, John of Salisbury and all the clerks, apart from Robert the canon, and William Fitzstephen, and Edward Grim, who had come to him recently, looking for protection, and concerned with their own safety, abandoned the bishop, and made for the altar, or other hiding-places' (*MTB* 3. 139). William of Canterbury admits how he took to flight, but at a slightly later stage (*MTB* 1. 133–4).

had hurried to the deadly spectacle – and in a spirit of fury the knights cried out, 'Where is Thomas Becket, traitor to the king and the kingdom?' When he did not respond they shouted with greater vehemence, 'Where is the archbishop?' To this call unafraid, and as is written, 'The righteous will be brave as a lion without fear',[40] he came forward from the steps where he had been carried by the monks in fear of the knights, and in a perfectly clear voice answered, 'Here I am, no traitor to the king, but a priest. What do you want from me?'[41] And he who had earlier already said that he did not fear them said, 'See, I am ready to suffer in the name of Him who redeemed me with His blood. Far be it that on account of your swords I flee or withdraw from righteousness.' This said, he turned to the right, under a pillar, with the altar of the blessed mother of God and ever Virgin Mary on one side, and on the other that of the holy confessor Benedict. By their example and support, now that he had been crucified to the world and its desires, he suffered and overcame whatever the butchers did to him with as much constancy of spirit as if he were not present in the flesh. Following him the butchers said, 'Absolve and restore to communion those you excommunicated, and return to office those you have suspended'. He said to them, 'No satisfaction has been made, so I will not absolve them'. 'Then', they said, 'you will now die and get what you deserve'. 'Then', he said, 'I am prepared to die for my Lord so that in my blood the Church may find liberty and peace, but I forbid you in the name of Almighty God to harm my men, whether clerk or lay, in any way.' How piously did the illustrious martyr provide for his men, how prudently for himself, lest a bystander be harmed, an innocent crushed, lest an unhappier outcome for a bystander obscure his glory as he hastened to Christ. It was quite fitting that the soldier martyr should follow in the footsteps of his Captain and Saviour, Who when he was being sought by the wicked said, 'If you seek me let these men go'.[42]

Therefore they rushed at him and laid their sacrilegious hands on him, roughly manhandling and dragging him, intending to kill him outside the church, or carry him away in chains, as they later admitted.

40 See Proverbs 28.1.

41 John of Salisbury and William Fitzstephen give the knights' answer as 'your death' (*MTB* 2. 319, 3. 140).

42 John 18.8. William of Canterbury and Benedict say that during this altercation one of the knights struck off the archbishop's cap (*MTB* 1. 133, 2. 12). According to William Fitzstephen, one of the knights struck Thomas between the shoulder with the flat of his sword, saying 'Flee, you are a dead man' (*MTB* 3. 141).

But since he could not easily be moved from the pillar, one of them attached himself and applied himself particularly fiercely. The archbishop pushed him away, calling him a pimp, and said, 'Do not touch me, Reginald, you who by right owe me fealty and obedience. You and your accomplices are acting like fools.'[43] But the knight was inflamed with terrible fury at this rebuff, and brandishing his sword against the consecrated crown said, 'I do not owe you fealty or obedience against fidelity to my lord king'. The invincible martyr seeing then that the hour was at hand when the miseries of mortal life would be ended, and that the crown of immortality prepared for him and promised to him by the Lord was now within reach, bent his head in the manner of prayer, joined his hands together and lifted them up, and commended his cause and that of the Church to God, St Mary and the blessed martyr Denis.[44]

Hardly had he said the words than the evil knight,[45] fearing that he would be snatched by the people and escape alive, suddenly leapt on him and wounded God's sacrificial lamb in the head, cutting off the top of the crown, which the oil of holy chrism had dedicated to God. The same blow almost cut off the arm of this witness who, as everyone fled, monks and clerks, steadfastly stood by the archbishop, and held him in his arms until his arm was struck. Behold the simplicity of the dove, behold the wisdom of the serpent,[46] in this martyr, who offered his body to the persecutors, so that he preserve unharmed his head, that is his soul and the Church, nor did he devise a defence or trap against the killers of the flesh! O worthy shepherd who, lest the sheep be torn to pieces, so bravely presented himself to the jaws of the wolves! Because he had abandoned the world, the world wishing to crush him unconsciously raised him up. Then he received another blow in the head but still remained immoveable.[47] But at the third blow he bent his knees and elbows, offering himself as a living sacrifice, saying in a low voice, 'For the name of Jesus and the well-being of the Church

43 Herbert of Bosham (not an eyewitness) writes that Thomas 'rebuked the gladiators with all authority for entering their mother church with such irregularity and profanity, and with his hand he quickly seized one of them, who had approached him, and shook him through his hauberk with such force, that he almost flattened him on the pavement. This was William de Tracy, as he later confessed' (*MTB* 3. 492–3).

44 Fitzstephen adds the name of Elphege (*MTB* 3. 141).

45 William of Canterbury agrees that this was FitzUrse, but Fitzstephen identifies William de Tracy as striking the first blow (*MTB* 1. 133–4; 3. 141).

46 See Matthew 10.16.

47 This seems to have been from de Tracy.

I am prepared to embrace death'. But as he lay prostrate the third knight[48] inflicted a grave wound. With this blow the sword was dashed on the pavement, and the crown, which was large, was separated from the head, so that the blood white from the brain, and the brain equally red from the blood, brightened the floor with the colours of the lily and the rose, the virgin and mother, and the life and death of the confessor and martyr.[49] The fourth knight[50] warded off those arriving on the scene so that the others could carry out their murder more freely and wantonly. But the fifth, not a knight but a clerk who had come in with the knights,[51] so that a fifth stroke was not lacking to the martyr who in other things had imitated Christ,[52] put his foot on the neck of the holy priest and precious martyr, and, horrible to say, scattered the brains with the blood over the pavement. 'Let us go, knights', he called out to the others, 'this fellow will not get up again.'

52. Aftermath to the murder (29–30 December 1170)

Benedict of Peterborough, *MTB* 2. 14–16.

Then the workmen of evil, driven no less by thirst for greed than intoxicated by the pouring of innocent blood, as quickly as possible ran back to the archbishop's palace with their accomplices. Some violently dragged horses out of the stables, others struck his servants, others turned over all the household goods, destroying chests and cabinets and dividing among themselves as they wished whatever they could find of gold or silver, clothes or various ornaments. In this way, then, it pleased divine piety, which powerfully and wisely arranges all things, that the imitators of those who divided Christ's clothes would liken more fully the passion of the servant to the passion of the Lord. In this way, by the manifest similarity of things, it would be recognised by all the faithful that the Church would be delivered from the servitude of the world through the blood of the martyr, just as it

---

48 Le Bret (*MTB* 3. 142).

49 Medieval writers identify two types of martyrdom: red, representing a violent death for Christ, and white, that of the 'confessor', who does not suffer such a fate, but in his life endures a 'living martyrdom'. A number of biographers refer to mingling of the two in Thomas's death: see J. O'Reilly, '"Candidus et Rubicundus", an Image of Martyrdom in the "Lives" of Thomas Becket', *Analecta Bollandiana*, 99 (1981), 303–4.

50 De Morville.

51 Hugh Mauclerk.

52 A reference to the five wounds of Christ.

was rescued from the power of the devil through the death of Christ. These men took all the church's deeds and privileges and handed them over to that son of perdition Ranulf de Broc, to be passed to the king in Normandy. This was so that any which seemed contrary to the customs of his realm, and to protect either the liberty of the universal Church or the privileges of the church of Canterbury, could at his pleasure be torn to pieces or shut up never to be seen. So much for the knights.

When the body had been raised from the ground, then, an iron mallet and a hatchet, left behind by the parricides, were found beneath him, of which the archbishop had taken possession when it fell on the ground, as if appropriated to himself. In this way he figuratively demonstrated that he was to be a hammer of the wicked, and that whoever did not turn to penitence could not escape the sentence of his vengeance. And while blood in the likeness of a crown, perhaps in a sign of sanctity, lay around his head, his face nevertheless seemed entirely free from blood, except for a thin line, which descended from the right temple to the left cheek crossing the nose. Indeed with this mark he later appeared in visions to many who knew nothing at all about this, who otherwise not mentioning it, described it as if they had seen it with their own eyes. As he still lay on the pavement then, some daubed their eyes with blood, others who had brought little vessels made away with as much as they could, while others eagerly dipped in parts of their clothes they had cut off. Later no one seemed happy with themselves unless they had taken something away, however insignificant, from this precious treasure. And indeed with everything disturbed and confused, everyone was able to do as he wished. But part of the blood which they had left to the church, was carefully collected in a most elegant vessel and replaced in the church to be preserved. His pallium and outer garment, as they were stained with blood, were given to paupers on behalf of his soul with indiscreet piety. They would have been happy enough, had they not ill-advisedly sold them immediately for a low price. So that lamentable night was spent in sorrow, in groans and sighs, and not for the moment either conscious of joy or ignorant of sadness, they awaited a greater evil the next day.

The next day, many armed men again gathered outside the city wall, and the rumour spread among the people that they had come together from everywhere with the intention of a greater atrocity: that they would seize the body from the bosom of the mother church and either pull it asunder through the city behind horses, or hang it on a gibbet, or tear it to pieces in bits or little particles and dispatch it in a swamp, or some other viler place which is not fitting to be named, more contemptible to God and the Church, saying that the body of a traitor ought not be interred among holy bishops.

The monks then, as fearful for themselves as for the saint, afraid that his body would be taken away to a filthier place, and that they would lose their precious treasure, took steps to bury him with great haste. Therefore they neither washed his most holy body, nor embalmed it according to the custom of the holy church of Canterbury. This came about less on account of human evil than divine piety, for what need has he for more common perfume, for whom the Lord has supplied the unction of his own blood? They were taking off his outer garments to put on his pontifical vestments when they discovered that his body was covered with a hairshirt. It was not only painful on account of its harshness[53] and – something we do not read about or hear of from any other saint – it went from his drawers right down to his knees, beneath a monastic habit. The monks looked at each other, and were astonished at this view of hidden religion beyond what could have been believed, and with their sorrow thus multiplied, so were their tears.

53. The beginning of the miracles (early 1171)

One of the earliest mentions of the miracles comes from John of Salisbury: 'In the place where Thomas suffered, and where he lay the night through, before the high altar, awaiting burial, and where he was buried at last, the palsied are cured, the blind see, the deaf hear, the dumb speak, the lame walk, folk suffering from fevers are cured, the lepers are cleansed, those possessed of a devil are freed, and the sick are made whole from all manner of disease, blasphemers taken over by the devil are put to confusion' (*LJS* no. 305, pp. 736–7; *MTB* no. 748, 7. 462–70; see Matthew 11.5; 10.8). Reports of miracles seem to have emerged immediately among the townspeople of Canterbury, but the cult really took off after Easter 1171.

William Fitzstephen, *MTB* 3. 149–50, 151–2.

Immediately after the observance of burial, on the same night that same week, the working of divine power showed itself, and such a great martyrdom was deservedly made known. For one of the townspeople of Canterbury, who was present among others as a spectator at his martyrdom, dipped part of his shirt in the saint's blood. His wife was

53 As reported by others, it was also covered with lice.

now long since paralysed. When the man returned home she learned from him – narrated with floods of tears and a confused voice – the extraordinary passion and constancy of the holy martyr, and she saw with her own eyes the holy blood on the man's clothes. With devoted faith in the Lord, greater hope for her health, and humble hope in the martyr, she asked to be washed, and the blood to be mixed in the water, so that she derive health and benefit. So it was done, and she was cured there and then. This was the first sign God performed on behalf of his martyr, immediately that very night. From this I believe it happened by God's inspiration, that the blood of St Thomas came to be dipped in water, and that mixture of blood and water came to distributed to the pilgrims to St Thomas in tin ampules to be carried back for the health of their infirm. I myself saw the inscription on many phials, *Bottle containing the blood of Thomas mixed with water.* And indeed with God working for the desire of the faithful, and with the support of the holy martyr, and deserving faith, for which nothing is impossible, that blood mixed with water not only succeeded in curing innumerable sick, but prevented the mortally ill from dying. Not only that, I say, and it should well be believed, but it also succeeded in bringing some back from the dead ...[54]

A great volume exists concerning his miracles in England, on the testimony of priests and good men, which is publicly read out in the chapter of the church of Canterbury. There are also others far and wide, in France, in Ireland and whatever lands to which St Thomas has devoted himself, which were committed to memory but not written down.

But these de Brocs made threats by day, and stood by night by the walls of the inns of Canterbury, so as to arrest anyone speaking well of the archbishop and summon them to their tribunal. At first the faithful did not dare to speak of the great works of God except privately, until in virtue of the Holy Spirit the cures and the throngs of people became so plentiful that charity banished fear. The plotters, who first had intercepted those visiting him during his life or after his martyrdom at the bridges and crossroads, said 'This is no use. No counsel can avail against the Lord.[55] See, all England goes to him.' There, for the glory of His name, for the consolation of His Church, to the corroboration of our faith, God shows how innocent blood shed cried out to Him from the pavement of the church, and so in miracles He glorifies His martyr and justifies his cause.

54 William relates some other early miracles.
55 Proverbs 21.30.

54. Miracles

The first two miracles included here are from Benedict of Peterborough's collection, the second two from William of Canterbury's. Both were custodians of the shrine, where they heard and recorded stories from those who claimed to have felt Thomas's posthumous power. Benedict was the first custodian, but William's collection came to be the official one, and was even presented to King Henry on behalf of the Canterbury monks. The miracles selected here illustrate some of the most common features of the collections as a whole: miracles of reward, protection, warning and vengeance; the inclusion of names and circumstantial detail; the association of Thomas with other saints; the central role of the shrine and the 'water of St Thomas'.

Benedict of Peterborough, *MTB* 2. 156, 224–5; William of Canterbury, *MTB* 1. 206–7, 308–9.

A young man from the port of Dover called Curbaran, who earned his living as a shoemaker, in his wonderful and pure innocence was accustomed to pray to God every day for the soul of the holy martyr, not knowing that to pray on behalf of a martyr is an insult. When he did not cease from doing so, the saint deigned him worthy to receive a visit from him in a dream, saying, 'Curbaran, are you awake or asleep?' When Curbaran replied that he was awake, the saint referred to a certain mill, and asked him, 'Do you know this mill?' 'Yes, I know it, sir', replied the youth, 'and who are you?' 'I', he replied, 'am Thomas archbishop of Canterbury. Go to that mill and take what you find under the elder-tree, for it is right that at least in some way I reward you for your devotion'. He got up at daybreak, and following the Lord's command, 'First seek the kingdom of God and his justice',[56] he went to church to pray. Leaving the church he remembered the vision, and made his way to the mill. Straight away he found under the elder-tree a heavy gold coin covered in rust. He thought it was made of brass or copper, but he showed it to one more astute, who bit it between his teeth and realised it was gold. When the rust was carefully cleaned off it was discovered to bear the image and inscription of Emperor Diocletian. Of the best and purest gold, and weighing as much as five silver coins, it was worth no doubt more than forty silver coins.

*   *   *

Among other things about the blessed and glorious friend of God Thomas that we also read about St Martin,[57] is that not only did Martin

56 See Matthew 6.33.

57 Martin of Tours (*c.* 316–97) was one of the most popular saints of the middle ages. His legend afforded certain comparisons with Thomas: he experienced a conver-

perform miracles, but also many were performed in Martin's name. Let me say first what happened to me. Necessity forced me to set out on a journey by night with only one companion attending me, when we were met by three dogs barking fearfully and following us in a menacing way, to our great terror. With God as my witness I say that I was very afraid that they would either harm me, or drag the boy off his horse and tear him to pieces, for it is natural for a dog to slaver for a bite more by night than by day. I happened to remember that in the Life of St Martin I had read of someone who stopped the mouths of barking dogs in his name,[58] so I turned to the dogs and said, 'In the name of St Thomas, be silent!' As I speak before God in Christ, so suddenly were all silent, that not one of them let out another bark – you would have thought that their mouths had suddenly been blocked up or their tongues cut out – and they fled as if with those words they had suffered lashes. I was astonished that the very same thing happened to me the following night. But, with God as my witness, I do not speak of this on my own account, nor do I seek my own glory but that of the martyr. For Roger the monk also, who had similarly been deputed to have custody of the holy body, found equally or more remarkable examples.

*   *   *

This is the story of a wounded boy who was freed from terrible danger. The boy, Geoffrey, a native of Winchester, son of Robert and Laetitia, was around sixteen months old when he began to burn up with fever. But when he drank the water of St Thomas, to his parents' delight, his temperature immediately dropped. But this unexpected happiness was clouded over with sorrow. For when the boy's mother was sitting on her own in the house, a wall of the house shook and collapsed from top to bottom on top of the child, who was asleep in his cradle. The wall was made of stone, and had measured thirteen feet in height, and it shattered the cradle, which was made of embossed and interwoven planks, into eighteen pieces. Some of the fragments splintered deep into the ground. It was thought that the wall had fallen because of a storm the previous day, but we believe that the Holy of Holies arranged it for the glorification of His saint. When the mother saw her child

---

sion from secular, as a bishop he retained the life of a monk, he was engaged in disputes with the secular power, and he was a prodigious miracle-worker. See C. Stancliffe, *St Martin and his Hagiographer; History and Miracle in Sulpicius Severus* (Oxford, 1983).

58 Sulpicius Severus, *Dialogues* iii, 3.

buried in the chasm, she cried out, 'St Thomas, save the boy whom you returned to me', and as she cried out, she fainted for sorrow. Wonderful is the kindness of the saint, wonderful the kindness of the unconquered martyr, who immediately took heed of the pious mother, and kept the boy safe from death, though covered by three or four cartloads of masonry. For as the boy was being snatched away from ruin, and his mother snatched away from sorrow, two men came in, put the mother back on her feet and heard the reason for her grief. They called for help, dislodged the heap of rubble, and found the cradle shattered into little pieces. They lifted out the boy, wonderful to report, unhurt in any way, and even laughing happily, with no sign of damage on his whole body, besides a small bruise next to his eye which could hardly be seen. Time went on, and the parents deferred their repayment of the bountiful favour of the martyr by which they were bound, when the boy, claimed in place of the debt, began to sicken. And it happened that one day a certain woman came to the boy's grandmother and said, 'It has been revealed to me that for the boy's sake you should go to visit the tomb of the blessed Thomas. Know that this revelation has come from God. For I do not say this for the sake of profit or any other dishonourable reason. Rather, I am an envoy of divine admonition'. So, after a little, the boy came to Canterbury, and we were told this story.

*   *   *

An Irish boy called Colonius, sought and received money from his presiding brothers for the blessed martyr Thomas. He left the monastery, intending to purchase a phial,[59] and stopped at the shop, when he came upon a phial which had by chance been dropped by the vendor. He stealthily picked it up, and retaining the money which he had received to buy the phial, he withdrew. He hung it, filled with holy water, around his neck, and made his way to his companions who were waiting to meet him in a cemetery, when suddenly a tumour grew on his neck. Finding it difficult to breathe, he put his hand to his neck, and was astonished at the growth of his swelling throat, not yet knowing the cause. Almost suffocated, he racked his brains, and eventually remembered the theft. The theft of that which belonged to someone else disquieted his conscience. 'What wretched thing have I done?' he said. 'The martyr is acting on the vendor's behalf: he persecutes the thief and does not know the pilgrim. Why do I delay? Delay in repenting the theft brings danger.' So he returned to the martyr, and on his

59 See above, p. 206.

return he met the dean of the Irish, to whom he said, 'Receive my confession. Look, I am suffocating, because I, a wretch, have hung this phial on my neck and there have developed this enormous tumour'. As he knew the order of the matter, he made penance before the martyr, and taking the stolen phial, the cause of the tumour, off his neck, he hung it where the martyr fell. And when the mediator prayed for him, he recovered.

55. Pilgrimage to Canterbury

On the growth of such shrines, see, for example, B. Nilson, *Cathedral Shrines of Medieval England* (Woodbridge, 1998); D. Webb, *Pilgrims and Pilgrimage in the Medieval West* (London, 1999).

The Lambeth Anonymous, *MTB* 4. 140–1.

Without question his glory came to be multiplied far beyond the injury inflicted. For, to be brief, the report of wonders not only reached the innermost and outermost corners of England, but also spread rapidly through many people of foreign races. It roused cities, towns, villages and even huts everywhere in England to such an extent that from the lowliest up to the greatest, few remained who did not come to see and honour the tomb of the famous martyr. Ordained and lay, poor and rich, commoners and nobles, fathers and mothers with children, lords with their households, all went there, drawn by the same spirit of devotion. The streets which led to Canterbury were so crowded with the throng of those working in stalls and shops and those coming and going, that almost everywhere it seemed as busy as a marketplace. Nights hardly less than days, winters hardly less than summers, slowed down the travellers' journey. For in a harsher time the more difficult it was, the sweeter it was considered to honour the promise to visit, because where the approach was more difficult the hope of reward was greater. Equally a great concourse of pilgrims went there from remote regions overseas, so that they differed little in number from the natives, and – as great men worthy of belief who visited holy places through-out the world witness – neither the seat of the blessed Peter, nor the memorial of James the Greater[60] or any other saint, nor indeed that glorious sepulchre of Christ, were so continuously or more crowded with men, or in offering was veneration more clear to be seen.

60 Santiago de Compostela.

56. The fate of the guilty (1171–72)

The young King Henry must have been one of the first to hear of Thomas's murder. His sorrow is said to have been mixed with relief that none of his men were involved. His father, who learned of the murder on New Year's Day had no such cause for relief, and his distress is well testified. Just after Christmas 1170 Henry had sent a mission to the pope. Negotiations were quickly halted when news reached the pope of the archbishop's death. Perhaps the first to inform the pope were Thomas's clerks Alexander Llewelyn and Gunter of Winchester, who travelled to Italy with letters from King Louis, Count Theobald of Blois, and Archbishop William of Sens. The pope is reported to have spent a week in mourning, during which time he was unable to bear even the sight of an Englishman. This is the fullest account of the fate of the murderers, but the details of their lives after 1170 remain sketchy. It seems that shortly after the murder they fled to London and then travelled to Yorkshire where they took refuge in Knaresborough Castle, which was held by Hugh de Morville. It was probably in August 1171 that they sought the king's advice. Then, after a period of consultation with the pope through the agency of Bartholomew of Exeter, they reached Rome by spring 1172.

The Lansdowne Anonymous, *MTB* 4. 159.

The world could not be silent about the passion of the most blessed Thomas, because even had men been silent, rocks and stones would have cried out. When they first heard of so great an act of wickedness, people shuddered at the report but did not immediately believe it until witness after witness confirmed that the fateful business had been done. As the common proverb puts it, 'What everyone sings about is rarely untrue'.

The very day of the passion of the blessed Thomas, some Canterbury monks approached the sea, and lest their journey be prevented by those who observed the ports, they immediately crossed the sea in order to announce to the most auspicious Pope Alexander the abominable deed unheard of in our time, indeed in any time. Their journey was steered so well by Thomas that they suffered not one injury. Nor were ministers of the devil lacking, who scoffed at his passion and reported the matter as a triumph, as if they were congratulating King Henry of England for a victory. But when the king heard the report he rightly suspected that the disgrace of the murder and betrayal of the archbishop would fester into a blemish on his person and disgrace to his descendents. For however much, as is said, he himself did not order it, it is clear nevertheless that he did not prohibit it, but rather by his words provoked his attendants to the act. For this reason then he was deeply grieved, just as David at the death of Saul or at the killing of Abner,[61] but for a different reason. For David grieved because his enemies fell, King Henry because he knew that the death of a friend, indeed his greatest friend, would be ascribed to him. For although the king was his enemy, he was the king's dearest friend, and although different things had caused them sorrow, the grief was the same. When, then, the king heard of the infamous death of the archbishop, whom he had granted peace on his return to England, and whom he had taken back into his friendship with witnesses and solemn promises, he was so upset that he neither gave an answer to this report, nor spoke to anyone that day, but withdrew to a chamber and did not take food until evening, and lamented like David lamenting his son Absalom,[62] so alarmed was he. But fresh sorrow tends to be more intense in the beginning, while the passage of time pardons men. Likewise, lingering infamy at first inspires shame, but when lasting and accustomed it is replaced by contempt. 'Guilt itself', says the poet, 'inspires wrath and insolence.'[63]

[...][64]

The king who, as we have said, was so distraught in the immediate aftermath of the murder, now, at the instigation of evil men, and as if it were appropriate for a king, he hardly sorrowed, or not at all, or else he hid his sorrow completely. For he ordered the sea ports and shores to be carefully watched, so no monk or clerk or other suspect person could leave England who would make this crime known, at Rome or elsewhere. But in a wonderful way, afraid to become known, the news became known more widely. Still, we would have preferred to excuse the king from this crime, had he not welcomed these abominable authors of death in his realm, had he not allowed them to go through his cities and towns, had he not permitted them to hunt in his forests and drives, had he not looked after them, had he not protected them. Perhaps he did this because he understood that these attendants had done what they had done out of love or fear of him.

When the king heard of the great works of God and the wonders which He was carrying out through His holy martyr Thomas, he did not believe them, but prohibited men by royal majesty from appealing to the holy martyr, arrested his men who went to the tomb, and had everyone who went to Canterbury observed. Nevertheless, since 'the

61 See 1 Samuel 1.11–27; 2 Samuel 3.31–9.

62 See 2 Samuel 18.33–19.4.

63 Juvenal, *Satires* vi. 285.

64 The Anonymous expands upon this point.

sin of many always goes unpunished',[65] he acquiesced eventually. But as is said — would that it were not said and it were not true — he threatened revenge on the body of the holy martyr or on the church of Canterbury, so far did the evil whisperers and serpentine instigators provoke him. But when He desired, God changed this counsel, or rather impulse, for the better, and as a wise prince he recoiled from such a plan. He did not threaten anything further of this kind, but instead ordered the prior of Canterbury[66] and the other brothers to give him some of the gold, silver and other offerings which had been brought to the holy martyr. But thanks to God, he quickly retreated from this exaction, for day by day the Lord softened the heart of the king to penitence and belief. Because, as Solomon said, he who is credulous is of paltry spirit,[67] and similarly he who never believes is obstinate, the king did not believe immediately, but nor did he never believe. Instead, wishing to examine how things would turn out, for the moment he held his counsel.

But how much discredit was incurred by everyone English on pilgrimage anywhere, how much infamy was heaped on us is not easy to say. They were called traitors, they were called rogues and assassins and killers of their bishops, and while a small portion of the English were guilty of such reproach, the crime rebounded on the whole mass. Clerical philosophers too were expelled from France with great dishonour and confusion, and that poetic reading was fulfilled, 'Kings go astray, and the Greeks are punished'.[68]

Indeed the most Christian king of France, and the archbishops and bishops and earls and barons, mediators and guarantors between the lord King Henry of England and lord Archbishop Thomas, sent letters and epistles containing complaint and calumny, demanding why such an outrage against their guarantee he had either himself committed or had allowed to be done through his attendants, since he neither condemned nor banished the contrivers of the crime when he could have done so. And now with threats, now with insistent warnings they instructed him either to purge himself of this charge or make appropriate satisfaction to the Catholic Church, and if he refused, he would have them as adversaries and common enemies for ever. The king answered that he had neither ordered nor wished the crime to be

65 Lucan, *Civil War* v. 260.

66 Odo.

67 Unidentified.

68 Horace, *Epistles* I. ii. 14.

committed, and that he sought to defend neither the deed nor the perpetrators, and in this matter he would do whatever he had to do. But since compurgation could not be undergone, nor compensation be settled without the pope, everyone waited on the wish and command of Pope Alexander. The king knew that he could not make amends to the Church or earn peace or forgiveness unless he punished these traitors and delivered them to Satan for the punishment of the flesh, so that their spirit may be saved in the day of the Lord,[69] but was unwilling to inflict this on them, because they had committed the crime, if not through him, at least on his behalf. Therefore he either ordered or advised them to withdraw into Scotland and to lie low there in peace according to the custom of the country. But when the guilty men went to Scotland, they were driven out by the king of Scotland and his men, good Christians, and if the dread and authority of the king of England had not stood in the way, they would have been hanged on the gallows. Returning to England and not knowing what would be his fate, one of them, William de Tracy, suddenly spurred and driven by profound penitence, promised that, as he had publicly sinned, he would make public satisfaction. Of his own accord, not forced by anyone, and going beyond what was required, he endured exile on the Continent, and without consulting his men or taking them with him, alone he hastened as a public penitent to the mercy of the pope. The other three also, stung by the same necessity promised the same, but first arranged to seek the king's advice, and do as he did. When they came to the king, and consulted him about this, they received the answer, 'They are old enough to speak for themselves, and he cannot protect them any further who also needs to purge himself'. Seeing then that there were only two options open to them, either to be punished or do public penance, they decided that it would be better to fall into the hands of the Lord than the hands of men,[70] and be subjected to divine rather worldly judgement. Stung and moved by penitence, they submitted themselves to the mercy of Pope Alexander.

But what could he do? If he spurned them completely, people would say that he lacked mercy; if he received them favourably, that he lacked justice. And, if he acted more leniently to them, others might be incited to a similar outrage. Acting more harshly towards them, or causing that expectation, he did not quickly grant an audience, but for

69 See 1 Corinthians 5.5.
70 See Ecclesiasticus 2.22.

all that, lest they despair, he did not withdraw his presence perman-
ently. For the Lord did not condemn the woman convicted of adultery,
lest he be considered a harsh physician, not did he absolve her completely, lest he act against the law. Eventually then, the pope, seeing
the constancy of the penitent sinners, received them with compassion,
but tried them strictly. He condemned their madness, and said that
they should be harshly punished, had the entreaty of so many holy
and faithful men not interceded on their behalf. For they had brought
with them pleas from the king of England and anyone else they could,
that they should be granted forgiveness on the condition of whatever
satisfaction. But later when the lord pope heard that they had subjected themselves entirely to his judgement, he proposed penance,
following Him who said, 'I seek mercy and not sacrifice'.[71] We heard
that the penance of these seditious men was that, apart from private
penance, which they would perform every day of their lives in fasting
and prayer and alms-giving, they were to go to the holy places of
Jerusalem, and perform military service there in the Temple for fourteen years fighting against the pagans. Otherwise, if the dignity of the
English, who had been sent into exile for no cause of their own, did
not prevent it, no penalty for their very grave sin would suffice without exile. But the lord pope considered it enough to be exiled and to
fight for so many years in Jerusalem, and that it was a necessary cause
because of the invasion of the pagans, which at that time was pre-
occupying the Christian world. Therefore he pronounced this penance
to them, they accepted it, and he dismissed them. When they had
completed the term of their penance in Jerusalem they were to return
to Rome, and submit to the counsel of whatever pope was then ruling
the Holy Roman Church. Immediately two of them gratefully took on
penance, but the other two, overcome by what they saw as the weight
of the penance, recoiled for a time; but later, they too acquiesced.

57. The settlement at Avranches (May 1172)

It took some time for Henry to be punished for his part in Thomas's murder.
A papal letter of 9 October 1170 had authorised an interdict on Henry's
continental lands, should he fail to fulfil the terms of the Fréteval agreement,
and on 25 January 1171 William of Sens and the French clergy imposed it on
him. After Easter the pope confirmed the interdict and the sentences imposed
by Thomas just before his death. In addition he prohibited Henry from

71 Matthew 12.7.

entering a church, and announced a comprehensive anathema against those who had assisted Thomas's murder. Henry showed no early signs of submitting, first sending a defiant letter to the pope in early 1170, then returning to England in August, before crossing to Ireland that winter to impose his authority on the nascent Anglo-Norman colony. At the same time the papal envoys Albert of San Lorenzo (later Pope Gregory VIII) and Theodwin of San Vitale, arrived in France and demanded Henry's return. Henry finally met with the envoys in May 1172 and conducted tortuous negotiations at Gorron on the 16th, Savigny on the 17th, and Avranches on the 19th. A ceremony of reconciliation was held at Avranches on the 21st, and it was confirmed at a larger assembly at Caen on the 30th. The pope confirmed the settlement on 2 September.

The Lansdowne Anonymous, *MTB* 4. 173–4.

So these gathered together at Avranches, and after the examination of the envoys the king swore, and attested in a clear voice persuasive to all, that he had never ordered or desired that Archbishop Thomas of Canterbury be killed, and that he had been no less alarmed by his unexpected death than if it had been his own son. But because he had often been moved to anger and had provoked his attendants against the archbishop whom he did not love as if he were a hostile enemy, he swore that these things had by no means been done through him, but did not deny that they had perhaps been done on his behalf. For which he promised not only to make amends but to give security according to the advice and judgement of Christianity. Regarding other things, upon which he had been called to account, vacancies in the English Church, and the rash decrees of Clarendon, or anything else that might demand correction, he would make appropriate remedy according to the counsel of his men.

These then are the terms of the peace and settlement between the most auspicious Pope Alexander and the most invincible King Henry of England, and the form of satisfaction of this king to the envoys Albert and Theodwin. The aforesaid king would abolish his Constitutions of Clarendon entirely, and none of them would be revived in the future.[72] He would allow every church its liberties and privileges, and within forty days of his arrival in England he would provide canonically

72 Henry does not, in fact, seem to have made an explicit renunciation of the Constitutions. He renounced all evil customs introduced to his churches during his reign, but as he wrote to the English clergy shortly afterwards, he did not believe that he had introduced many evil customs. He did allow for appeals to Rome in cases of ecclesiastical jurisdiction, should they involve no damage to his person, but the issue of criminous clerks was not settled in favour of the Church until Cardinal Hugh of Pierleone visited England in the winter of 1175–76.

elected pastors to those thus deprived.[73] In addition, he would pay for two hundred knights to fight against the pagans in Jerusalem in defence of the Christians. And finally, the king himself would fight against the pagans in person with every effort, unless he were diverted by another intervening necessity, and was given licence by the pope to remain.[74]

58. The king's penance (12 July 1174)

Thomas's canonisation was announced on 21 February 1173. In April 1173 Henry faced a large-scale rebellion led by his wife Eleanor and his sons Henry, Richard and Geoffrey, in alliance with King Louis of France, King William of Scotland and others. By summer 1174 the rebellion was well on its way to being crushed, and the support of the Church had remained firm, but Henry's visit to the saint's tomb certainly served to strengthen his position.

Edward Grim, *MTB* 2. 445.

Even though the shedding of innocent blood had not been done by him or through him, the king bore responsibility for it on account of his anger. Finally, shown through a vision that there was no other way of obtaining peace except by placating and reconciling the martyr, in whose revenge such great confusion of things now seized the whole realm, so that without much blood no one might hope for peace, the king put aside his pride for a time, and with a contrite and humble heart he came to the tomb of the precious martyr to beg pardon for his presumption. While he was hastening there, and was already near the town, so that he might make clear with how much love he was devoted to the saint of God, with how much penitence he was moved on account of what he had done to him, he advanced through the town, in bare feet and ordinary clothes, weeping as he walked, wherever the road appeared roughest, from the church of our blessed father Dunstan, which is the first one meets on entering Canterbury, to the great church where the body of the blessed martyr rests. He did not think of the harshness of the path, or the tenderness of his feet, or the spectacle to the common people all about, but only the danger to his soul, and the scar on his conscience.

---

73 He was to restore in full the lands of Canterbury, and those men dispossessed during Thomas's exile.

74 This was later commuted to founding three religious houses.

It was indeed customary to precede kings in a festive manner and to show obedient reverence in a solemn manner. But he prohibited all such displays, being nourished more by grief that joy, saying 'My lyre is turned to mourning, and my pipe to the voice of those who weep'.[75] Coming then to the door of the church he fell prostrate and prayed, but when he went in he drenched the place of martyrdom, where the saint fell, with tears and kisses. He said confession before the bishops present, and with much trembling and reverence he approached the tomb. There he prostrated his entire body, and intent on prayer in an extraordinary way, what sobs he emitted, what sighs, with what a copious shower of tears he flooded the marble, cannot be estimated.

But later, after he had prayed for a long time, the bishop of London began to speak in these words, making amends on the king's behalf to the monks and the multitude that had gathered: 'Since it is known that some think otherwise, may the integrity of deeds show itself before God, to whom all are naked and open. Before Christ the Lord Who may be worshipped here in faith and truth in the presence of your brotherhood by pure confession, our lord king recalls that the venerable archbishop was killed by evil men neither on his order nor with his knowledge. For when he learned of the murder, it provoked such sorrow of spirit, as we then present could see, as he had never before suffered from any occurence. But because of the words that anger brought forth, which it is believed gave an occasion for profane rashness to carry out the killing, and because he harassed the archbishop during his life so unyieldingly, he proclaims himself blameworthy and begs forgiveness, and is prepared to give satisfaction in every way according to your judgement. Therefore he begs the influential support of your community, so that his abject penance may be acceptable in the sight of our Lord and Saviour, who does not scorn the contrite and humble heart, and to the blessed martyr Thomas. Today he restores in full the privileges and rights of this church, whatever the Catholic Church is recognised to have had freely from past times either in this land or in any other. But also from his own account he offers £30 as a gift to the martyr, so that with your intercession he may be well disposed and forgetful of injuries. Besides, he abandons all ill-feeling in his heart to all those who seemed to have offended him in the cause of the venerable archbishop, and all who were the archbishop's people, whether clerks or relatives or servants, whom he saddened in any way, more than he ought have, he restores

75 Job 30.31.

today to his former favour.'

The bishop proceeded in this way, and when he ceased speaking the king graciously conceded all, and he publicly declared its confirmation for the future. After this he removed his outer clothes, and leaned his head and shoulders into one of the openings of the tomb with very humble devotion, so much so that it provoked everyone to tears, and he was whipped five times by the bishops, then three times more by each of the eighty monks, and thus was solemnly absolved. That done, he remained on the bare ground, with the mud not even washed from his bare feet, fasting as he had come, for sorrow of penitence did not allow him any break. He spent the whole night in prayer, his downcast expression and the posture of his whole body well enough conveying the transformation of the mind, the work of Him, Who looks on the earth and it trembles.[76] Not easily is there found in any history of Christian times anyone either humbler or more devoted in penance than this king. And lest it be doubted that through the satisfaction of the king the sentence of divine severity, which the merits of the blessed martyr Thomas had inspired, had been remitted, an obvious sign was now shown. For the day the king came to Canterbury to make amends for those things he had done to offend the saint, the count of Flanders, who with an immense army had blockaded the coast of the sea so as to invade England without warning, suddenly changed his mind and retreated. Likewise, the next day, as was discovered when they counted the days, the king of the Scots, who was attacking and laying waste and robbing the Northumbrians, was captured in battle.[77] In short enemies fell silent and those disturbing the peace were humiliated. And just as when the king was under accusation in revenge for blood innocently shed, and the anger of God raged equally against the king and the realm, so in reverse the humbled king, through the intervention of the venerable martyr, divine favour now restored, both subdued the enemy and restored more abundant favour of peace. Hence we offer ourselves to you, distinguished martyr, the fruit of our lips and the labour of our hands, praying that if anywhere our utterance departed from the limits of truth, by your intercession and merits we may achieve indulgence and life.

76 Psalm 104.32.

77 On 13 July 1174 Scots forces were surprised at Alnwick and King William the Lion was captured, thereby effectively ending the rebellion against Henry.

VI: DISSENTING VOICES

59. The bishops' appeal

This letter, *Quae vestro*, was written around 24 June 1166 in response to Thomas's excommunications at Vézelay. Its authorship was quickly attributed to Gilbert Foliot.

CTB no. 93, pp. 372–83; *LCGF* no. 167, pp. 222–5; *MTB* no. 205, 5. 408–13.

To their venerable father and lord Thomas, by grace of God archbishop of Canterbury, the suffragan bishops of the same church, and the beneficed clergy established in different places throughout their dioceses, due submission and obedience.

We had hoped, father, that the things disturbed by the novelty of your unexpected distant separation,[1] would, with God's favour, be returned to the serenity of former peace by your humility and prudence. It was certainly a comfort to us when we all heard after your departure that you were doing nothing across the sea that smacked of arrogance[2] and were planning no insurrection against our lord king or his realm. Instead, we heard that you were modestly bearing the burden of poverty which you had voluntarily adopted, were applying yourself to reading and prayer, were making up for the waste of lost time[3] in fasting, vigils and tears, and, occupied in spiritual exertions, you were ascending towards perfect virtue with blessed steps.[4] We rejoiced that you were applying yourself with such effort to the restoration of peace, which gave us hope that you might summon divine favour from on high and instil it in the heart of the king, so that in royal piety he might grant you a reprieve from his anger, and forget about the injuries inflicted by your departure and its consequences. While these things were being reported about you, your friends and well-wishers had some access to him, and whenever people pleaded for his reconciliation towards you, he listened with good nature. But now we learn from certain people, and we recall it with anxiety, that you have sent him a menacing letter, in which you omitted the greeting, offered no

---

1 I.e. Thomas's flight and exile.

2 See Romans 11.20; 12.16.

3 See Ephesians 5.16.

4 A reference, probably satirical, to Thomas's retreat to Pontigny.

counsel or entreaties to gain favour, did not write or express yourself in a friendly manner, but very sternly threatened him with the imminent imposition of an interdict or sentence of excommunication against him.[5] Should this be carried out with the same severity with which it was promised, we are no longer confident that what has been disturbed may be restored to peace, but fear that it would be inflamed into a permanent and inexorable hatred. Holy prudence considers the end of things, and diligently strives to bring a good beginning to fruition. Therefore, if it pleases, may your discretion consider the course you are taking, and whether it is possible to achieve the desired result by this approach. These recent happenings have dashed our great hope, and we who once ventured to believe that peace was in our grasp, have been thrown back from its threshold in grave desperation. The sword has been drawn and the battle joined, and no place can be found to plead on your behalf. Therefore we write to you, in charity, as our father, and advise you not to add trouble to trouble, injury to injury, but to drop your threats and devote yourself to patience and humility, committing your cause to divine clemency and the merciful favour of your lord, and by these actions accumulate and heap burning coals upon the heads of many.[6] In this way charity may be kindled, and perhaps by the inspiration of the Lord and the persuasive counsel of good men, piety alone may achieve what threats could not.

It is better to be praised for voluntary poverty than to be publicly accused by everyone of ingratitude for kindness. Our lord king's generosity towards you is deeply imbedded in the minds of all. He raised you to glory from a lowly position and welcomed you into his friendly favour with such a generous spirit, and all the lands in his dominion, which stretch from the North Sea to the Pyrenees, he subjected to your power to such an extent that in these places the only people thought blessed were those who could win sympathy in your eyes. Then, lest worldly fickleness impair your glory, he sought to root you immoveably in the things which are God's. So, with his mother advising against it, the kingdom crying out against it, the Church of God, as much as it could, sighing and groaning, he took great pains to raise you to your present dignity, hoping that from then on he would reign happily, and that through your labour and counsel he would

---

5 *CTB* no. 74, pp. 292–9; *MTB* no. 154, 5. 278–82. This, *Desiderio desideravi*, was one of the letters of mounting severity sent to Henry in May 1166 which begins with, instead of the traditional greeting, the words, 'These are the words of the archbishop of Canterbury to the king of England'.

6 See Romans 12.20.

enjoy the greatest security. If, then, he found a battle-axe where he looked for security,[7] what do you think the world's verdict will be on you? What will it remember about such an unprecedented example of repayment? Spare your reputation then, if it pleases, and spare your glory, and take care to win your father over with humility and your son with charity. If our advice fails to move you, at least the love and fidelity of the pope and the Holy Roman Church ought to prevail. It should be easy to persuade you not to do anything that might increase the labours of your mother[8] already labouring for so long, or augment sorrow at the disobedience of many through the loss of the obedient. For what if (God forbid!) by your provocative actions our lord king, who by God's gift is followed by people and nations, should turn away from the lord pope, and refuse to follow him because he will not satisfy the king by going against you?[9] And how many entreaties and gifts, how many promises of great things tempt him to take this course! Yet, up to now he has been steady as a rock, and he has high-mindedly spurned all the world can offer. But there is one thing we must fear: that he who refused to be turned by offers of riches and everything precious in men's eyes, may alone be subverted by his anger. If this should happen through you, you will fall into deep mourning, and nothing from now on will stem the font of tears from your eyes. Therefore, if it pleases your highness, retreat from your course, which, should it proceed, would be entirely damaging to the lord pope and the Holy Roman Church, and to yourself, if you would care to give heed.

But perhaps the arrogant among you will not allow you to follow this path. They urge you to prove yourself by wielding the power by which you rule against our lord king, and everything that belongs to him. This power is certainly to be feared by the sinner, and should strike terror into the one who refuses to make satisfaction. We do not say that the king has never sinned, but we say with confidence that he has always been prepared to make amends to the Lord. The king, being established by God, provides peace in every way for his sub-jects, and in order to preserve this peace for the churches and peoples committed to him, he requires and demands that the dignities owed and enjoyed by kings before him, be also enjoyed by him. When a dispute arose between him and you over this – and he was petitioned

---

7 A pun: *securim accipit unde securitatem sperabat.*

8 I.e. the Church.

9 I.e. if Henry should abandon Alexander and support the imperial side in the papal schism.

and warned in fatherly grace by the pope through our brothers the
bishops of London and Hereford – he did not set his mouth against
the heavens,[10] but regarding any demonstrated grievances to the
Church or to ecclesiastics, he mildly and humbly answered that he did
not seek the things of others, and was prepared to accept the judgement of the English Church. He is prepared to make satisfaction even
through deeds, and considers obedience sweet when he is warned to
correct whatever offence he might have committed against God. Not
only is he prepared to repent but, if right demands it, to make amends.
Therefore, since he is willing not only to repent but to make amends,
not flinching from the Church's judgement regarding the things that
belong to the Church, and submitting his neck to the yoke of Christ,
by what right, by what law, or by what canon will you either inflict
interdict upon him or (far be it!), cut him off with the evangelical
axe?[11] To be carried away by impulse is not praiseworthy, but to rule
oneself with prudent judgement is. Therefore it is our common
petition that you do not by rash counsel continue to scatter and
destroy, but instead with fatherly grace take steps to provide life,
peace and security to the sheep committed to your care ...[12]

60. Gilbert Foliot's case against Thomas

This is an answer to two in particular of Thomas's letters of 1166. In *Frater-
nitas vestro*, to the clergy of England (*CTB* no. 95, pp. 388–425; *MTB* no. 223,
5. 490–512), Thomas refers to their letter of appeal as 'more caustic than
consoling'. He goes on to accuse them of turning back in the day of the battle
and of failing in their zeal for the Church. God will judge between us, he says
– while he has suffered conscription on their behalf, they have abandoned him
– and he urges them to stand bravely in the battle. *Mirandum et vehementer*, to
Gilbert (*CTB* no. 96, pp. 426–41; *MTB* no. 224, 5. 512–20), is a more personal
attack in which he expresses his astonishment that a prudent, learned and
religious man should stand against truth and justice, confound right and
wrong, and wish to subvert the Church. In these letters Thomas also reviews
the question of Gilbert's cupidity towards the office of archbishop, the Council
of Northampton, the exile, and the excommunications at Vézelay. What
follows is Gilbert's reply.

CTB no. 109, pp. 498–537; *LCGF* 170, pp. 229–43; *MTB* 5, no. 225, pp. 521–44.

10 See Psalm 73.9.
11 See Matthew 3.10; Luke 3.9.
12 The bishops go on to appeal against the censures against Jocelin of Salisbury and
John of Oxford.

To his venerable lord and father in Christ Thomas archbishop of
Canterbury, Gilbert, servant of the church of London, greeting.

Manifold and extensive, father, is the subject of your profound and
eloquent letter, and anxious though I am to see through the appeal to
the lord pope, you compel us by grave necessity to reply to your
highness. For among the reproaches you have fired off in a scattered
manner, you single me out for reproof from the whole college of your
brothers,[13] so that you pile up shame and disgrace upon me individually, even though it is unjustified. It is astonishing that a man of
moderate disposition, an ecclesiastic of venerable gravity, a master
respectfully answerable to truth by reason of his position and scholarship, should become so inflamed at the utterance of truth; that roused
to anger he should not only spurn the innocent and pious advice of a
son to his father, but should also see in this advice a certain malice of
which the one who gave it is unaware. Therefore, when I am publicly
accused in writing of subverting the Church of God, of confounding
right and wrong,[14] of insanely wishing to overthrow that mountain,
the Church, the pillar of the living God, of seeking to obtain what is
yours, of recklessly disturbing your peace and that of the Church of
God because I failed in this ambition, and of turning tail in the battle
of the Lord, it is difficult to remain silent. To approve this accusation
with silence would act as a confession, so that it would either be
accepted now, or be transmitted unchallenged to posterity.

Since, then, covetousness is the root and source of all evil,[15] and lest
those easily led come to suspect us of this, we must begin here. The
Apostle said, 'What person knows a man's thoughts except the spirit
of the man which is in him?'[16] For men conceal the inner things of men,
and the Lord observes the abyss of the heart from heaven. Unknown
things do not pass Him by, hidden things do not escape His notice.
'For the word of God is living and active, sharper than any two-edged
sword. Before him no creature is hidden.'[17] To Him and before Him I
speak. Under His examination I answer confidently and freely, and I
declare truthfully and unequivocally, with all my conscience as a witness, that never for an instant did ambition spur me towards that which

13 *MTB* no. 224, 5. 512–20.

14 Thomas made this accusation against Gilbert, *CTB* no. 96, pp. 426–7; *MTB* no.
   224, 5. 512.

15 See 1 Timothy 6.10.

16 2 Corinthians 2.11.

17 Hebrews 4.12–13.

is yours. Never did I envy your honour.[18] To nobody did I offer gifts, service, grace or favour so as to be rewarded with this honour, and prepare for myself in whatever way a sacrilegious path to that summit. Who, father, can judge this better than you, who at that time was archdeacon of that church, and chosen of our lord king from thousands, not only as a counsellor but as a friend, without whose influence it was not easy, in fact impossible, to achieve that promotion. What favour did I try to gain before you? Did I ever, either in person or through someone else, try to win your favour with gifts and services, so as to use your influence to advance to promotion, without which influence it could not have been achieved? From this, father, your prudence may gauge how I behaved towards others. I did not entreat advantage from your exalted eminence, nor did I ever attempt to flatter you in the smallest way to seek favour. To sum up, let me confidently take on this burden, that it may be stored up against me on the day of reckoning, if my heart finds me guilty of this blame in any way. It was not my rejection, father, that I lamented in your promotion. Indeed that day I longed with all my heart not for my interests but those of Jesus Christ, and that glory be shown in every way not to me, but to His name.[19] It was when I saw that matters had turned out otherwise that I grieved. Seeing the law of the Church subverted, the pinnacle of that great mountain that you speak of bowed down, the bride of Christ shamelessly deprived of the liberty which she had always before enjoyed with reverence, I groaned with loud sighs to the Lord, and many of us, no doubt influenced by the divine spirit, felt presentiments and forewarnings of the sorrows which we now experience unremittingly. Indeed it should have been remembered that it is written, 'It is difficult to bring to a good conclusion what had a bad beginning'.[20] For, to return to that beginning, who in all of our world is so backward that he does not know that you obtained the office of chancellor by several thousand marks, and by force of this breeze[21] you sailed into the port of the church of Canterbury and eventually entered upon its rule. How piously, how blamelessly, how canonically, by what merit of life, this was done, is known to many, and is inscribed with the pen of sorrow on the hearts of the good.

That good father of ours of happy memory, Theobald, had ended his

18 Thomas makes this charge, *CTB* no. 96, pp. 434–5; *MTB* no. 224, 5. 517.

19 See Philippians 2.21; Psalm 113.1.

20 See Gratian, c. I, q. I, cc. 25, 28: Leo I, *Epistle*, 12.

21 *Aure huius impulso*: a pun on gold and breeze.

days, and you, who had not closed the ever-watchful eyes of your heart to this eventuality, immediately returned from Normandy to England.[22] After a while the king sent as his representative the great and wise justiciar of the realm, Richard de Lucy, whom today you reward with the chain of anathema. He had full authority of the king to have the Canterbury monks and the suffragan bishops of that church seek you out, elect you, and adopt you as father and pastor, without any pause for deliberation. Otherwise, they would not escape the king's anger, but would undoubtedly find evidence that they had made themselves his enemies. What I say I know for certain. For seeing that the Church was being suppressed severely, I raised an outcry on behalf of its liberty, and then heard the sentence of proscription, by which not only myself, but also my father's house and all my friends and relations were banished. Others indeed had to drink from this cup. It is written, 'The lion had roared; who will not fear?',[23] and, 'The dread wrath of the king is like the growling of a lion'.[24] Who would deny this proposal? The king had ordered it with such vigorous intention, he had insisted it would be fulfilled through such a great envoy, everyone knew you had set your heart on it, and all your men energetically promoted it with threats and warnings, promises and flattery. Who would resist the torrent of royal will and command? The sword of the realm rested in your hand, terrible with its flashing fire of unbearable anger towards anyone upon whom you laid the evil eye. Not long before, you had plunged this same sword into the heart of the holy mother Church, when you despoiled it of so many thousand marks to pay for the expedition to Toulouse.[25] Lest you use the sharpened sword to wound again, the Church obeyed orders, avoided what it feared, and pretended it desired what it did not. How far were the hearts of all good men from this! How different were their wishes! Nevertheless, what had been ordered with most ominous menaces was fulfilled with insistence and pressure. In this way, then, you ascended into the sheepfold not through the door, but by another way,[26] and in this entrance, father, you took away the Church's liberty which it had enjoyed for so long. If this, as you write, is its life, you have rendered it lifeless. Good God, what horror seized

22 The biographers present the events differently: see above, pp. 59–60.

23 Amos 3.8.

24 Proverbs 20.2.

25 See above, p. 57.

26 See John 10.1 ff.

us all that day, when that prognostic was glimpsed as accustomed and shown to those present! That prognostic from Matthew the evangelist was proffered as prophesy of things to come: 'the Lord said to the fruit-less fig tree, "May no fruit ever come from you again!", and immedi-ately it withered'.[27] That improper day we should have replied to the king's mandate that one ought to obey God rather than men.[28] If only that day our hearts had been fully filled with fear of Him who can kill not only the body but the soul in hell.[29] Because it was otherwise, this sin brings forth blushes, blushes bring confusion, and confusion penitence, which may give rise to worthy work, and amends to the Lord, so that the ever-flowing tears do not cease from our cheeks until the Lord restores the fortunes of Zion,[30] and consoles those mourning in Jerusalem, and looks again with mercy on Jerusalem's desolate.

Meanwhile, to follow briefly what happened, let us hear what fruit arose from your elevation. From the accession of our pious king up to that day, Holy Church had flourished in great peace, except, as we have said, that it had already experienced the weight of your hand to fund the expedition to Toulouse. Otherwise, under our good king, all rejoiced, everyone lived happily. The crown with holy devotion observed obedience to the priesthood, and the priesthood gave steadfast and useful support to the crown. The two swords served the Church, rendering obedience to the Lord Jesus: they did not stand in opposi-tion, they did not struggle with each other by pulling in different directions. The people were as one and, as is written, spoke one language,[31] striving to punish sins and vigorously root out vice. Peace thrived between the crown and the Church: each promoted favour to the other, and were united in their intention. Indeed with your pro-motion we hoped for and expected an increase in favours, when, for our sins, everything was thrown into confusion. It is a virtue to counter sin when it arises, and to dash against the rock which is Christ the perverse productions of the mind as soon as they appear. Therefore your prudence ought to have taken steps lest disputes between you

---

27 See Matthew 21.19, and above, p. 66 n. 81. This seems to be the only explicit record of Thomas's prognostic, though William of Canterbury may be referring to it whan he writes, 'If a bad tree cannot bear good fruit, as God declares, it follows that a harmless seed cannot grow from a poisonous root', above, p. 191.

28 See Acts 5.29. This and the following line echo *CTB* no. 95, pp. 388–9; *MTB* no. 223, 5. 491.

29 See Matthew 10.28.

30 See Lamentations 1.2; Psalm 126.1.

31 See Genesis 11.1.

and the crown from a small beginning grow great, and from a small spark there rise up a great fire to the ruin of many. It happened otherwise, and for reasons tedious to enumerate the disputes increased, anger was inflamed, and hatred strongly secured. This was the cause, from here emerged the opportunity, for our lord king to apply his energy and counsel to inquire about royal dignities and have them recorded publicly. He demanded their observance from you and the suffragan bishops of your church, but, because certain of them seemed to oppress the liberty of the Church of God, we refused to give our assent, except to those which could be seen to save God's honour and our order. Our lord king vehemently demanded our categorical promise of obedience to them but could in no way obtain from us what was contrary to the liberty of the Church, and fidelity to the lord pope. For this reason meetings were assembled, and councils convoked.

What need is there to mention what happened at London and later at Oxford?[32] Let us call to mind what happened at Clarendon, where for three continuous days the sole aim was to secure our promise to observe the customs and dignities of the realm. There we stood with you, who we thought was standing bravely in the spirit of the Lord. We stood immobile, we stood unafraid. We stood to the ruin of fortunes, to the torment of our bodies, prepared to suffer exile, to suffer also, if the Lord allowed it, even the sword. What father ever had sons more united in his testimony, or more unanimous? We were all enclosed in one chamber. But on the third day, when all the princes and nobles of the realm had already blazed up in the greatest anger, roaring and brawling, they entered the chamber where we were sitting, threw back their cloaks, stretched out their arms and said to us, 'Look, you who despise the statutes of the realm, you who do not perform the king's bidding. These hands that you see are not ours, nor are these arms or these bodies: they belong to our lord king, and are now ready to enforce his every command, his every act of retribution, his every wish, whatever it may be. His mandate, whatever it may be, at his wish alone will be law to us. Change your intention, turn your minds to his command, so that you may avoid, while you can, the danger which very soon you will not be able to escape'. What was the result? Who fled? Who turned tail? Who was broken in spirit? Your letter accuses us of being turned in the day of the battle, of not rising up against adversity, of not opposing ourselves as a wall

---

32 The Council of Westminster, October 1163 (see above, no. 18), and the meeting later that year which Garnier and 'Roger of Pontigny' place at Woodstock (see above, p. 87), but Herbert of Bosham, probably correctly, places at Oxford.

for the house of the Lord.[33] Let God be a witness between us.[34] Let
him judge on what account we could not be turned by the threats of
princes; let him judge who fled, who was a deserter in the battle.[35] To
be sure, the noble Henry of Winchester, most constant of spirit in the
Lord, stood firm; Nigel of Ely stood firm; Robert of Lincoln stood
firm, Hilary of Chichester stood firm, as did Jocelin of Salisbury,
Bartholomew of Exeter, Richard of Chester, Roger of Worcester,
Robert of Hereford and Gilbert of London. The assassin failed before
all of these, but courage did not fail them. Considering temporal things
dross, for Christ and the Church they laid themselves and their
possessions bare. Therefore let the truth be told, let the light be shone
on what we witnessed and saw: the leader of the army turned tail, the
commander of the battlefield ran away, the archbishop of Canterbury
departed from the common counsel and association of his brothers.
After a pause for private reflection he returned to us and burst out in
these words, 'It is the wish of my lord that I perjure myself, and for
the present I submit and incur perjury, so that I will be able to repent
in the future.' Hearing this we were astounded, and rooted to the spot
we looked at each other and sighed and groaned at this fall from the
height – as we thought – of virtue and constancy. There is no 'yes' and
'no' with the Lord,[36] nor did we think his disciple could be moved like
that. When the head grows weak the rest of the body quickly becomes
weak and its infirmity is rapidly spread to the other members. He
agreed to our lord king's demands and promised henceforth to observe
faithfully, truthfully and absolutely the royal privileges and the ancient
customs of the realm which had been announced according to the
memory of the elders of the realm and put in writing, and constrained
us to pledge ourselves to a similar promise of obedience.

At this the dispute was put to rest, and peace was made between the
clergy and the crown. Israel descended into Egypt, and we read that
it later came out with much glory. We also still retained a strong
hope that with our lord king's former anger driven out and his spirit
calmed, good might be restored again to his honour and the glory of
God. But that old disturber of concord envied the delicate peace, and
just as we had sailed away from the storm and now hoped to reach

33 See Ezekiel 13.5.

34 See Genesis 31.49.

35 See Ezekiel 13.5; Genesis 31.49, cited by Thomas, *CTB* no. 95, pp. 390–1; *MTB* no.
223, 5. 491, 493–4.

36 See 2 Corinthians 1.18, quoted by Thomas, *CTB* no. 96, pp. 428–9; *MTB* no. 224,
5. 513.

port, we were driven back into the depths by the north wind. Only recently you had promised the king in the word of truth not to leave the kingdom without his licence. It is written, 'The words of a priest should always have truth as a companion', and 'Whatever anyone says ought to be truthful, and what he promises, faithful'.[37] Nevertheless after a few days you committed your sails to the wind, and made provision to leave the realm, without the king's knowledge. When he learned of it, no one was more surprised and saddened than he. He was surprised that a promise given by a pontiff in the manner of an oath had not been fulfilled; he was saddened, knowing the scandal that this would seriously provoke against him, and that this flight would most gravely damage his reputation, previously unharmed, among peoples and kingdoms. What would those ignorant of the truth think, except that the king, ignoring royal piety, had flared up into the fury of a tyrant, and hating Christ had expelled his servant from his realm and dominions. He would rather have received a grievous wound to his flesh at your hand than to have incurred the damage which you and your people brought to his fame before the whole Christian world. What happened? With the north wind filling your sails, the voyage looked secure, until a stronger wind arose from the south and spoiled your plan, blowing you safely back to the port that you had left. Now, by this turn of events finding yourself within the king's power, did he direct anger or force against you or even speak to harshly? Not at all. Instead, he received you well and sent you home with due reverence, to rule over the church committed to you.

But hardly had the south wind ceased to blow, when the north wind struck. Hardly had the disturbed feelings on both sides settled down when they burst out again more fervently. A certain noble of the realm claimed an estate from your church and on the king's mandate you were meant to show him justice. But after the required period he returned to the king and claimed that though he had made his case before you according to the statutes of the realm with the appropriate oath and that of witnesses, he failed to receive justice from you. He continued to pursue the king, and to plead with him every day that he show justice to him, so eventually you were summoned by the lord king to show yourself before him on a fixed day, so that the suit would be settled according to his judgement, and you would fulfil what you failed to do on his earlier mandate. But you did not heed his

---

37 Both quotations are unidentified, though the first is cited by Thomas, *CTB* no. 95, pp. 402–3; *MTB* no. 223, 5. 498.

summons, and the response you sent him showed your disobedience. The lord king considered this a grave detraction from his right and authority, and he ordered the Church of the realm to be summoned to a council at Northampton.[38] The people came together as one man, and before those who had attended, according to their dignity and rank, he reported, with fitting moderation and grace, what had been said of his spurned mandate in the suit against you. Without waiting for or seeking the counsel of your brothers, you confessed your fault, adding that you did not obey the summons because that John, who had delivered the king's mandate to you, in your presence swore not on the gospel but on a troper which he had produced.[39] It was commonly said that this was no reason to ignore the royal mandate, and for such an offence the customary penalty was a fine, at the mercy of the king. Your highness obeyed the royal judgement, providing bail in full. Nevertheless you did not observe that apostolic decree, 'No bishop, whether for a civil or criminal case, should appear before any judge, either civil or military', and again, 'If a clerk is impleaded before a secular judge, he should not answer or speak' ... [40]

But you say that it is unheard of for an archbishop of Canterbury to be compelled to such a thing in the court of the king. You could have also said it was unheard of for an official of the court to have risen to the Church by such a sudden transition: that one day he is managing the court, the next day the Church, one day involved with hawks and hounds and other pleasant pastimes, the next attending at the altar and ministering in spiritual matters to the bishops and priests of the whole realm. Therefore, adopting perverse counsel, you entered the royal house carrying the cross in your hands, and instilled the suspicion in everyone present that the king was guilty of some hateful wickedness. Nevertheless, his patience fully proclaimed his innocence, when he suffered the distress of the cross being carried against him without exceeding the bounds of royal modesty. He did not boil over into rage, nor did he act or speak with malice, but sought to conclude the case in which he was plaintiff within the appropriate limits of justice. But you refused to be judged and appealed to the pope. As in your entrance, so in your leaving, the king's great mildness and tolerance towards you could be recognised by signs of evident peace. For

38 See above, pp. 100–15.
39 See above, p. 101.
40 Gratian, *Decretum* C. II, q. I. cc. 8, 17. Gilbert then goes into a lengthy and detailed digression on the question of when a churchman should submit to secular judgement. See Morey and Brooke, pp. 174–9.

just as regarding Absalom, as the army was advancing, paternal piety cried out, 'Deal gently for my sake with the young man Absalom',[41] immediately his command was publicly announced, that if you or your people should be put in any distress, the person guilty would be put to the avenging sword.

You went further, and as if an ambush were being contrived against your life or your blood, you took to flight by night, changed your dress and lay low for a while, before crossing the sea. With no one pursuing and no one expelling you, you chose a dwelling-place for a time in another place outside the king's dominions. From there you arranged to steer the ship which you had left without an oarsman amidst the waves and the storms. Now you order us and encourage us to turn to you and we will be saved.[42] You tell us to follow in your footsteps, to submit to death, and not fear to lay down our lives to liberate the Church. Undoubtedly, if we give heed to all that is promised to us in heaven, the soul ought to give little value to whatever we can possess on earth. For tongue cannot tell nor mind grasp the joys of the heavenly city, to be present with the choir of angels, with the most blessed spirits to witness the glory of the Creator, to come face to face with God, to be affected by no fear of death, and to rejoice in the gift of eternal life. The sufferings of the present time do not compare to the glory that will be revealed in the saints.[43] And the light and momentary afflictions of the present prepare for the elect an eternal weight of glory beyond all comparison.[44] For a long time these things have rested heavy on my senses. For a long time these promises have driven my efforts. Would that the head which sits upon my shoulders had been cut off by the sword of the executioner for the common good, provided that I had fought a good battle, pleasing to God. But it is the cause, not the penalty, that makes the martyr.[45] To endure hardships in a saintly manner is glorious; to do so perversely and obstinately is ignominious. To submit to the sword on God's behalf is a perfect commendation and victory; to provoke it rashly is perfect madness. And, father, considering not only your words but your deeds, I should not rush to death rashly or lightly. You bent the knee at Clarendon, took to flight at Northampton, changed your dress and

41 2 Kings 18.5.

42 See Isaiah 45.22.

43 See Romans 8.18.

44 See 2 Corinthians 4.17.

45 Found in various patristic sources, e.g. Augustine, *Epistles* 89.

hid for a time, and secretly left the king's lands, and what did you
achieve? What did you gain in doing this, except to evade studiously
that death which no one had deigned to threaten? Therefore, with
what effrontery, father, do you invite us to death, which you have
shown to the whole world with such manifest signs to have shrunk
from and fled? What charity persuades you to impose the burden on
us which you have thrown away? The sword which you fled hangs
over us. You have chosen to combat it with a sling, instead of fighting
at close quarters. Perhaps you invite us to flee in the same way, but to
us the sea is closed, and since your flight all ships and harbours have
been shut off. An island is a king's strongest prison, from which it is
almost impossible to escape or release oneself. If we must fight, we
will fight hand-to-hand. If we join battle with the king, and we strike
with the sword, he will strike back; if we inflict a wound, we ourselves
will be unable to avoid wounds. Do your annual revenues mean so
much to you that you wish to acquire them even through your
brothers' blood? Even the Jews spurned Judas's silver, because they
recognised it as blood money.[46]

But perhaps you propose another position to us. Let us turn aside, then,
so as to consider more fully why you urge us to our death. Thanks to
the Lord, there is no dispute beween us regarding faith, nor regarding
the sacraments, nor morals. Good faith flourishes before the king, the
prelates and the people, and the Church of this kingdom is sound in
its adherence to all the points of right doctrine. Nobody is divided
from obedience to the pope by the folly of the present schism. Everyone respects and honours the sacraments of the Church, adopting
them for themselves and communing with others in a pious and holy
manner. As for morals, we all offend a great deal.[47] Still, no one praises
or defends his error, but through penance hopes to efface what he has
admitted. The entire dispute with the king and regarding the king,
then, is about certain customs which he claims were observed, and
enjoyed by his predecessors, and he wishes and expects to enjoy.
Though your highness threatened him over this matter, he did not
desist from his purpose, and would not renounce these things which
he claimed were ancient and long-held customs of the realm. This is
why you hastened to arms, and pressed forward to suspend the sword
over his holy and noble head. As very many people say, and the whole

46 See Matthew 27.3 ff. In *CTB* no. 96, pp. 434–5; *MTB* no. 224, 5. 216, Thomas
   repudiates his identification with Judas.
47 See James 3.2.

history of the realm testifies, he did not himself set up these customs:
this is how he found them. It is more difficult to root something out if
it is deeply established: the plant clings on more tenaciously that has
its roots immersed deeply for a long time. If one wishes to transplant
it, one should not root it up, or it will wither away immediately.
Instead, one should dig around it and take out some soil, and bare the
root entirely, so that in this way prudent diligence may achieve what
the incompetent application of force did not. One ought to adopt the
example of good men, and attend to their works more diligently.
Your predecessor Father Augustine rooted out many evils from this
realm, and filling that king with the light of the faith he eliminated no
few depravities from those customs;[48] not with reproaches, but with
blessings and praise, and steady encouragement, and in this way
strongly inclined the souls of the powerful to good. In our time John
of Crema was sent to these parts by the Holy Roman Church and in
the long period which he spent here changed customs of the realm,
not with reproaches or threats, but with sound doctrine and holy
exhortations.[49] Blessings he sowed, and from blessings he reaped. If
these men had hastened to arms they would have achieved little or
nothing. When divine inspiration granted the pious king of France
the child he had long wished for,[50] he remitted many of the Church's
grievances which antiquity had established, and up to then lay undis-
turbed. This, as we have heard, was achieved at the suggestion and
advice of the Church, not by assailing an elected ruler with threats.
Who can recount how many privileges, liberties, immunities and
possessions have been conferred on us by pious kings the world over,
driven by piety alone, not forced by taunts? Certainly there is not
enough time, for this is the commendable nobility of kings. From
these the supplicant obtains what the haughty man and his threats
would never obtain, no matter what the effort. They consider money
cheap and worthless, but anyone who tries to take it away from them
with violent force will be disappointed, soon finding that they are well
able to defend even what is of little value to them.

You should have approached these matters with mature counsel, not
the passion of a novice.[51] You ought to have sought out the counsels

---

48 Augustine of Canterbury's mission to England resulted in the conversion of King
   Aethelbert of Kent in 601, who went on to promulgate a new law code: see Bede,
   Historia Ecclesiastica i. 26; ii. 5.

49 See *Councils and Synods*, pp. 733–41.

50 His son Philip was born in 1165.

51 See *Regula S. Benedicti*, c. 1.

of your brothers and others, and paid attention to the works of wise Fathers, and balanced the Church's losses against its gains. Then eventually, perhaps, if no hope of remedy remained, you might have given this judgement. And when you gave it, according to the procedures of the sacred canons, you ought to have noted to whom it is given, why it is given, how it is given, how the Church would benefit if it were given, and what would tell against it if it were not given. May we remind you that the one whom you attack is none other than he whom his dear children, his noble and honourable wife, all the realms subject to him, the crowds of friends and throngs of subjects, and whatever worldly delights, could hardly detain, could hardly dissuade with flattery, from rejecting all these things and, naked, taking up his cross and following the Lord Jesus. And contemplating the poverty he had adopted, he would strive to fulfil by his actions the teaching of Christ, 'He who does not take up his cross and follow me is not worthy of me'.[52] Such is his obstinacy of mind, such is his aggressive and abusive cruelty, such is his illwill towards the Church of God which the whole world declaims! If you inflict insults on this man, the Church will truly grieve that its most noble part has been injured by its own missiles. And when he is wounded, it will be a source of lament not only to a few, but to a great number of people, about which holy authority teaches: 'In such cases where, through serious schism, the danger is not that of one man or another, but extends to the devastation of a people, one should remove severity, so that with greater evils allayed, sincere charity might bring relief', and again, 'Correction by the many cannot be beneficial, if he who is corrected has many allies'.[53] For what cure is useful that heals one wound, and inflicts one far greater, far more dangerous? What kind of prudence is it to desert the Church in this way and rise up against one's lord, because of some matters which could have been obtained more easily and more efficiently, and then, when the peace of the whole realm has been disturbed, to neglect the souls and the bodies of one's charges when they are in danger? Ambrose left his fields, but did not approve of abandoning his church.[54] What, father, can prudence not hope for from your good prince, whom it knows has been stung by the divine spirit and is zealous for Christ? Whatever temporal benefit these customs might hold, they mean nothing to him, for whom worldly glory of whatever proportion has now lost almost all its value, and the desire

52 See Luke 14.27; Matthew 10.38.

53 Gratian, *Decretum* D. 50, c. 25; C. 23, q. 5, c. 32.

54 See Ambrose, *Epistles* I, 20, 8.

of whose heart is so distant from such glory that speaking to the Lord
he would more often say, 'O Lord, you know I hate the sign of honour
on my head'.[55] Surely this should have been fostered, and the holy
doves allowed to continue building their nests, until, with Christ fully
formed in him, his hidden things be drawn forward into the light, and
the liberties of the Church, not only these in question, but also those
far more important, he grant of his own accord? In this matter, we
speak of what we know, and what we know, we confidently assert.
Our lord king would have already rejected in their entirety the customs
about which you are most indignant, had not two things seriously
impeded this intention: first, he feared that if anything which had
fallen to him from his predecessors were to be removed or threatened,
it would be a matter of shame to him; and second, whatever he might
give up for the Lord's sake, he would not wish this to seem to have
been extorted from him by force. Nevertheless, he had already
trodden on the first with the foot of sanctity, and fear of God, natural
goodness, the holy advice of the lord pope, and the incessant prayers
of many had already led him to this: that on account of reverence for
the One through whom he has been exalted far beyond all his
predecessors, he would call together the Church of God, and on his
own initiative, with much devotion of spirit, he would change and
correct the customs of the realm which he knew had caused grievance.
And if the humility which had begun within you had persevered,
happiness would already have widely gladdened the Church of God in
this realm, for your goal had already been achieved by entreaty, when
your recent disturbance set up an evil obstacle to everything. For
when Britanny had not yet recognised his authority, and this people,
never before subdued, raised up their heel against him,[56] you sent
terrible letters to him, in no way redolent of either the devotion of a
father or the modesty of a pontiff. And by flinging threats, you
destroyed almost everything that had been achieved by humble and
earnest devotion, in the form of the pope's admonition and that of
many others, and you cast both the king and the realm into the
greatest scandal.

May God avert what we fear might result if things continue like this!
Lest it erupt in our time, for the sake of God's honour, and reverence
for the Holy Church, and, if it pleases, for the sake of your well-being,

55 See Esther 14.16.

56 Henry besieged Fougères in June–July 1166, and eventually successed in replacing
    Duke Conan IV with his own son, Geoffrey.

for the sake of the common good of peace, for the sake of reducing scandals, and with God's help recalling what has been disturbed of its former peace, I appeal to the lord pope. In this way the violent impulse of your course, of your destruction to the king and the realm, may at least temporarily be checked. In which matter it would be good for your zeal to remain within the bounds of modesty, lest from over-arching pride it subvert the law of the king, and likewise despoil due reverence to the pope by not accepting appeals to him. If it pleases you to note that the Lord did not lodge in the house of Zacchaeus, until he had descended from the sycamore tree,[57] perhaps you also will descend, and take steps to soothe with peaceful words the one you have exasperated with threats, not only determining, but also offering humble satisfaction, even if perhaps you have suffered injury. The Lord gave to his apostles the example of a boy, who when hurt does not become angry, quickly forgets the injury, nor is roused by any malice, but is very fully compensated for all this by the reward of an innocent and happy life.[58] He is a remarkable model of virtue, who forgave those who crucified him, and with great charity ordered the persecutors and haters to be loved, and, if a brother sins against us, orders forgiveness to be given, not only seven times, but seventy times seven.[59] What can such humility not achieve before our lord king? What can this perfect path not achieve? This is the right track[60] which leads directly to peace. When you enter upon it, father, you will find peace there, and when the clouds of sorrow have been dispelled you will replace them with full peace, full joy, and you will be able to obtain from our most pious king and dearest lord not only what you now seek, but far more, with his heart kindling the spirit of the Lord, and ever expanding into love for Him.

61. Doubts about Thomas's sanctity

Caesarius's work on the nature of miracles was written in the early thirteenth century. The reference to Thomas's subsequent miracles suggest that this debate occurred very early after his death. It is discussed by J. Baldwin, 'A Debate at Paris over Thomas Becket between Master Roger and Master Peter the Chanter', *Studia Gratiani* 11 (1967), 119–32.

57 See Luke 19.2 ff.
58 Unidentified.
58 See Matthew 18.21–2.
60 See Isaiah 26.7.

Caesarius of Heisterbach, *Dialogus Miraculorum*, ed. J. Strange (Cologne, 1851), II, pp. 139–40.

Novice: Why is it that certain martyrs work more wonders after death than others? Is it because of some distinguishing sanctity?

Monk: As said above, miracles are not of merit in themselves, but as signs of sanctity. Certain saints work many miracles in their life-time, but cease when they die. Others, on the other hand, because they produced no signs of sanctity while alive, are wonderful in miracles after death.

The blessed Thomas, archbishop of Canterbury, who in our time fought even to the death, during his persecutions did not shine with miracles, and after his death there was much disagreement about him. Some said that he was a damnable traitor to his king-dom; others that as a defender of the Church he was a martyr. This question was debated at Paris among the masters. For master Roger, judging the constancy of the man as obstinacy, swore that he had been worthy of death, even if not such a death. On the other hand, Peter the Chanter judged him to be a worthy martyr to God, in as much as he had been murdered for the liberty of the Church. Christ himself answered the question when he glorified him with so many signs. Nevertheless, he should not be considered superior to the apostles or the other great martyrs who we do not read performed such great and frequent miracles. The same applies to St Anno, archbishop of Cologne.[61] After his death many detracted from him, saying that he was a schismatic, and had put out the eyes of his citizens, but in his translation the Lord showed by many signs what a saint he was.

62. A critical view of Thomas's life

William, an Augustinian canon, began writing his history in or around 1196. It breaks off suddenly, suggesting that he died in 1198.

William of Newburgh, *Historia Rerum Anglicarum, Chronicles of the Reigns of Stephen, Henry II and Richard*, ed. R. Howlett (London, 1884), pp. 139–43, 160–5.

Thomas was a Londoner by birth, a man of keen intellect and corres-ponding eloquence, refined of appearance and manners, and second to none in efficient administration. He was foremost in the service of the

61 Anno II (1056–75).

archbishop of Canterbury, and when Roger was appointed archbishop of York, Theobald appointed him as archdeacon. But when, as has been discussed above, Henry II succeeded to the throne on Stephen's death, unwilling to pass over such a suitable assistant, he made him royal chancellor. So outstanding was his secular service in this distinguished office that he earned the privilege of such love and honour before the king, that he seemed to share the throne. But when he had spent a number of years in secular service he was enrolled in the service of the Church, and at the king's desire he was elected archbishop of Canterbury. Immediately, with pious and wise deliberation, he gave himself to such consideration of this great honour that some said, 'This is the hand of the Lord', and others, 'This is the transformation of the hand of the Almighty'.[62] In the second year of his archiepiscopate he attended the Council of Tours, where, as is said, his conscience stung by his irregular and uncanonical promotion, effected by the king's will and power, he secretly resigned his office into the hands of the pope. The latter approved this action and restored the burden to him by the ecclesiastical hand, and cured the attack of troubled conscience in the scrupulous man.[63] After the bishops had returned from the council to their own sees, the crown and the priesthood of England began to argue, and a considerable disturbance regarding the prerogatives of the clerical order arose. Royal justices informed the king, who had his hands full with ordering the cares of the realm and rooting out evil-doers without exception, that many violations of public discipline – theft, rapine and homicide – were regularly being committed by clerks, to whom the sanction of lay jurisdiction could not be extended. Finally it is said to have been reported in the king's hearing that more than a hundred homicides had been committed in England by clerks since his accession. Roused to fiery anger, furious with clerical evil-doers, he enacted laws, which were certainly driven by zeal for public justice, although his fervour exceeded appropriate bounds.

But the bishops of our time share the blame for this royal excess, in as much as they also contributed to it. For the holy canons order that not only criminous clerks, those involved in serious crimes, but also those accused on less serious charges, ought to be purged of their office. The English Church contains thousands of such, like so much chaff among the grain, but how many have been deprived of their office in

62 Psalm 76.11.

63 The Council of Tours occurred in May 1163, but Thomas's resignation is said to have occurred at Sens in November 1164.

so many years past? The bishops, being more intent on defending clerical liberties and privileges than correcting and curtailing their vices, believe they render obedience to God and the Church if they protect criminous clerks from public discipline, whom by virtue of their office they refuse or neglect to coerce with the vigour of ecclesiastical censure. In this way clerks, who have been called to the province of the Lord as stars fixed in the firmament of heaven, and ought by life and word shine above the world, have licence and liberty to do whatever they wish with impunity, give reverence neither to God, whose judgement seems a long way away, nor men in power. This is especially so when episcopal solicitude towards them is languid, and the prerogative of holy order exempts them from secular jurisdiction.

So, the king set up certain new laws against the chaff of the holy order, so that criminous clerks should either be tried or punished, in which, as has been said, he went too far. He believed that these would eventually come into effect if they were supported by the consent of the bishops. Therefore he called the bishops together so as to elicit their assent in whatever way, and he managed either to inveigle them with flattery or break them down with menaces, so that they submitted and subdued themselves to the royal will, and affixed their seals to the written draft of these new laws. All except one he managed to persuade, for the archbishop of Canterbury was not turned, but stood firm to every pressure. But then royal fury erupted so violently against him, according as he seemed indebted to him by reason of royal bounty given and received. So the king began to grow hostile to him, and pursuing every possible opportunity to injure him, he demanded an account of his time as chancellor. He answered with fearless frankness that when he had fulfilled his secular service, he had been fully discharged by the king to the Church, and that old things ought not be dragged up for reasons of opportunism rather than truth. Day by day the causes of royal anger became aggravated, until on the day on which he was to respond fully to this charge, he ordered that solemn office of St Stephen, 'Princes sat and spoke against me, and the evil have persecuted me', to be sung in solemn celebration of the sacrifice. Soon after he entered the court, carrying in his own hands the silver cross normally carried in front of him, and when some of the bishops present offered to carry the cross before their metropolitan, he refused, nor would he allow anyone else carry it, no matter how much he was asked. This caused the king's already kindling fury to blaze, and the following night the archbishop fled secretly and crossed the sea. He was welcomed with honour by the king, the nobles and the bishops of

France, and remained with them for a time. The king of England, however, raged unreasonably at his departure, and indulged in unbridled fury, more than is fitting to a monarch, and in an act of quite unbecoming and petty revenge he expelled all the archbishop's relations from England.

Many people, driven more by affection than prudence, tend to approve everything that is done by those they love and praise. But these actions of the venerable man, although they proceeded from praiseworthy zeal, by no means do I consider praiseworthy, as they brought no profit but only incited the king to anger, from which so many evil things are later known to have derived. Similarly do I regard the action of the most blessed prince of the apostles, who, when he had already reached the height of apostolic perfection, forced the Gentiles by his own example to become Jews, which the teacher of the Gentiles declared reprehensible, although it is agreed that it was done out of praiseworthy piety ...[64]

In the year of our Lord 1170, which was the seventeenth of King Henry II,[65] the same Henry had his young son Henry solemnly consecrated and crowned king in London at the hand of Roger archbishop of York. For the venerable Thomas of Canterbury was still in exile in France, as the king had not yet made his peace with him, despite the efforts of the pope and the French king towards a reconciliation. When news of the coronation reached him, jealous on behalf of his church, he speedily informed the pope, by whose favour and support he had been sustained. Claiming that the coronation had been celebrated in prejudice to him and his church, he obtained very severe letters of correction addressed to the archbishop of York, who had performed the ceremony in another's province, and the bishops who had approved it by their presence. At this, the king of England, who had spent a short time in England after his son's coronation, crossed the sea again. And, urged by the frequent warnings of the lord pope and the importunate pleas of the illustrious king of France, that at least now after seven years of separation he deign to be reconciled to this distinguished exile, he eventually agreed. So a solemn agreement was made between them, and was all the more pleasing for its delay in coming. The king therefore remained across the sea, and the archbishop returned to his church with royal blessing and favour. But,

64 William continues with the secular affairs of the 1160s before returning to the Becket dispute.

65 Actually the sixteenth.

unknown to the king, he had with him papal letters condemning the archbishop of York and the other bishops who had been present at that most inauspicious coronation, which proved an irritant to the peace just made, and a provocation to future anger. The archbishop sent these letters of suspension ahead of him, and himself followed, raging with zeal for justice, but whether fully aware of the situation, God knows.

It is not for one as lowly as me to dare to judge the actions of so great a man. Still, I think Pope Gregory would have acted more softly towards the king's reconciliation which was tender and as yet young, and for reasons of time and compromise would have chosen to pass over certain things which could be tolerated without danger to the Christian faith,[66] according to the saying of the prophet, 'he who is prudent will keep silent in such a time, for the days are evil'.[67] Therefore I neither declare the archbishop's actions praiseworthy, nor do I presume to disparage them. But this I say, that if perhaps through the slightly excessive force of praiseworthy zeal, the holy man went a little too far, he was purged by the fire of his holy passion which we know followed. So, though we ought to love and praise holy men, whom we know to be far superior to us, we should nevertheless by no means either love or praise the actions which they committed through human weakness, but only those which we ought to imitate without reservation. For who can say that they ought to be imitated in their every deed, when the apostle James says, 'For we all err in many ways'?[68] Therefore we ought not praise them for everything they do, but wisely and cautiously, so that God, Whom no one can praise enough, no matter how hard we try, should have His dignity preserved.

Therefore, for the aforesaid transgression – would that it had been passed over at the time – at the instigation of the blessed Thomas, by the authority of the apostolic see, the bishops were suspended from the privilege of the episcopal office in its entirety. When some of them complained of this to the king, he raged in exasperation, flew into terrible anger, and unable to control himself enough, as his agitated heart overflowed he spat out unreasonable words. Then four magnates standing by, men of noble birth and famous in warfare, jealous of the temporal rights of their lord were incited to a terrible crime. They

66 Gregory I gave such instructions in 601 to his missionaries to the English: see Bede, *Ecclesiastical History* i. 30.

67 Amos 5.13.

68 James 3.2.

quickly left his presence, and crossed the sea with as much speed as if they were hastening to a solemn banquet. Spurred on by the fury they had conceived, they came to Canterbury on the fifth day of Christmas, and found the venerable archbishop intent on the celebration of the festival with religious joy. They entered his palace as he was eating and sitting with his honourable men, but they did not greet him. Instead they threatened him in the king's name, and ordered more than requested or advised, that since by suspending the bishops for obeying the king he had brought contempt and insult on the king himself, he ought to relax the suspension immediately. The archbishop answered that the sentence of a higher power could not be overruled by a lower power, and that it was not his concern to absolve those who had been suspended, not by himself, but by the pope. At this they spoke in loud roars, but he, unafraid at their frenzy, spoke with wonderful frankness and confidence. So, all the more inflamed, they went out and took up arms, for they had entered unarmed, and prepared themselves with great clatter and noise for a most atrocious crime. The venerable archbishop was persuaded by his men to retire to the holy church, and thereby escape their savage rage. But he, ready to throw himself into the battle, would not easily acquiesce, so eventually, when his enemies rushed in and pressed forward, his men dragged him with friendly violence to the protection of the holy place. Monks were singing vespers to Almighty God as he, soon to be the evening sacrifice, entered the venerable temple of Christ. The attendants of Satan, showing Christian reverence neither to holy order, nor the holy place and time, attacked the great priest as he stood in prayer before the venerable altar. In the very festival of Christ's nativity the most worthless Christians killed him most cruelly with their swords. When the deed had been done, they withdrew as if in triumph, and left with unfortunate joy. But considering that perhaps what had been done should displease him on whose behalf they had been jealous, they withdrew into the northern parts of England for a time until they gauged more fully how the king felt towards them.

Thereafter how precious was the death of the blessed pontiff in the eyes of the Lord, and how great the atrocity of the crime committed against him in terms of the time, the place and the person, the frequency of the signs that followed him declared. In fact as soon as the report of such a great sacrifice had been quickly spread through all the lands of the Latin world, the illustrious king of the English was so disgraced and his distinguished reputation so tarnished before Christian kings that, since it could hardly be believed that it had been carried out without his wish and command, he was assailed with the curses of nearly everyone, and judged fitting for rebuke by public contempt. And when he heard what had been done by his men, and understood that a blemish had been cast on his glory and an indelible blot branded on him, he grieved so much that it is reported that he tasted no food for a number of days. But whether he spared these murderers or not, he considered that it would be easy for men to think ill of him. For if he spared these most wicked men, it would seem that he had given initiative or authority to such evil. But, on the other hand, if he punished them for what they were thought to have done at his command, he would be accused of great wickedness. Therefore he decided they should be pardoned, and looking to his reputation as much as their safety, he ordered them to present themselves to the apostolic see to receive solemn penance. This they did. For their con-sciences stung, they set out for Rome, where the pope ordered them to do penance in Jerusalem. And there it is said, that after many years making satisfaction in no sluggish way, all ended their lives. But more of this later.

Then the same king, while almost everyone was attributing the murder of the blessed man to him, and especially the nobles of France, who had always been jealous of his good fortune, were inciting the Holy See against him, as the true and certain author of such great outrage, he directed envoys to Rome, so that they might temper the fervent illwill with reverend entreaty. When they came to Rome, with everyone cursing the king of England, they were hardly admitted. But insisting constantly that the great crime had not been committed by the command or consent of their lord, they eventually succeeded in having legates sent to France as the pope's representatives with full powers. They, once they had enquired into and investigated the matter diligently, would either allow the king to absolve his reputation, or if they found him guilty they would correct him with ecclesiastical cen-sure. So this was done. For two envoys from the apostolic see, namely the venerable Albert, who later presided over the same see,[69] and Theodwin, came to France. And in his own dominions, the king humbly presented himself to a solemn gathering of ecclesiastics and nobles, and firmly declared that neither by his wish nor his command did that deed happen which had tarnished his reputation, and that he had never grieved more over anything else, and he solemnly undertook absolution. Indeed he did not deny that these murderers had perhaps

69 As Gregory VIII, October–December 1187.

taken the opportunity to dare such madness, when, having heard report of the suspension of the bishops he was filled with immoderate anger and spoke without moderation. 'And on this account', he said, 'I do not shrink from Christian punishment: make whatever judgement you please, with devotion I will embrace and comply with the decree.' He said this, and having taken off his clothes, according to the custom of public penance naked he submitted himself to ecclesiastical discipline. The cardinals were overcome by the humility of so great a king, and cried for joy, the crowds wept and praised God, the king's conscience was soothed and his reputation somewhat restored, and the council dissolved. Richard prior of Dover then succeeded the blessed Thomas in the cathedral church of Canterbury.[70]

---

70 Richard of Dover was elected 3 June 1173, consecrated 8 April 1174 and died 16 February 1184.

SELECT BIBLIOGRAPHY

The Latin Lives and letters are published, without translation, in seven volumes in the Rolls Series (the Lives vols 1–4, letters 5–7), in *Materials for the History of Thomas Becket, archbishop of Canterbury*, eds J. C. Robertson and J. B. Sheppard (London, 1875–85). The Icelandic Saga, with English translation, is published in two volumes of the Rolls Series, *Thómas Saga Erkibyskups*, ed. E. Magnússon (London, 1875–83). Garnier's Life is published in French in *Guernes de Pont-Sainte-Maxence*, ed. E. Walberg (Lund, 1922) and is translated into English by J. Shirley, *Garnier's Becket* (Llanerch reprints, 1996). Only a small proportion of the Latin Lives has been published, and none of the Lives in its entirety. For selections from the Lives and letters, see *English Historical Documents*, II, eds D. C. Douglas and G. Greenaway (London, 1981), pp. 749–828; G. Greenaway, *The Life and Death of Thomas Becket* (London, 1961); W. H. Hutton, *St Thomas of Canterbury* (London, 1889); G. Giles, *The Life and Letters of Thomas Becket*, 2 vols (London, 1846).

The publication of *The Correspondence of Thomas Becket, Archbishop of Canterbury, 1162–70*, 2 vols, ed. A. Duggan (Oxford, 2000), has made a great contribution to the subject. Now it is possible to read his correspondence as archbishop in a translated and fully annotated form. For scholarly editions of the correspondence of two of the most important figures in the dispute, see *The Letters of John of Salisbury*, vol. II, eds W. J. Millor and C. N. L. Brooke (Oxford, 1979, with English translation), and *The Letters and Charters of Gilbert Foliot*, eds A. Morey and C. N. L. Brooke (Cambridge, 1967).

There are numerous modern biographies of Thomas. F. Barlow's *Thomas Becket* (London, 1986, repr. 1997) is indispensable, providing a comprehensive narrative of Thomas's life and death based on a thorough analysis of the available evidence. D. Knowles, *Thomas Becket* (London, 1970) is also very valuable, and probably provides the most accessible introduction to the subject. Though not really a biography, B. Smalley's *The Becket Conflict and the Schools* (Oxford, 1973) provides a wide-ranging and learned discussion of the issues involved in the dispute in the light of contemporary thought. For a scholarly biography of Henry II, and a critical assessment of Thomas, see W. L. Warren, *Henry II* (London, 1973).

For background reading on the period, see, for example, R. Bartlett, *England under the Normans and Angevins, 1075–1225* (Oxford, 2000), F, Barlow, *The Feudal Kingdom of England* (London, 1956) and R. Mortimer, *Angevin England, 1154–1258* (Oxford, 1994). On the Church and the crown, see Z. N. Brooke, *The English Church and the Papacy* (Cambridge, 1931), C. R. Cheney, *From Becket to Langton* (Manchester, 1956), R. Foreville, *L'église et la royauté en Angleterre sous Henri II Plantagenet 1154–1189* (Paris, 1943) and W. Urry, *Canterbury under the Angevin Kings* (London, 1967).

A vast amount of literature exists on different aspects of the Becket dispute. On Thomas's personality, see D. Knowles, 'Thomas Becket: a Character Study', in his *The Historian and Character and Other Essays* (Cambridge, 1963), pp. 98–128. For a detailed discussion of Thomas's early life, see L. B. Radford, *Thomas of London Before His Consecration* (Cambridge, 1894). On Archbishop Theobald, see A. Saltman, *Theobald, Archbishop of Canterbury* (London, 1956). On Thomas's accession to Canterbury, see M. Staunton, 'Thomas Becket's Conversion', *Anglo-Norman Studies*, 21 (1999), 193–211.

For Henry's early career, see E. Amt, *The Accession of Henry II: Royal Government Restored 1149–1159* (Woodbridge, 1993). On the world of his court, see E. Türk, *Nugae curialum: le règne d'Henri II Plantagenêt (1145–89) et l'éthique politique* (Geneva, 1977). R. W. Eyton, *Court, Household and Itinerary of Henry II* (London, 1878) is still very useful, but is likely to be surpassed by the publication of *The Acta of Henry II*, eds J. C. Holt, N. Vincent (Cambridge, forthcoming). For the English bishops, see D. Knowles, *The Episcopal Colleagues of Thomas Becket* (Cambridge, 1951), and for Gilbert Foliot, see A. Morey and C. N. L. Brooke, *Gilbert Foliot and his Letters* (Cambridge, 1965). For John of Salisbury, see *The World of John of Salisbury*, ed. M. Wilks (Oxford, 1984).

On the issues at stake in the dispute, C. Duggan, *Canon Law in Medieval England: the Becket Dispute and Decretal Collections* (London, 1982) provides an informed analysis of the canon law tradition. A particularly useful commentary on the Constitutions may be found in *Councils and Synods With Other Documents Relating to the English Church, I AD 871–1204*, Part 2, 1066–1204 (Oxford, 1981), eds D. Whitelock, M. Brett, and C. N. L. Brooke. For the general development of administration and record, of which the Constitutions were a part, see M. Clanchy, *From Memory to Written Record* (1993) and W. L. Warren, *The Governance of Norman and Angevin England 1086–1272* (1987). On canon law and the exile, see E. M. Peters, 'The Archbishop and the Hedgehog', in *Law, Church and Society: Essays in Honour of Stephan Kuttner*, eds K. Pennington and R. Somerville, (1977), pp. 167–84.

A detailed discussion of the murder, with particular attention to its Canterbury context, may be found in W. Urry, *Thomas Becket: His Last Days* (Stroud, 1999). The accounts of the murder and the miracles which followed are discussed by A. Abbott, *St Thomas of Canterbury, His Death and Miracles*, 2 vols (London, 1898). For the miracles, see also B. Ward, *Miracles and the Medieval Mind* (Aldershot, 1982). On the cult, see D. Knowles, 'Thomas Becket: the Saint', *Canterbury Cathedral Chronicle* 65 (1970) and A. Duggan, 'The Cult of St Thomas in the Thirteenth Century', *St Thomas Cantilupe, Bishop of Hereford*, ed. M. Jancey (Hereford, 1982), pp. 21–44. On the history of Thomas's relics, see J. R. Butler, *The Quest for Becket's Bones* (London, 1995).

The fullest analyses of the Lives, in terms of datings and interconnections, are E. Walberg, *La tradition hagiographique de saint Thomas Becket avant la fin du XIIe siècle* (Paris, 1929) and R. Foreville, *Thomas Becket dans la tradition hagiographique* (London, 1981). For a stimulating discussion of the Lives as literature, see J. O'Reilly, 'The Double Martyrdom of Thomas Becket: Hagiography or History?', *Studies in Medieval and Renaissance History*, 7 (1985), 185–247. See also, for the Lives, A. Gransden, *Historical Writing in England c. 550 to c. 1307* (London, 1974), A. Duggan, *Thomas Becket: a Textual History of His Letters* (Oxford, 1980) is an important analysis of the correspondence. For visual representations of Thomas see *The Becket Leaves*, eds J. Backhouse and C. De Hanes (London, 1988) and T. Borenius, *Thomas Becket in Art* (London, 1932).

A number of relevant articles are published in *Thomas Becket: Actes du Colloque International de Sédières, 1973* (Paris, 1975), ed. R. Foreville. For a bibliography up until 1970, see J. W. Alexander, 'The Becket Dispute in Recent Historiography', *Journal of British Studies*, 9 (1970), 1–25.

INDEX

Note: numbers in **bold** refer to authorship of chapters; 'n.' after a page reference indicates a note number on that page. Subentries are listed in chronological order.